SIMPLE FORM	PAST	
get	got	
give	gave	given
go	went	gone
grind	ground	ground
grow	grew	grown
hang	hanged	hanged (people)
hang	hung	hung (things)
have	had	had
hear	heard	heard
hide	hid	hidden
hit	hit	hit
hold	held	held
hurt	hurt	hurt
keep	kept	kept
know	knew	known
lay	laid	laid
lead	led	led
leave	left	left
lend	lent	lent
let	let	let
lie	lay	lain
lie	lied	lied
light	lit	lit
lose	lost	lost
make	made	made
mean	meant	meant
meet	met	met
pay	paid	paid
prove	proved	proven
put	put	put
quit	quit	quit
read	read	read
rid	rid	rid
ride	rode	ridden
ring	rang	rung
rise	rose	risen
run	ran	run
say	said (pronounced like *led*)	said (pronounced like *led*)
see	saw	seen
seek	sought	sought
sell	sold	sold
send	sent	sent
set	set	set
sew	sewed	sewn
shake	shook	shaken

GRAMMARGUIDE
ENGLISH GRAMMAR IN CONTEXT

Janet M. Bing
Old Dominion University

PRENTICE HALL REGENTS, Englewood Cliffs, NJ, 07632

Library of Congress Cataloging-in-Publication Data

BING, JANET MUELLER,
    Grammarguide: English grammar in context / Janet M. Bing.

    Includes index.
    ISBN 0-13-362310-6
    1. English language—Grammar—1950- I. Title.

PE1112.B48 1989   89-3463
428.2—dc19   CIP

Editorial/production supervision and
    interior design: CAROLE BROWN and TÜNDE A. DEWEY
Cover design: LUNDGREN GRAPHICS, LTD.
Manufacturing buyer: PETER HAVENS and LAURA CROSSLAND

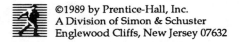
Printed in the United States of America

10 9 8 7 6 5 4

ISBN 0-13-362310-6

PRENTICE-HALL INTERNATIONAL (UK) LIMITED, London
PRENTICE-HALL OF AUSTRALIA PTY. LIMITED, Sydney
PRENTICE-HALL OF CANADA INC., Toronto
PRENTICE-HALL HISPANOAMERICANA, S.A., Mexico
PRENTICE-HALL OF INDIA PRIVATE LIMITED, New Delhi
PRENTICE-HALL OF JAPAN, INC., Tokyo
SIMON & SCHUSTER ASIA PTE. LTD., Singapore
EDITORA PRENTICE-HALL DO BRASIL, LTDA., Rio de Janeiro

To my father, Dr. Albert Christian Mueller

Contents

Chapter **1**

KINDS OF WORDS AND HOW THEY ARE USED 1

Chapter **2**

NOUN PHRASES AND NOUN CLAUSES 11

Chapter **3**

PRONOUNS AND OTHER PROFORMS **40**

Chapter **4**

VERBS AND VERB TENSES **59**

Chapter 5

MODALS AND SEMIMODALS 113

Chapter 6

SPECIAL KINDS OF VERBS 147

Chapter **7**

ADJECTIVES AND ADJECTIVALS 178

Chapter **8**

ADVERBS AND ADVERBIALS 211

Introduction

This is an easy-to-read grammar for students and teachers of English as a second language. It is written primarily for students to use independently outside of class so that class time can be spent practicing English rather than discussing rules of grammar. It should also be useful for teachers. Most English teachers have a good understanding of English grammar, but cannot always communicate this understanding to students. The simple, non-technical explanations in this book may help teachers answer student questions in ways students can understand.

The rules in this book are for American English unless otherwise noted. Some rules were not included because they were judged too complicated for beginning and intermediate students. Deciding which rules to leave out was difficult, and users will not all agree with my choices.

Language always occurs in some context. In most sections of **GrammarGuide** the examples are from a single context so that readers do not have to imagine a new situation for each example sentence. The first example sentence usually suggests the context. Many of the structures explained in **GrammarGuide** can be practiced in the companion workbooks, **GrammarWork** 1-4 by Pamela Breyer.

I would like to thank Leslie Levine Adler, Pamela Breyer, Louis Carrillo, Deb Davia, Mark Landa, Eric Nelson, Cheryl O'Brien, David Tillyer, and Margaret Segal for comments on early versions. Pamela Breyer and Eric Nelson were particularly generous with both time and ideas. Louis Carrillo did most of the editing of this version and simplified, clarified, and generally improved the entire book. Tünde Dewey was most helpful in the final stages of editing.

I dedicate this book to my father, Dr. Albert Christian Mueller, who retired from practicing medicine and successfully taught English to a Thai student (who now also calls him Dad). I hope that this book will help him with his next student.

Janet Bing
Department of English
Old Dominion University
Norfolk, VA 23508

TO THE STUDENT: How to Use *GrammarGuide*

This book is an easy grammar for beginning and intermediate students. Chapter 1 includes very brief descriptions of the parts of speech for people who do not know how to identify them. In some cases it is possible to look up something in the index even without knowing the part of speech. For example, to learn about the use of *must* or *have to*, the reader can look up these words directly in the index. Not all English words are in the index, of course, but many words which are important to English grammar can be found there.

Even if you do not understand everything in the explanation, study the examples. Sometimes examples can be more helpful than explanations. It is also sometimes helpful to compare examples in the charts.

The organization of this book is:

Table of Contents

Helpful Charts

LIST OF CHARTS AND TABLES

Chapter 1

Kinds of Words and How They Are Used

1.1 Parts of Speech and Parts of a Sentence

When you use a grammar book, it is useful to know the parts of speech. It is also useful to know how words and phrases are used in sentences. Words can be both parts of speech and parts of a sentence. Look at the following:

My new camera has fallen off the table.

When you ask, "What is the word *camera*?" the answer is a part of speech. *Camera* is a noun. When you ask, "How is the word *camera* used in this sentence?" the answer is that *camera* is the subject of the sentence. A subject is a part of the sentence.

1.2 Recognizing Parts of Speech

Here are several ways to identify a part of speech:

1. Learn a definition for each part of speech. One traditional definition of a noun is "the name of a person, place, or thing." A camera is a thing; the word *camera* is a noun.
2. Decide if the word is similar to another word that you know. If you know that *good* is an adjective, you can guess that *new* is an adjective, too, because it fits into the same part of the sentence.
3. Look up the word in a dictionary. A dictionary tells which parts of speech a word can be. After the word and the pronunciation, the part of speech is given. *Adj.* is the abbreviation for "adjective."

new (no͞o) *adj.*

PARTS OF SPEECH

1.3 Nouns

Photography is fun.

Nouns name people, places, actions, and ideas and include anything that can be touched, smelled, heard, felt, or seen. Nouns answer questions that begin with *what* or *who*. Names of particular people, places, or things are proper nouns. A noun phrase is a group of words that includes a noun or a pronoun as the main word.

I have a *new camera from Japan.*

In the following sentences, words that can fit into the blanks are nouns and noun phrases:

He is thinking about _____.

> his camera
> photography
> a new camera from Japan

_____ can be interesting.
Photography
Taking pictures

1.4 Determiners

The camera is gone!

The first word in a noun phrase is usually a determiner. There are several kinds of determiners.

Articles: the, a, an
Demonstratives: this, that, these, those
Possessives: my, your (singular), his, her, its, our, your (plural), their

1.5 Pronouns

I can't find *it.*

A pronoun is a substitute word. Pronouns are used to avoid repeating nouns or noun phrases, and they have different forms depending on how they are used. Pronouns such as *I, you,* and *she* are personal pronouns. They refer to particular people. Pronouns such as *anybody, everyone, anything,* and *nobody* are indefinite pronouns. They are used when the speaker has no particular thing or person in mind. The demonstrative pronouns *this, that, these,* and *those* are used in place of noun phrases such as *this camera.*

1.6 Adjectives

It was a *new* camera.

Adjectives tell something about nouns. *New* in the preceding example describes the camera; it tells what kind of camera it was. An adjective phrase is a group of words that includes an adjective as the main word.

The camera was *very expensive*.

Many adjectives and adjective phrases can be used in the blank in the following sentence:

We took pictures of some _____ things.

beautiful
green
important
very unusual

1.7 Verbs

Someone *stole* my camera.

Verbs are words that show action. The action in the example above is *stealing*. Verbs also describe a state or condition.

It *was* a very expensive camera.
It *cost* $200.
I *feel* very upset.

A verb phrase can be one verb, or it can have auxiliary verbs and a main verb. The main verb is the last verb in the verb phrase. The verbs that precede the main verb are auxiliary verbs.

	AUXILIARY VERB	MAIN VERB	
She	has been	sweeping	the patio.
She	was	working	when I called.
She	started		early.

The auxiliary verbs in English are *be, have,* and *do* in all their forms. The modals, *can, could, may, might, shall, should, must, will, would,* and *ought to,* are also auxiliary verbs.

Linking verbs are used in sentences where the words following the verb tell something about the subject of the sentence. It is usually possible to replace a linking verb with a form of *be* and keep the general meaning.

This fruit	is	a mango.
Mangoes	are	delicious.
They	taste	wonderful.

1.8 Adverbs

There was an accident *yesterday.*

Adverbs tell something about verbs, adjectives, other adverbs, or an entire sentence. Adverbs answer *where, when,* or *how* questions.

Where did it happen?	It happened *outside.*
When did it happen?	It happened *early this morning.*
How often does this happen?	It *rarely* happens.
How fast were the cars going?	*Very fast.*
How much damage was there?	One car was *completely* destroyed.

1.9 Prepositions

We're moving *into* the house now.

Prepositions are words that show many kinds of relationships, such as time, place, and direction. In the following examples, the prepositions *on* and *under* show two different place relationships between the suitcase and the table:

Put the suitcase *on* the table.
Put the suitcase *under* the table.

In the next examples, the prepositions *before* and *after* show two different time relationships between moving the sofa and eating dinner.

Let's move the sofa *before* dinner.
No, let's move it *after* dinner.

A prepositional phrase is a preposition followed by a noun or noun phrase. *On the table* and *before dinner* are prepositional phrases.

1.10 Conjunctions

Take this list *and* go to the drugstore.

Conjunctions are words that connect a word with a word, a phrase with a phrase, or a clause with a clause. (A clause contains a subject and verb and is part of a sentence.)

Coordinate conjunctions are single words that join parts of a sentence. *And, or, nor, but, so, yet,* and *for* are coordinate conjunctions. (*So* and *yet* are sometimes called conjunctive adverbs.)

Correlative conjunctions are conjunctions used in pairs.

Both Sarah *and* Tom graduated from college this year.
Graduation is on *either* the twenty-fifth *or* the twenty-sixth of May.

Subordinate conjunctions, such as *before* and *after,* are words that introduce adverbial clauses.

Before they went shopping, they went to the bank.
After they finished their shopping, they went home.

1.11 *Wh*-words

Where did they go?

The *wh*-words in English are *who, whom, what, where, when, which, why, whose, whether,* and *how.* These words are often used at the beginning of a sentence to ask a question.

When did they go shopping?

All the *wh*-words can be used to introduce clauses.

I wonder *why* they left so early.
I'm not sure *when* they'll be back.

1.12   Interjections

Ouch!

Interjections are words and phrases that express strong emotion. They occur independently of sentences and are common in spoken conversation. They are rarely used in formal writing. Many interjections are impolite. Some mild ones follow.

Wow!   Good Grief!   Gee!   Darn!   Oh no!

PARTS OF SENTENCES

1.13   Subject and Predicate

Their children watch too much television.

The subject of a sentence is a word or group of words that the rest of the sentence is going to comment on. It often identifies the doer of an action. In short sentences, the subject is often the first noun or noun phrase. The predicate of a sentence is the verb and the rest of the sentence.

SUBJECT	PREDICATE
Maria	watches football games on television.
Her brothers	like to watch tennis matches.

1.14   Subject-Verb Agreement

She *likes* football, but they *like* tennis.

The subject and the first verb in the predicate must agree; that is, singular nouns are used with singular verb forms, and plural nouns are used with plural verb forms.

SUBJECT	VERB	
She	doesn't play	football.
They	don't play	tennis.

Two or more subjects that are joined by conjunctions are compound subjects. Compound subjects joined by *and* are used with the plural form of the verb.

Tony and Mark *are* watching the late movie.

In compound subjects joined by *or* or *nor,* the verb agrees with the noun or noun phrase that comes after *or* or *nor.*

Neither Maria *nor* her sisters *are* watching the movie.
Neither her sisters *nor* Maria *is* interested.

The introductory word *there* is sometimes used in the subject position of a sentence. When *there* is in the subject position, the first verb agrees with the noun that follows the verb.

There *is* a good *movie* on Channel 4.
There *are* several good *programs* on TV tonight.

1.15 Predicate Nouns and Predicate Adjectives

Predicate nouns give another name for the subject. Predicate adjectives describe the subject. Predicate nouns and adjectives follow linking verbs. Sometimes predicate nouns and adjectives are called subject complements.

"Miami Cops" is a *crime show.* (predicate noun)
It is *very exciting.* (predicate adjective)

1.16 Modifiers

I bought a *new* cookbook *of Greek dishes.*

Words, phrases, and clauses that give information about other words are called modifiers. Adjectives and adverbs are modifiers. Prepositional phrases, participial phrases, relative clauses, and adverbial clauses are also modifiers.

The modifiers in the following examples tell something about the noun *shelf.* When the modifier is short, it usually comes before the noun. When it is long, it usually follows the noun.

I need a *new* shelf.
I would like a *glass* shelf.
It would be a shelf *for flowers.*
A shelf *built into the wall* would be nice.
A shelf *that fits under the window* would look the best.

The modifiers in the following examples tell something about the verb.   Like adverbs, adverbial modifiers answer the questions *where, when,* and *how.*

> We can put it *over there.* (where)
> I will build it *later.* (when)
> You can attach it *with three screws.* (how)

1.17   Direct and Indirect Objects

> She gave *her father a book* for his birthday.

Nouns that follow verbs are usually objects. A direct object usually answers the questions *what* or *who.*

> Barbara invited *her relatives.*
> She ordered *flowers.*
> She baked *some cookies.*

Some verbs can have two objects: a direct object and an indirect object. If a verb is followed by one object, it is usually a direct object.   If it is followed by two objects, the indirect object usually answers the question *to whom* or *for whom.*   The direct object usually answers the question *what.*

	INDIRECT OBJECT	DIRECT OBJECT
She gave	her father	a present.
She offered	her aunt	some cookies.

1.18   Object Complements

> Her new baby made her family *happy.*

A few verbs, such as *choose, elect, make,* and *name,* can be followed by a direct object and words that describe or rename the direct object. These words are called object complements.

Object complements refer to the object, just as subject complements refer to the subject.

	OBJECT	OBJECT COMPLEMENT
The baby made	his father	proud.
They named	the boy	Antonio.
We call	him	Tony.

Chapter 2
Noun Phrases
and Noun Clauses

NOUN CLAUSES

COMPARING NOUN PHRASES

2.1 Defining Nouns, Noun Phrases, and Noun Clauses

Nouns name people, places, and many things, including emotions, ideas, and activities. They answer questions that begin with *what* or *who.* The words *house, building,* and *city* are nouns. A **noun phrase** is a group of words that includes a noun or pronoun as the main word. Noun phrases can include determiners, such as *the, this,* or *a* and modifiers, such as *famous.*

I just visited *a famous theater.*

A **noun clause** is a group of words that includes a subject and a verb and is used as a noun.   Noun clauses usually begin with *wh*-words or *that.*

I don't know *which one you're talking about.*
I thought *that you were studying today.*

THE NOUN PHRASE: NOUNS

2.2 Common and Proper Nouns

Orson Welles directed the movie *Citizen Kane.*

A **proper noun** is the name of one particular person, place, animal, or thing. It begins with a capital letter. All other nouns, called **common nouns**, begin with small letters.

PROPER NOUNS		COMMON NOUNS
Jane Fonda	is	an actress.
Los Angeles	is	a city.
George Lucas	directs	movies.

a.   Names and Titles of People

English speakers usually have two or three names.

FIRST NAME	MIDDLE NAME	LAST/FAMILY NAME
Martin	Luther	King
John	Fitzgerald	Kennedy

Titles are used before names in formal English. A title begins with a capital letter and (except for *Miss)* ends with a period.

Mr. Jesse Jackson (a man)
Ms. Bella Abzug (a woman)
Mrs. George Bush (a married woman using her husband's first name)
Mrs. Barbara Bush (a married woman using her own first name)
Miss June Adams (an unmarried woman)
Dr. Christiaan Barnard (a doctor)

b. Names of Places

The names of specific places begin with capital letters. *The* is usually not capitalized in place names, unless it begins a sentence.

My aunt comes from *the* Philippines.
She now lives in *Paris, France.*

2.3 Singular and Plural Nouns

Do you want an *apple?*
Apples are only eighty-nine cents a pound.

Common nouns can be countable or uncountable. Countable nouns are either singular or plural. Regular noun plurals end in *-s, -es,* or *-ies*.

Banana*s* are seventy-nine cents a pound today.
Tomato*es* are ninety-nine cents a pound.
How much are the cherr*ies*?

Irregular noun plurals are not covered by a general rule. Many common words for people have irregular forms.

SINGULAR	PLURAL
a child	several *children*
a man	some *men*
a person	several *people*
a woman	five *women*

When a singular noun ends in *-f* or *-fe*, the *-f* is often changed to *-v* and followed by *-es*. Following are some examples. The second group of words contains exceptions.

SINGULAR	PLURAL	SINGULAR	PLURAL
knife	knives	handkerchief	handkerchiefs
scarf	scarves	roof	roofs
wife	wives		

For some nouns, the vowels in the singular and plural forms are different.

SINGULAR	PLURAL
foot	*feet*
goose	*geese*
mouse	*mice*
tooth	*teeth*

For a few names of animals and fish, the singular and plural forms are the same.

SINGULAR	PLURAL
deer	*deer*
fish	*fish*
sheep	*sheep*
trout	*trout*

a.   Plurals with No Singular Forms

There are some nouns that have only a plural form. Some examples are *jeans, scissors,* and *(eye)glasses.* They can be made singular by using the phrase *a pair of.* Notice the form of the verbs in the following examples.

Jeans *are* expensive.
A pair of jeans *costs* seventy dollars here.

Glasses *are* very fashionable these days.
A pair of glasses *changes* a person's looks.

Other nouns that usually take the phrase *a pair of* are *clippers, binoculars, pants, pajamas, pliers, shorts, slacks, trousers,* and *tweezers.*

b. Singular Nouns That Look Plural

Some nouns end in *-s* but are not plural nouns. These nouns are used with singular verbs. The pronoun *it* is used to replace them.

The *Philippines* is a group of islands.
Honduras is in Central America. *It* is next to Nicaragua.

General Motors is an automobile manufacturer.
It uses robots in its plants.

Some uncountable nouns, such as *mathematics,* end in *-s* but are not plural. These nouns are used with singular verbs.

Politics	requires dedication.
Economics	is a field of study.
Measles	is a childhood disease.
Checkers	is a game.
The news	begins at seven o'clock.

c. Collective Nouns

Some nouns that refer to groups of people are often grammatically singular in American English. They are called collective nouns.

The committee *is* meeting. The government *is* in danger.
  group   nation
  class   team

Collective nouns can also be plural.

The committees *are* meeting now.

d. Numbers and Measurement

Large numbers before nouns usually do not end in *-s*. Words such as *dozen, hundred,* and *thousand* are used in the plural form only when they refer to an indefinite number and are followed by an *of*-phrase.

A truck carrying five *hundred* chickens had an accident.
About two *dozen* chickens were killed.
Hundreds of chickens were running around.
Dozens of eggs were broken.

Nouns of measurement are sometimes used directly before a noun *(a two-foot board),* and sometimes before the preposition *of (two feet of wire).* When the measurement word comes directly before a noun, it is never plural.

A six-*foot* pole was sticking through a truck window.
The forty-*gallon* gas tank was ruptured.
I saw at least twenty *feet* of chicken wire on the road.
Thirty *gallons* of gasoline were spilled on the road.

In the following examples, the subjects of the sentences are the nouns in the measurement phrases. Therefore, the verbs agree in number with these words. They do not agree with the nouns that follow the preposition *of*.

The *load* of chickens *was* expensive.
Two *bags* of chicken feed *were* also lost.

2.4 Countable and Uncountable Nouns

We'll need *toothpaste* and *toothbrushes* for the trip.

A countable noun can be used after numbers. An uncountable noun cannot be used with numbers.

CORRECT	INCORRECT
one toothbrush	
toothpaste	*one toothpaste (uncountable)
three forks	
silverware	*four silverwares (uncountable)
six chairs	
furniture	*two furnitures (uncountable)

Knowing if a noun is countable or uncountable is important for subject-verb agreement, the use of articles *(a, an, the)*, and the use of quantifiers *(much, many)*.

Most dictionaries do not indicate whether nouns are countable or uncountable. However, nouns that fit the following categories are usually uncountable.

Liquids: milk, coffee, water
Gases: air, oxygen
Solids: chalk, soap, string, rope, bread
Substances composed of particles: flour, rice, dust
Actions or states: swimming, living
Abstractions and emotions: love, hate, honesty
General classes: money, furniture, food
Fields of study: astronomy, mathematics

Specific concrete nouns, such as *chair* and *cow*, are usually countable, but general or abstract nouns, such as *livestock* or *happiness*, are usually uncountable. Compare these countable and uncountable nouns.

COUNTABLE (concrete)	UNCOUNTABLE (abstract)
letter, package	mail
dollar, coin	money
cow, chicken, horse	livestock
table, sofa, chair	furniture
portrait, drawing	art

Uncountable nouns can be counted when a countable noun plus *of* is used before them.

milk	a quart of milk
helium	two tanks of helium
string	three balls of string
bread	eight loaves of bread

The pronoun *it* replaces uncountable nouns.

The furniture is on the moving van. *It* is all tied down.

Some nouns are countable when they have one meaning and uncountable when they have another meaning.

COUNTABLE

The auto *companies* (businesses) lost money.
Your *papers* (documents) are in your briefcase.
Don't make any *changes* (alterations) in the contract.

UNCOUNTABLE

We are having *company* (guests) for dinner.
Paper (a material) is made from wood.
I need *change* (coins) for the phone.

Sometimes a noun is countable or uncountable with no change in meaning.

This store has excellent *fruits* and vegetables.
The *fruit* is from many different countries.

THE NOUN PHRASE: DETERMINERS

2.5 Demonstrative Adjectives: *This, That, These,* and *Those*

Demonstrative adjectives agree in number with the nouns they modify. *This* and *that* are used with singular nouns and uncountable nouns. *These* and *those* are used with plural nouns.

> *This dress* is washable. (singular noun)
> Put *that laundry* in a bag. (uncountable noun)
> *Those socks* aren't wool. (plural noun)

This and *these* are used to refer to objects that are close to the speaker; *that* and *those* are used to refer to objects that are distant from the speaker.

> I bought *this dress* two years ago. (close)
> I like *that dress* in the window. (distant)

2.6 Articles: *A, An, Some,* and *The*

Use *a* and *an* with singular countable nouns. With plural countable nouns, use *some* or no article.

> I went to *a* sale today.
> The shopping center often has sales.
> *Some* sales at the shopping center are very good.

A, one or *some* is usually used for the first mention of a noun.

> I bought *a* shirt and *some* shoes at the clothing store.
> The shirt is white, and the shoes are black.

A and *an* are usually used when one is referring to a choice made from several possibilities.

> Four black shirts and one white one were on sale.
> I bought *a* black one.

Some is generally used with uncountable nouns, but no article is used when a general statement is being made.

> I bought *some* candy for my sister.
> She likes candy.

Use *the* after the first mention of something.

> I bought a dress and some stockings.
> *The* dress was expensive, but *the* stockings weren't.

Speakers use *the* when they believe that listeners know which person or thing they are talking about.

> Four black belts and one brown one were on sale.
> *The* brown one was not well made.

The is used with identifying modifiers.

> Maria: Do you see those two clerks?
> Roberto: *The* tall one looks familiar.
> Maria: Do you know *the* one with the red hair?

Sometimes it is clear from the situation or from knowledge of the world that only one choice is possible.

> How do you like *the* weather? (the weather here)
> I wish *the* sun would come out. (the sun in our solar system)

Because it is usually clear which one is meant, the following words are usually used with *the*.

the earth	the sky	the universe
the equator	the stars	the world
the moon	the sun	the weather

For the same reason, people who know each other well use *the* to refer to something when it is clear which one is meant or when there is only one possibility.

> Did you feed *the* cat? (our cat)
> *The* aspirin is in the medicine cabinet. (our supply of aspirin)

The word *the* usually comes before *radio, newspaper,* and *news,* but it is not used before *television* or *TV* unless the word refers to the television set.

> I read about the fire in *the* newspaper.
> It wasn't on TV.

The is used when a superlative word —that is, a word ending in *-est* or preceded by *most*— comes before a noun. A superlative modifier usually tells which one of several things the speaker means.

Flying is *the* fastest way to travel.
It is also *the* most expensive way.

a.   Articles with General Statements

When we speak of general classes or groups, plural nouns are used without the article *the*. Uncountable nouns are also used without *the* in general statements.

CORRECT	INCORRECT
Sharks are fish.	*The sharks are fish.
Whales are mammals.	*The whales are mammals.
Food is plentiful in the ocean.	*The food is plentiful in the ocean.

It is also possible to use singular nouns with *a, an*, or *the* to refer to a group or class. The singular noun refers to all the members of the class.

A butterfly is an insect. (Butterflies are insects.)
The alligator is a reptile. (Alligators are reptiles.)

b.   Articles with the Names of Illnesses

Articles are not used with the names of most illnesses.

I had bronchitis.
Have you ever had pneumonia?
Do you have arthritis?

However, articles are used with the names of some illnesses and ailments.

A, AN	*THE*
He has *a* headache.	She has *the* flu.
I may have *a* cold.	Have you had *the* mumps?
She has *a* toothache.	I had *the* measles as a child.
Does she have *a* sore throat?	

2.7   *A* or *An*

My sister is *an* opera singer.
She's *a* very famous singer.

A and *an* are two forms of the same word. *An* is used before a word that begins with a vowel sound. In written English, these words usually begin with the letters *a, e, i, o,* and *u.* Some words that begin with a silent *h* actually begin with a vowel sound, so these words are used with *an.*

an attorney	an exterminator
an interior designer	an optician
an unusual gardener	an agent
an X-ray technician	an honest man
(*X* begins with vowel sound)	(*honest* begins with silent *h*)

Use *a* before words that begin with consonant sounds. *A* is also used before words beginning with *u* when *u* sounds like *y.*

a bank	a delicatessen
a yellow tablecloth	a hardware store
a tennis match	a university (*u* sounds like *y*)

2.8 *A, An,* or No Article

He has *a* good job. It is interesting work.

A and *an* are not used with proper nouns. Use them only before common nouns.

That is Julia Peterson. She's *a* doctor.
Hugh works for Nabisco. He's *an* engineer.

A and *an* are used only before singular countable nouns. Use *some* or no article before uncountable nouns and plural nouns.

SINGULAR	PLURAL/UNCOUNTABLE
He has *a* good job.	It has many benefits.
He got *a* new desk.	He was given new furniture.
He put *a* painting on the wall.	He likes modern art.

Do not use *a* or *an* after the words *kind, sort,* or *type.*

A pediatrician is a kind of doctor.
An appendectomy is a type of operation.

A and *an* are used in the following expressions of price. The word *per* can also be used.

Milk is $1.50 *a* quart.   Eggs are $1.35 *a* dozen.
Apples are $.99 *a* pound.   Yeast is $.75 *per* ounce.

2.9   *The* or No Article

We sat in *the* fifth row.
Our friends sat in row 6.

a.   Numbers

The is used with ordinal numbers *(first, second, third)* and related words, such as *next* and *last,* when these words are used before nouns. *The* is not used before nouns that are followed by cardinal numbers.

Do you have *the* fifth book?   Do you have book five?
Look in *the* second chapter.   Look in Chapter 2.
It may be on *the* last page.   It may be on page 144.

Do not use *the* in the idioms *at first* and *at last.*

I found the right page *at last.*

b.   Parts of the Day

The is not used in expressions with parts of the day when they include the prepositions *at* and *by.* However, it is used in expressions beginning with the preposition *in.*

in *the* morning   at dawn   by day
in *the* afternoon   at midnight   by night
in *the* evening   at noon

c.   Directions

When *north, south, east,* and *west* are used in prepositional phrases, use *the.* Otherwise, do not use *the* with the names of the four points of the compass.

The sun rises in *the* east. My home faces east.

When the points of the compass name parts of the world, they are capitalized and take *the*.

The Civil War was between *the* North and *the* South.

d. Special Comparatives

Some shortened comparative expressions use *the*.

The more, *the* merrier. (The more people that come, the merrier the group will be.)
The sooner, *the* better. (The sooner something happens, the better I will like it.)

e. Languages and People

The is not used with the names of languages unless the word *language* is used. However, *the* is used with nationalities.

I am studying *French* (language) because I want to learn about *the French* (people).
Chinese (language) is difficult to read.
The Chinese (people) have a new writing system for their language.
He speaks *Italian*.
The Italian language sounds very musical.

f. Institutions

Some nouns refer both to a building and to an institution or activity. Use *the* when referring to the building but not when speaking of the institution or activity.

INSTITUTION OR ACTIVITY

My son goes to *school*.
We go to *church* on Sunday.
My oldest daughter is in *college*.

BUILDING OR PLACE

I visited *the school* last week.
The church is on Main Street.
The college is in Massachusetts.

In American English, *the* or *a* is always used with the word university whether the institution or the building is meant.

g. *The* or No Article with Proper Nouns

In most cases, articles are not used with proper nouns; however, there are many exceptions to this rule.

Use *the* with proper nouns that contain *of*-phrases.

NO ARTICLE	*THE* + *OF* + NOUN
China, France	the Republic of China
Utah, Nebraska	the state of Utah
Atlanta, Seattle	the city of Atlanta
Yale University	the University of the Pacific
Clark Hall	the Hall of Science
Christmas, Halloween	the Fourth of July
Time, Newsweek	the *Journal of the American Medical Association*
Hudson Bay	the Bay of Biscay
Fifth Avenue	the Avenue of the Americas

If a proper noun is plural in form, use *the*.

NO ARTICLE	THE + A GROUP
Mark Ryan	the Ryans
Poland	the United States
Easter Island	the Virgin Islands
Lake Superior	the Great Lakes
Mount Fuji	the Rocky Mountains

The is sometimes used with a proper noun if the name includes the category. *The* is always used with names that include *union* or *republic*.

NO ARTICLE	*THE* + NAME + CATEGORY
Alpha Centauri, Sirius, Vega	the North Star
French	the French language
General Motors	the Ford Motor Company
Samoa, Thailand	the Soviet Union
	the Dominican Republic

Other categories often used in this pattern are rivers (the Amazon River), canals (the Erie Canal), bridges (the Brooklyn Bridge), tunnels (the Holland Tunnel), zoos (the San Diego Zoo), deserts (the Gobi Desert), poles (the North Pole), forests (the Black Forest), gulfs (the Persian Gulf), and newspapers (the *St. Louis Post-Dispatch*).

However, do not use *the* before the names of parks (Rock Creek Park), streets (Olympic Boulevard), squares (St. Mark's Square), beaches (Jones Beach), or schools (Cantwell High School).

Most names of geographical areas do not use *the* unless they are based on the points of the compass.

No Article	*The*
Asia, Africa	the Middle East
Spain, Thailand	the Far East
Vermont	the Midwest (U.S.)
Putnam County	the South (U.S.)

Most oceans, seas, and rivers use *the* in their name. Lakes, ponds, and bays generally do not use *the* unless they are modified by an *of*-phrase.

No Article	*The*
Lake Titicaca	the Indian Ocean
Lake Victoria	the Adriatic Sea
Hudson Bay	the Bay of Fundy
Walden Pond	the Mediterranean Sea

Some uses of *the* with a proper noun are idiomatic and should be memorized as part of the name.

the Ukraine   the Sudan   the Hague (the Netherlands)

The is used with eras and with time words modified by an *of*-phrase.

No Article	*The*
	the Middle Ages
	the Stone Age
March	the month of March
Wednesday	
July 10 (tenth)	the tenth of July

2.10 Possessive Adjectives

His work is fun.

Words such as *my*, *your*, and *his* are usually called possessive adjectives. They refer to the owner or possessor of the noun being described.

Maria works here.
These are *her* books.
Her father bought them.

Tom and Angelo work over there.
That's *their* office.

Teruo isn't here.
He's visiting *his* mother.

These adjectives have different forms that agree with the owner of the noun being described.

SUBJECT PRONOUNS	POSSESSIVE ADJECTIVES
I work in an office.	*My* work is easy.
He works in a theater.	*His* work is fun.
She works in a bank.	*Her* work is difficult.
We go to school at night.	*Our* schoolwork is interesting.
They work at the airport.	*Their* work is exciting.
Where do *you* work?	Is *your* work interesting?

The singular pronoun for nonhumans and babies is *its;* the plural form is *their.*

The monkey hurt *its* tail.

Although possessive nouns have an apostrophe *(the monkey's tail),* possessive adjectives do not. Compare the following sentences.

It's (it is) very sad.
Its (the monkey's) tail has a bandage on it.

The possessive adjectives are used with parts of the body and family relationships.

I washed *my* hands.
My sister washed *her* hands, too.

THE NOUN PHRASE: OTHER COMPONENTS

2.11   Ordering Words in Noun Phrases

All of the three young children began to scream.

A noun phrase can be a single noun or pronoun, or it can be a group of words.

NOUN PHRASE	VERB PHRASE
Mac	
A police officer	
Two old men	went into the bank.
The two old men in raincoats	
Both of the women	

The following chart shows a common order for words in noun phrases. Words do not always appear in this order, but this order is always correct.

1 quantifier or cardinal number
2 *of*
3 determiner or possessive
4 ordinal number
5 cardinal number or quantifier
6 adjective
7 noun
8 prepositional phrase

1	2	3	4	5	6	7	8
one	of	the		many	old	men	in raincoats
both	of	those		two	strong	guards	
		my	first	few	difficult	years	on the job
		the	first	few		people	
		those	last	two		women	

As can be seen from the chart, quantifiers can occur in position 1, where they are usually followed by *of*. However, they can also occur after the determiner, in position 5.

2.12 Quantifiers

Some of the apples are gone.

Quantifiers are words that tell how much or how many. Different quantifiers are used with uncountable, singular, and plural nouns. For example, the word *much* is used before uncountable nouns such as *milk,* but the word *many* is used before plural countable nouns such as *apple.*

How *much* milk is in the refrigerator?
How *many* apples do we have?

When quantifiers are used at the beginning of a noun phrase before the determiner, they are pronouns.

Some of the apples are gone.

The following examples show the use of quantifiers with different kinds of nouns.

UNCOUNTABLE NOUNS

How *much* of the sand is black?
How *much* is black?
All of the sand is black.
None of the sand is white.

Most of the sand is black.
Some of the sand is white.
There's not *much* white sand.
There's only a *little.*

Half of the sand is white.

SINGULAR NOUNS

How *much* of the pail is black?
How *much* is white?

The whole pail is black.
None of the pail is white.

Most of the pail is black.
Part of the pail is white.
Not *much* of the pail is white.
Only a *little* of it is white.

Half of the pail is white.

Each pail is white.
Every pail is white.

Neither pail is white.

PLURAL NOUNS

How *many* of the pails are black?
How *many* are white?
All of the pails are black.
None of the pails is white.

Most of the pails are black.
Some of the pails are white.
There aren't *many* white pails.
There are only a *few* white pails.

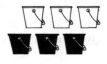

Half of the pails are white.

Both of the pails are white.

The following chart ranks quantifiers on a scale from more (the top) to less (the bottom).

UNCOUNTABLE NOUNS	SINGULAR NOUNS	PLURAL NOUNS
all	the whole	all
most	most	most
much	much	many
half	half	half
some	part	some
a little	a little	a few
none	each	both
	every	none
	neither	
	none	

2.13   Possessive Nouns

> There was a fire at *Bill Smith's* house.
> The roof *of the house* was ruined.

Possession can be shown with an apostrophe (') and *s*, or with *of*. When the owner or possessor is a person or an animal, the apostrophe -*s* form is usually used.

> *Bill Smith's* house was badly damaged.

If the possessor is not a person or an animal, the *of* form is usually used.

> Several parts *of the house* were burned.
> The roof *of the house* was ruined.

The apostrophe is used in the following ways:

a.   Nouns That Do Not End in -*s*

When a noun does not end in the letter -*s*, add -*s* to show possession.

> *Bill's* desk was burned.
> His *wife's* jewelry was ruined.
> The *children's* clothes were soaked.
> His *father-in-law's* papers were lost.

b.   Plural Nouns That End in -*s*

When a plural noun ends in -*s*, add only an apostrophe to show possession.

> The *girls'* clothes were new.
> The *boys'* rooms were not damaged.
> The *Smiths'* friends helped them after the fire.

c.   Singular Nouns That End in -*s* or -*z*

When a singular noun ends in -*s* or -*z*, the possessive can be formed with either an apostrophe alone or an apostrophe and -*s*.

> *Charles's* room was on the first floor.
> *Charles'* room was on the first floor.

> *Mr. Jones's* house was also damaged.
> *Mr. Jones'* house was also damaged.

The possessive with apostrophe -s is used with time expressions such as *second, minute, hour, day, night, week, month,* and *year.*

It was a *week's* work to clean up the mess.

2.14 Nouns as Modifiers

We bought an old *brick* farmhouse.

Nouns can be used to modify other nouns. The first noun always modifies the second one. A noun used as a modifier is always in the singular form, even when the second noun is plural.

We wanted to buy a *country* house.
We looked at several *country* houses.

When a noun is used as a modifier, it comes after any adjectives in the noun phrase (between positions 6 and 7 in the chart in section 2.11).

3 determiner or possessive
6 adjective
7 noun

	3	6		7
The builders used	old	oak		beams.
There is	a	new	stainless-steel	sink.
We need to replace	the	worn out	cupboard	doors.

2.15 Noun Compounds

The *garden tools* are on sale.

Noun compounds are made of two or three words put together. A noun compound looks like a noun modifier plus a noun when written, but it usually has a different stress pattern when spoken.

I need to buy a *kitchen curtain.* (noun modifier + noun)
I should buy a *coffee table,* too. (noun compound)

Compounds can be written as one word, a hyphenated term, or as two words. Check your dictionary for the correct forms. Here are some examples:

She's in the *rose garden.*
She's wearing a *rose-colored* dress.
She's near the *rosebush.*

We'll have a *tea party.*
Do you know the correct *tea-brewing* procedure?
Where's the *teapot*?

Don't sit near the *water spout.*
The chair is *water-logged.*
It isn't *waterproof.*

Two common kinds of compounds include words that end in *-er* and *-ing.*

He dances with a local ballet company.
He's a *ballet dancer.*
Ballet dancing is strenuous.

She smokes cigarettes.
She's a *cigarette smoker.*
Cigarette smoking is dangerous.

She climbs mountains.
She's a *mountain climber.*
Mountain climbing is difficult for smokers.

A compound that ends in *-er* is often but not always a person. Some that aren't are the following:

The machine opens cans. It's a *can opener.*
The machine sharpens pencils. It's a *pencil sharpener.*
The machine makes coffee. It's a *coffee maker.*

The second element of a compound is the more important. A *racehorse* is a horse. A *horse race* is a race. A *house dog* is a dog. A *doghouse* is a house. Here are some more examples of compounds with their meanings:

salad bowl	a bowl for salads
garden party	a party in a garden
periodical index	an index to periodicals
biology lecture	a lecture about biology

2.16 Appositives

Our neighbors, *the Broskys*, have a beautiful garden.

An appositive is a noun or noun phrase that gives more information about a preceding noun or noun phrase.

Their son, *Roger*, works very hard at their parties.

Appositives may be either essential or nonessential. Nonessential appositives add information that is not necessary to identify the noun that they describe. Nonessential appositives are separated from the sentence by commas (,). However, when an appositive indicates *which one* about the preceding noun, it is essential, and no commas are used.

Their daughter *Jane* makes the cookies.
Their daughter *Joanne* cleans the house.

The Broskys have two daughters. In the sentences above, the appositives are essential. They indicate which daughter does which job.

Their nephew, *George,* often stays with them.

They only have one nephew; incidentally, his name is George.

When appositives contain pronouns, the pronouns agree with the noun they refer to. If the appositive refers to the subject, use subject pronouns. If the appositive refers to an object, use object pronouns.

The best piano players, Eric and *I,* are always invited to
    their parties.
They always invite the best piano players, Eric and *me.*

2.17 Gerunds and Gerund Phrases

Making movies is hard work.

A group of words used as a noun is called a nominal. A nominal usually names a person, place, or thing, but it can also name an activity or condition. The *-ing* form of a verb, a gerund, is sometimes used as the name of an activity or condition. Gerunds and gerund phrases are used anywhere that a noun phrase can be used.

Acting is my profession.
Making movies is what I like to do best.
Do you enjoy *acting*?
Do you like *signing autographs*?
Are you tired of *having your picture taken*?

2.18   Infinitives and Infinitive Phrases

She likes *to listen* to music.

An infinitive is the simple form of a verb. It often begins with the word *to*. Infinitives can sometimes be used as noun phrases. For example, an infinitive phrase can be the object of a verb.

OBJECT

Roger wants	to work in a city.
He wants	to go to New York.
He hopes	to work in the theater.

Some verbs can be followed by infinitives but not by gerunds.

Roger wants *to be* (not *being*) an actor.
He expects *to go* (not *going*) to New York.

Some verbs can be followed by gerunds but not by infinitives.

She enjoys *being* (not *to be*) a star.
She can't imagine *doing* (not *to do*) anything else.

To name an activity after a preposition, use a gerund or gerund phrase. Never use an infinitive or infinitive phrase.

How do you feel about *acting* (not *to act*) in movies?
Do you get nervous before *filming* (not *to film*) a scene?

Infinitives can also be used in special sentences that begin with *it*. In these sentences, the infinitive is a delayed subject.

It's important *to solve* these problems. (To solve these
    problems is important.)
It's foolish *to start* so late. (To start so late is foolish.)

Sentences that begin with an infinitive and sentences with an infinitive as the delayed subject have similar meanings; however, those with delayed subjects are more common. Infinitives as delayed subjects may have subjects themselves, that is, the person or thing that will do the action of the infinitive. A prepositional phrase with *for* is used for the subject of the infinitive; it comes before the infinitive.

It's important *for you* to solve these problems.
It's foolish *for us* to start so late.

NOUN CLAUSES

2.19 Noun Clauses as Objects

Do you know *how far it is from here*?

Sometimes a noun clause can be used as the object of a verb, just as a noun phrase can.

OBJECT

I know
- that actor. (noun phrase)
- who played the part. (noun clause)
- the theater. (noun phrase)
- where the movie is playing. (noun clause)

Noun clauses can begin with *wh*-words; however, unlike questions that begin with *wh*-words, noun clauses use statement order (subject before the first verb).

QUESTION WORD ORDER		STATEMENT WORD ORDER
Who is the actor?	I know	who the actor is.
What was the movie?	I forgot	what the movie was.
Where is it playing?	Let's find out	where is it playing.
How far is it?	I don't know	how far it is.

Some noun clauses begin with the word *that,* and they are often found in sentences with verbs of communication.

The movie character
- admitted
- confessed
- swore
- whispered
- said

that he was a thief.

It is sometimes possible to leave out the word *that* without changing the meaning of the sentence.

> He said *that* he would go.
> He said he would go.

Noun clauses that are based on yes-no questions begin with the words *if* or *whether*.

> We asked *if* he could go to the movies with us.
> We didn't know *whether* he had enough money.

Noun clauses can also begin with indefinite pronouns, such as *whoever* or *whatever*.

> We can see *whatever you want to see.*

2.20 Noun Clauses as Subjects and Delayed Subjects

> It surprises me *that Louise invited us to her party.*

Noun clauses, like noun phrases, can be used as subjects of sentences.

SUBJECT

> That Louise would give herself a party   surprises me.
> Whoever goes to the party   will have fun.

When noun clauses are long, they are usually moved to the end of the sentence, and *it* is used as the subject. Sentences with *it* have the same meaning as sentences without *it;* however, sentences with *it* are more common.

> It really surprises me that she's giving herself a party. (That she's giving herself a party really surprises me.)
> It's well known that she's very shy. (That she's very shy is well known.)

Noun clauses beginning with *whoever* and *whatever* can be used to refer to someone or something that is not known at the time of speaking. In the following examples, *whoever* means "the person who," and *whatever* means "the thing that."

> *Whoever* arrives at the party first can help her get ready.
> *Whatever* you buy for a gift is all right with me.

COMPARING NOUN PHRASES

2.21 Comparison of Nouns and Noun Phrases

This store has *fewer* salespeople than the others.

One way to compare nouns is with the words *more, less, fewer, least,* and *fewest.*

They have *more* women's clothes in this store.
However, they have *less* furniture.
They have *fewer* books in the book department.

There are many other words and phrases that can be used for comparing things.

This dress is *the same* color as the jacket.
That shirt is *similar to* the one I bought last week.
That coat *looks like* a designer coat.
All those skirts are *alike.*

To contrast things that are different, negatives can be used.

This dress is *not the same* color as the jacket.
That shirt is *not similar to* the one I bought last week.
That coat *doesn't look like* a designer coat.
All those skirts are *not alike.*

In addition, contrasts can be made with words and phrases.

The blue blouse is *different from* the others.
This material is *inferior to* cotton.
These two colors *differ* quite a bit.

Certain nouns refer to size, measure, and quantity. Use *greater* rather than *more* when making affirmative comparisons about size, weight, height, cost, and population. *Higher* can also be used when comparing cost.

The weight of this desk is *greater* (not *more*) than the weight of that one.
The price of this book is much *higher* than the price of that one.

The comparative and superlative forms of adjectives are often used to compare nouns.

> This desk is *cheaper* than the others, but the *cheapest* ones are downstairs.

Chapter 3
Pronouns and Other Proforms

3.1   Defining Proforms

My neighbor has *a wonderful garden.*
He works in *it* every evening.

A proform can replace any part of a sentence, not just a noun or noun phrase. A pronoun, such as *it,* is one kind of proform. The verbs *do* and *does* are another kind.

He *works until five.*
His wife *does,* too.

The proform *does* is a substitute for the phrase *works until five* in the example above.

Personal pronouns have different forms for the first, second, and third persons. The term *first person* refers to the speaker(s). *Second person* refers to the listener(s). *Third person* refers to anything or anyone else.

PERSON	SUBJECT	OBJECT	POSSESSIVE ADJECTIVE	POSSESSIVE PRONOUN	REFLEXIVE
1	I	me	my	mine	myself
2	you	you	your	yours	yourself
3	he	him	his	his	himself
	she	her	her	hers	herself
	it	it	its		itself
1	we	us	our	ours	ourselves
2	you	you	your	your	yourselves
3	they	them	their	theirs	themselves

3.2   Demonstrative Pronouns

That's my camera.

There are four demonstrative pronouns in English. *This* is used for a single thing or person that is near the speaker; *these* is the plural form of *this. That* is used for a single thing or person that is far from the speaker; *those* is the plural form of *that.*

Look at *these* cameras. They're really excellent.
That's a good camera over there, but it's expensive.

That's is a contraction (shortened form) of *that is. This is, these are,* and *those are* do not have contracted forms.

Those are (not *Those're)* our best cameras.

The phrase *this is* (plus a name) is often used to identify the caller at the beginning of a telephone conversation. *This* and *that* can refer to something that will follow. They can also refer to something that has been said or written previously, as in the following telephone conversation.

Hi! *This* is Bill. Listen to *this!* There's a big sale at the camera store. Cameras are half price. *That's* quite a saving.

3.3 Subject and Object Pronouns

They're watching *us.*

Subject pronouns are usually used as the subject of a sentence. When they are followed by *am, is,* or *are,* the subject pronouns and the verbs are often contracted (shortened).

I'm (I am) from a large family.
You're (You are) lucky. I brought some pictures.
That's (That is) my brother. *He's* (He is) fourteen.
That's (That is) my sister. *She's* (She is) only six.
It's (It is) small, but *it's* (it is) home.
They're (They are) my parents.

The forms *it's* and *they're* sound the same as the possessive adjectives *its* and *their* but have different meanings.

It's (It is) a beautiful horse.
Its (The horse's) name is Sarwar.

They're (My parents are) very old now.
Their (My parents') home is in Beirut.

It is important not to omit the subject pronouns in a sentence.

CORRECT   Everyone admires Sarwar because *he* is a
            beautiful horse.
INCORRECT *Everyone admires Sarwar because is a
            beautiful horse.

Object pronouns are used for direct objects, indirect objects, and objects of prepositions.

My sister is in Germany. I miss *her.* (direct object)
My parents are in Beirut. I worry about *them.* (object of
   preposition)
My parents are too old to work. I send *them* money every
   month. (indirect object)

Subject pronouns usually come near the beginning of sentences
and clauses; object pronouns usually come near the end of
phrases and clauses.

SUBJECT PRONOUN		OBJECT PRONOUN	
I	write to	them	frequently.
They	write to	me	quite often, too.

In very formal English, a subject pronoun is used after the linking
verb *be,* as in the following telephone conversation:

Student: May I speak to Professor Miller, please.
Professor: This is *he.*

However, in informal spoken English, most people use an object
pronoun after the linking verb *be.*

Jane: Who's there?
Mary: It's *me.*

In formal English, *one* and *one's* are used for people in general.
In informal English, *you* and *your* are used this way.

FORMAL   One should choose *one's* courses carefully.
INFORMAL   You should choose *your* courses carefully.

When making comparisons, a subject pronoun sometimes comes
at the end of a sentence because part of the sentence is omitted.

Professor Sato knows more about biology than I *do.*
Professor Sato knows more about biology than I.

3.4 Possessive Adjectives and Pronouns

You can carry *your* packages, and I'll carry *mine.*

Possessive adjectives agree with the possessor and not with the
thing possessed. Possessive pronouns are used in place of the
possessive adjective and noun.

		POSSESSIVE ADJECTIVE + NOUN		POSSESSIVE PRONOUN
		my packages.		mine?
You		your packages.		yours?
He		his packages.		his?
She	can carry	her packages.	Are these	hers?
We		our packages.		ours?
They		their packages.		theirs?

Although possessive nouns have apostrophes, possessive adjectives and pronouns do not.

Yoko: Isn't that your *mother's* package?
Maria: It's probably *her* new dress. Then again, it may not be *hers*.

3.5 Introductory *There* and *It*

a. *There*

There's a fireplace in the living room.

The introductory *there* usually comes at the beginning of a statement and is followed by a linking verb, usually a form of *be*.

There's (There is) a nice apartment available near here.

The introductory *there* cannot be omitted.

CORRECT   *There* is a new refrigerator in the kitchen.
INCORRECT   *Is a new refrigerator in the kitchen.

In sentences with the introductory *there*, the verb agrees with the noun that follows the linking verb.

There is one window in the bedroom.
There are two windows in the living room.
There was a mop in the kitchen.
There were some dishes in the sink.

In written English, the linking verb *is* can be contracted to -'s after the introductory *there*, but *are, was,* and *were* are not contracted.

CORRECT   There's a big bathtub in the apartment.
            There are two sinks in the basement.
INCORRECT   *There're two dishes on the table.

Note the use of introductory *there* in yes-no questions and short answers.

Is	there	a shower?	Yes, there is.
Are	there	any closets?	Yes, there are.
Is	there	a dishwasher?	No, there isn't.

Note the use of introductory *there* in the question-word questions.

| How many outlets | are | there | in the living room? |
| How much wood | is | there | in the shed? |

The introductory *there* is spelled the same as the adverb *there*, but there is a difference in stress. The adverb *there* is stressed, but the introductory *there* is not.

Sally: Where's the BROOM?
Kate: It's over THERE.
Sally: Do you have a MOP?
Kate: There's one in the CLOSET.

There is sometimes confused with the words *their* and *they're*. These words sound the same but have different meanings.

There are new tiles in the bathroom. (introductory *there*)
They're (They are) going to rent the apartment to me.
Their (The owners') son lives downstairs.

b. *It*

When *it's* Monday in New York, *it's* Tuesday in China.

The introductory *it* is a pronoun that is used in the subject position of a sentence. It does not stand for a noun in the same way that other proforms do.

James: Mark, is *it* really you?
Mark: Yes, *it* is.
James: How is *it* in China?
Mark: *It's* exciting.

The introductory *it* is often used to describe the weather.

It's really hot in Beijing today.
It was nice yesterday.

The introductory *it* can also be used in sentences about time, days, dates, temperature, or distance.

Mark: Hello. I'm calling from my hotel. What time is *it* in New York?

James: *It's* one o'clock in the morning. What day is *it* in China?

Mark: *It's* Tuesday. *It's* July 17 here.

The introductory *it* is often used with adjectives such as *easy, difficult, important, impossible, enjoyable, fun, hard,* and so on. These words often describe the opinion of the speaker.

It's difficult   to learn Chinese.
It's important   for me to be here.
It's strange   that there are no telephones in the room.

The true subjects of these sentences follow the adjectives. These subjects are called delayed subjects. All the sentences can be restated with the delayed subjects coming first.

To learn Chinese   is difficult.
To be here   is important for me.
That there are no
    telephones in the room   is strange.

3.6 Quantifiers and Numbers Used as Pronouns

All of the furniture is on the truck.

Quantifiers and numbers sometimes function as pronouns and come before prepositional phrases beginning with *of*. The noun phrases in the prepositional phrases usually begin with determiners such as *the, this,* or *my*.

Three of these chairs are broken.
Lots of our things are very old.
Much of this furniture belonged to my mother.

Different quantifiers are used depending on whether the noun that follows is countable or uncountable.

COUNTABLE   Not many of the *dishes* match. (Few of the dishes match.)

UNCOUNTABLE   Not much of that *furniture* is new. (Little of that furniture is new.)

The following chart shows which of the quantifiers are used with countable nouns, singular and plural, and with uncountable nouns.

COUNTABLE—SINGULAR

Each
Either } of the rooms is going to be painted.
Neither

COUNTABLE—PLURAL

All
Half } of the chairs are old.
None
Both

A lot } of the dishes were missing.
Lots

A few
Many
Some
Several } of the plates are broken.
A couple
Five
Not many

UNCOUNTABLE

All
Half } of the furniture is new.
None

A lot } of damage was done.
Lots

A little
Much } of the china was damaged.
Not much
Some

Except when *each, either,* or *neither* is used, the verb agrees with the noun in the *of* phrase.

| A lot of the | dishes | were | damaged. |
| A lot of the | furniture | was | very dirty. |

For formal English, a singular verb is always used after *each, either,* and *neither.*

| Each | of the cups | was | wrapped in paper. |
| Neither | of the new chairs | is | here. |

The word *of* can be omitted after *all, half,* and *both* before a noun, but not before a personal pronoun, such as *them.*

Both of those chairs are broken.
Both those chairs are broken.
All of them should be checked.

When the noun in the prepositional phrase has already been mentioned, the entire prepositional phrase can be omitted.

Look at these cups.
Several (of the cups) are broken.

3.7 *Wh*-words

Who did it?

The words *who, whom, whose, what, which, when, where,* and *why,* are called *wh*-words. *How* is also a *wh*-word. These words are used in questions.

Why did he do it?
What did he take?

They are also used as introductory words for noun, adverbial, and relative clauses (dependent clauses).

Tell me *what* you know.
When you get to the house, call me.
The person *who* robbed you must know the house.

The word order after *wh*-words is different in questions and in dependent clauses.

QUESTION WORD ORDER

WH-WORD	AUXILIARY VERB OR *BE*	SUBJECT	MAIN VERB
What	did	the robber	steal?
When	did	the robbery	occur?
Where	were	you?	

STATEMENT WORD ORDER

	WH-WORD	SUBJECT	VERB
I'd like to know	what	he	stole.
Do you know	when	the robbery	occurred?
I need to know	where	you	were.

It is incorrect to use question word order in dependent clauses.

INCORRECT   *I'd like to know what did he steal.
            *Do you know when did the robbery occur?

Different *wh*-words have different uses. The pronouns *who* and *whom* refer to people. In conversation, *who* is generally used except directly after prepositions.

Officer: Who saw the man buy the radio?
Kim: I did.
Officer: Is the *man* to whom you sold it in this room?
Kim: Yes, he is.

In formal written English, *whom* is used to replace all direct objects, indirect objects, and objects of prepositions.

FORMAL   The woman *whom* I called is a lawyer. (direct
           object)
INFORMAL   The woman *who* I called is a lawyer.

Whose is the possessive form of *who*.

Officer: Whose jewelry was stolen?
Mrs. Jones: *My* necklace was. The people *whose* money was
             in the safe are very upset.

Whose is pronounced the same as the contraction *who's*. Do not confuse these two words.

Officer: Whose purse is this? (Who does this purse
             belong to?)
Mrs. Jones: It's mine.
Officer: *Who's* usually at home in the evening? (Who is
             usually home in the evening?)
Mrs. Jones: My sister.

What is usually used to refer to things or events.

Officer: *What* was taken from this room?
Mrs. Jones: They took a *silver teapot.*
Officer: What were you doing at the time?
Mrs. Jones: We were *sleeping.*

The expression *what . . . for* often means "why" or "for what purpose."

What do you need an assistant *for?* (Why do you need an assistant?)
What did you close the door *for?* (Why did you close the door?)

In questions, *which* is used when there is a choice to be made. Use *which* when choosing from a specific number of things or people.

Officer: You had three TV sets, but I see only two. Which one is missing?
Mrs. Jones: The Sony.

What can also be used for choices, but the speaker usually does not have a limited number of possibilities in mind. Compare these questions:

What is missing?
All three purses are here. *Which* one is yours?

In relative clauses, *which* refers to things rather than to people (see 7.10).

CORRECT   The *stereo system,* which is very heavy, was stolen.
INCORRECT   *The thief, which is very strong, was caught the next day.

When refers to time.

Officer: When did you hear a noise?
Mrs. Jones: I heard footsteps *at five o'clock.* Ask the cook when she went to the kitchen.

Where refers to places.

Officer: Where were you last night?
Mrs. Jones: We were *at a concert.* It was at the Music Center.
Officer: *I don't know where* the Music Center is.

Why refers to causes or reasons.

Officer:	Why did you take out new insurance last week?
Mrs. Jones:	We did it *because our neighbors were robbed.*
Officer:	Why did you turn down the heat last night?
Mrs. Jones:	*We did it to save money.* I wonder *why* the thief came last night.

How, when used alone, tells in what manner or to what degree.

Officer:	*How* did he get in?
Mrs. Jones:	He entered *by breaking a window.* The police discovered *how* he did it right away.
Officer:	*How* did he open the safe?
Mrs. Jones:	He cut it open *with a blowtorch.*

How much and *how many* ask about quantity. *How much* is used before uncountable nouns, and *how many* is used before countable nouns.

Officer:	*How much* money was in the safe?
Mrs. Jones:	There was at least *four thousand dollars.*
Officer:	*How many* people were here last night?
Mrs. Jones:	There were *ten people* in the house.

How is also used before adjectives and adverbs.

Officer:	*How often* are you away in the evening?
Mrs. Jones:	We go out *every Wednesday.*
Officer:	*How long* are you away?
Mrs. Jones:	We are usually gone *for four or five hours.*
Officer:	*How tall* is that fence?
Mrs. Jones:	It's about *ten feet high.*

3.8 Reflexive and Reciprocal Pronouns

I looked in the mirror and laughed at *myself.*

Reflexive pronouns usually refer to someone already named in the sentence.

He hurt *himself* right before the hockey game.

Singular reflexive pronouns end in *-self,* and plural ones end in *-selves.* In the first and second persons, the first part of the reflexive pronoun is similar to the corresponding possessive adjective. In the third person, the first part of the reflexive pronoun is similar to the corresponding object pronoun.

POSSESSIVE ADJECTIVES	REFLEXIVE PRONOUNS	OBJECT PRONOUNS
my	myself	
your	yourself	
	himself	him
	herself	her
	itself	it
our	ourselves	
your	yourselves	
	themselves	them

A phrase containing *by* and a reflexive pronoun means "alone" or "with no one else." Sometimes the word *by* can be omitted.

She made the goal *by herself* (alone).
She did it *herself* (by herself).

Sometimes reflexive pronouns are used to give emphasis to a noun. These reflexive pronouns come right after the noun or at the end of the sentence.

The manager *himself* yelled at the referee.
The manager examined the ice *himself.*

The reciprocal pronouns *each other* and *one another* have a different meaning from those of reflexive pronouns.

The manager and the referee yelled at *each other.* (The manager yelled at the referee, and the referee yelled at the manager.)
Finally, they laughed at *one another.* (The manager laughed at the referee, and the referee laughed at the manager.)

The pictures below show the difference in meaning between *themselves* and *each other* or *one another.*

The players poured champagne on *themselves.*

They congratulated *one another.* Then they poured champagne on *each other.*

3.9 Indefinite Pronouns

My suitcase is broken. I need a new *one.*

Use the indefinite pronoun when you do not have a particular person or thing in mind. Pronouns such as *somebody, everything,* and *whoever* are indefinite pronouns. *One* is sometimes an indefinite pronoun and sometimes a definite pronoun.

a. *One*

Use the indefinite pronoun *one* when you are referring to a kind of object or person in general, not a particular object or person. *One* is used only with singular, countable nouns.

Kim: I need a suitcase. I'll look for *one* today.
Lee: I like this suitcase. How much is *it* (not *one*)?

The pronoun *one* can also be preceded by adjectives and definite determiners. When definite determiners, such as *the, this,* or *my,* and adjectives precede *one,* a particular noun is referred to.

Kim: Which *one* do you like?
Lee: I like the leather *one.* It looks like my old *one.*

The plural form *ones* can also come after a determiner or a determiner and an adjective. *Ones* can occur after *the* and *which* but not directly after *these* and *those.*

CORRECT *Which ones* have you looked at?
I looked at *the ones* over there.
Those big ones are expensive.

INCORRECT *Did you see those ones?

b. Compound Indefinite Pronouns

The following words are compound pronouns that do not refer to a particular person or thing.

everyone	someone	anyone	no one
everybody	somebody	anybody	nobody
everything	something	anything	nothing
everywhere	somewhere	anywhere	nowhere

Singular verbs are used with compound pronouns. This is true even with *everyone* and *everybody*, which mean "all the people."

> Everyone *is* waiting.
> *Is* everything ready?

Compound pronouns beginning with *any* are usually used in questions and negative sentences. Compound pronouns beginning with *some* are used in affirmative sentences and sometimes in questions.

> Kenji: I need *something* to write with. Do you have *anything*?

> Yoko: I have a pen, but I don't have *anything* to write on. Do you have *something* to write on?

Modifiers come after compound indefinite pronouns. Notice the position of the modifiers in the following sentences.

> I hope he talks about *something interesting*.
> Did I miss *anything important*?
> There was really *nothing new*.

Else means "in addition" or "other" and is often used after compound indefinite pronouns.

> I know you want to meet Dr. Wong, but there's *somebody else* (another person) I want you to meet first.
> Let's not talk about school; I have to talk to you about *something else* (another subject).
> We had to meet in the gym; we couldn't hold the conference *anywhere else* (another place).

c. *Wh*-compounds

The following compound pronouns have meanings very similar to those of the *wh*-words that they begin with.

Whoever (the person who) wrote that article isn't a very
good writer.
Buy *whatever* (anything that) you want, but don't forget to
buy me a newspaper.
Buy *whichever* one (anyone that) you find at the newsstand.
You can have the comics *whenever* (any time that) you want
them.
Wherever (every place that) I look, I find stories about
murders.

In questions, the *ever* compounds are emphatic (stronger) forms
of the *wh*-words. For example, the words *whoever* and *whatever*
cause the following questions to be more emphatic or to show
surprise.

Who wrote that story? *Whoever* wrote that story? I can't
imagine!
What are they trying to do? *Whatever* are they trying to do?
They must be crazy!

Sometimes *whatever* or *whatsoever* are used to make a negative
statement more emphatic.

They had no business *whatever* writing that story.
You shouldn't believe a word of it *whatsoever*.

In adverbial clauses, the *ever* forms imply the idea "it doesn't
matter . . ."

Whatever happens, don't talk to any reporters. (It doesn't
matter what happens, . . .)
Whoever calls, tell them I'm not here. (It doesn't matter who
calls, . . .)

d. *Another, others, the other,* and *the others*

Another and *others* can be used as pronouns without a noun after
them. They should be used when the speaker has no definite person or thing in mind.

Karen: Have a cookie.
Eric: Thanks.
Karen: Please take *another*. There are plenty of *others* in the
kitchen.

The other and *the others* are used when specific people or things
are referred to.

Karen: There are two cookies left. Someone ate *the others.*
Eric: If you eat one, I'll eat *the other.*

3.10 Pronouns in Indirect Speech

She said that *she* wanted to see *me.*

Pronouns are used differently in indirect speech (words that are reported to someone) than they are in direct speech (the exact words). Compare the examples in this conversation between a police officer and a lawyer.

Carlos: What did Ms. Mendoza say to you on the telephone?
Maria: She said that *she* wanted to see *me.*
Carlos: What were her exact words?
Maria: She said, "*I* want to see *you* today." *She* asked *me* to go to *her* house.
Carlos: What were her exact words?
Maria: She asked, "Can *you* come to *my* house at three o'clock?"

In direct speech, the exact words of the speaker are used. In indirect speech, the pronouns are changed to reflect the point of view of the person who reports the speech.

She said, "*I* want to see *you.*" (direct speech)
She said that *she* wanted to see me. (indirect speech)
She asked, "Can *you* come to *my* house at three o'clock?" (direct speech)
She asked *me* to go to *her* house at three o'clock. (indirect speech)

In addition to the changes in pronouns, there are often differences in verb tenses (see section 6.5b).

3.11 Pronoun Agreement

Maria will be here soon. I want you to meet *her.*

Pronouns must agree with the nouns that they replace; that is, they must be the same in person, number, and gender (male or female).

Maria is a wonderful woman. *She* will be here soon. I want
you to meet *her.* (*she* and *her* = Maria)
Jaime is *her* husband. (*her* = Maria's) *He* will arrive later.
You can meet *him,* too. (*he* and *him* = Jaime)
His store closes at five o'clock. (*his* = Jaime's)

Some pronouns, such as *he* and *she,* refer to people and not to
things. Sometimes these pronouns are also used for animals,
especially pets. Other pronouns, such as *it,* are used for things
and most animals, and sometimes babies.

Maria painted this picture. *She* (Maria) is very good. *It* (the
picture) is very professional.

The pronouns *they, their,* and *them* are used for both people and
things.

Maria and Jaime live in Los Angeles. *They* (Maria and
Jaime) enjoy the city.
Jaime sells musical instruments. He repairs *them* (the
musical instruments), too.

The *wh*-words *who, whom,* and *whose* refer only to people.

Maria is the artist *who* painted this picture.

In relative clauses, *which* is used for things and animals.

Her first picture, *which* she painted when she was nineteen,
now hangs in a museum.

The pronoun *one* replaces noun phrases that begin with *a* or *an.*

Would you like a *picture* of the museum, or would you like
like *one* (not *it* or *that*) of the downtown area?

The demonstrative pronouns *this, that, these,* and *those* replace
noun phrases that begin with *the.*

Do you like *the photographs* by Cunningham or *those* by
Adams?

3.12 Proforms *So, Not,* and *Do*

Luis: Can you find the construction company easily?
Maria: I hope *so.*

Proforms are words that are used so that phrases and clauses do not have to be repeated. The proform *so* is often used after verbs such as *say, think, believe, hope,* and *expect.*

Luis: Is the construction company hiring people today?
Maria: I think *so*. (I think that the construction company
            is hiring people today.)
Luis: Do they need any laborers?
Maria: I believe *so*. (I believe that they need some
            laborers.)
Luis: Will there be any jobs next week?
Maria: I don't think *so*. (I don't think that there will be
            any jobs next week.)

The proform *not* is used like *so*, but it replaces negative phrases and clauses.

Luis: Are they going to hire anyone else today?
Maria: I guess *not*. (I guess they are not going to hire
            any one else today.)
Luis: Is this the only company hiring today?
Maria: I hope *not*. (I hope this is not the only company
            hiring today.)

The proform *do* replaces a verb or verb phrase.

I need a job, and my friend *does,* too. (My friend needs a
    job, too.)
I worked on construction last year, and he *did,* too. (He
    worked on construction last year, too.)

Chapter 4

Verbs and Verb Tenses

PAST TIME

POSSIBLE OR IMAGINARY EVENTS

PASSIVE VERBS

4.1 Names and Forms of Verb Tenses

a. Traditional Tenses

The traditional names of the verb tenses are listed as follows. According to traditional grammar, the imperative is a mood, not a tense; however, it is listed with the tenses for convenience. In these sentences, all the verbs are in the active voice. The passive verbs are discussed in sections 4.24–4.30.

IMPERATIVE	*Enjoy* yourself.
SIMPLE PRESENT	Mr. Tanaka *enjoys* classical music. His children *enjoy* jazz.
SIMPLE PAST	They all *enjoyed* last week's concert.
PRESENT CONTINUOUS	He *is traveling* in the United States. His children *are traveling* with him.
PAST CONTINUOUS	When I talked to him, he *was enjoying* the trip. The children *were enjoying* it, too.
PRESENT PERFECT	He *has traveled* to many cities. They *have been* to many concerts.
MODAL PERFECT	They *could have traveled* by plane.
FUTURE	They *will travel* by plane the next time.
FUTURE CONTINUOUS	They *will be traveling* with friends.
MODAL CONTINUOUS	They *must be enjoying* the concert now.
PRESENT PERFECT CONTINUOUS	Mr. Tanaka *has been traveling* too long.
PAST PERFECT	Before he left, he *had planned* to travel for two weeks.
PAST PERFECT CONTINUOUS	They were sorry to leave because they *had been enjoying* the concert.
FUTURE PERFECT	They *will have visited* fifteen states by August.
FUTURE PERFECT CONTINUOUS	By September they *will have been traveling* for twelve weeks.
MODAL PERFECT CONTINUOUS	They *could have been traveling* by plane, but they weren't.

b. Main Verbs and Auxiliary Verbs

Verb tenses made up of more than one word are called verb phrases. Verb phrases are made up of main verbs and auxiliary (helping) verbs. The main verb is always the last verb in the verb phrase. There may be one, two, or three auxiliary verbs before the main verb.

	AUXILIARY VERBS	MAIN VERB	
That mechanic		repairs	cars.
She	is	repairing	a car.
She	has been	working	for a long time.
She	will have been	working	for two hours soon.

There are only a few auxiliary verbs. The auxiliary verbs are *be, have, do,* and the modals. The modals are *can, could, will, would, shall, should, may, might,* and *ought to* (see Chapter 5).

Be, have, and *do* are auxiliary verbs, but they can also be main verbs if they are the only verb or the final verb in a verb phrase.

	AUXILIARY VERB	MAIN VERB	
My mechanic		*has*	an old garage.
She	*has*	fixed	my car many times.

c. Verb Forms

Verb forms combine to make the verb tenses. Most verbs have five forms. Here are the forms for the regular verbs *practice, work,* and *study.*

SIMPLE FORM	PRESENT -S	PAST -ED	PAST PARTICIPLE -ED/-EN	PRESENT PARTICIPLE -ING
practice	practices	practiced	practiced	practicing
work	works	worked	worked	working
study	studies	studied	studied	studying

The simple form is the basic verb form. All other forms are made by adding -s, -ed, or -ing to the simple form. The past form and the past participle form are the same for regular verbs. They are usually different for irregular verbs.

SIMPLE FORM	PRESENT -S	PAST -ED	PAST PARTICIPLE -ED/-EN	PRESENT PARTICIPLE -ING
have	has	had	had	having
do	does	did	done	doing
eat	eats	ate	eaten	eating

d.   Order of Verb Forms in Verb Tenses

In active sentences, the order of verb forms in a verb phrase is very predictable.

1 PRESENT/ PAST/ MODAL	2 SIMPLE FORM	3 PAST PARTICIPLE	4 PRESENT PARTICIPLE
He eats.			
He ate.			
He has		eaten.	
He has		been	eating.
He might	have	been	eating.

Remember the following rules for the order of verb forms:

1. The first verb in a verb phrase is always a present, past, modal, or simple form.

      1   4
Martha Robles is working on gymnastics.

      1
She practiced for four hours yesterday.

      2
Gymnasts practice hard.

2. When the auxiliary verb is *do, does,* or *did* or a modal, the next verb is in the simple form.

     1   2
Martha did not practice this morning.

    1   2

Does she usually practice in the morning?

        1   2

She should practice this afternoon.

3. When the auxiliary verb is *have, has,* or *had,* the next verb is always the past participle.

    1   3

She has practiced for ten hours this week.

     1   2   3

She could have gone to the gym this morning.

4. In active sentences, when the auxiliary verb is a form of *be* (*am, are, is, was, were, been*), the next verb is the present participle.

    1   4

She was leaving school when I saw her.

    1   2   3   4

She might have been going to the gymnasium.

4.2 The First Auxiliary Verb

    Masayo: *Do* they live in Los Angeles?
    Yoko: Yes, they *do.*

The first auxiliary verb is important. In questions, the first auxiliary verb comes before the subject.

    Masayo: My brother *has* been living in Seattle.
    Yoko: *Has* he been living there long?

In short answers, the first auxiliary is used as a proform (substitute) for the complete verb phrase.

    Masayo: No, he *hasn't.*

In negative statements, the word *not* comes after the first auxiliary verb.

    Masayo: He has *not* been living there long.

Since the simple present and the simple past tenses do not have auxiliary verbs, the auxiliaries *do, does,* or *did* are used in negative sentences, questions, and short answers.

Masayo: He likes Seattle. He *does* not like the rain.
Yoko: *Does* he like Los Angeles?
Masayo: No, he *doesn't*.

a.   Negative Sentences

He *isn't* going to sing.

In negative sentences, *not* comes after the first auxiliary verb.

	FIRST AUXILIARY		
Sam	is	not	singing well.
He	was	not	singing before.
He	is	not	going to sing.
He	will	not	sing anymore.
He	will	not	be singing here.
He	has	not	sung here before.
He	had	not	sung that song.

	CONTRACTION	
He	isn't	good.
He	wasn't	there.
He	isn't	ready.
He	won't	listen.
He	won't	have time.
He	hasn't	practiced.
He	hadn't	tried.

When the only verb is *be (am, is, are, was, were)*, use *not* after it in negative sentences.

He is a singer.
He is *not* a good singer.

When there are no auxiliary verbs, add the auxiliary verb *do (does, did)* in negative sentences (except when the verb is *be*).

He sings badly.
He *does* not sing well.
He sang five songs last night.
He *did* not sing them in English.

When the main verb in negative sentences follows *do, does,* or *did,* it is in the simple form, not in the present form ending with *-s* nor in the past form with *-ed.*

b. Yes–No Questions

Is she studying French?

Yes-no questions usually begin with the first auxiliary verb. Notice the form of the yes-no questions in these tenses.

	FIRST AUXILIARY			
PRESENT CONTINUOUS	Is	she	studying	Italian?
PAST CONTINUOUS	Was	he	studying	Italian?
GOING TO FUTURE	Is	she	going to study	Spanish?
WILL FUTURE	Will	they	study	Greek?
FUTURE CONTINUOUS	Will	you	be working?	
PRESENT PERFECT	Has	she	spoken	to you?
PAST PERFECT	Had	they	said	anything?
PRESENT PERFECT CONTINUOUS	Has	he	been studying	English?

When the only verb is a form of *be (am, is, are, was, were)*, it usually comes before the subject of the yes-no question.

He is a North American.
Is she a North American?

In a yes-no question, add the auxiliary verb *do (does, did)* to other verbs that do not have an auxiliary.

Naima:	She speaks many languages.
Fatima:	*Does* she speak French?
Naima:	He spoke Finnish as a child.
Fatima:	*Did* he speak Swedish at home?

The main verb is in the simple form after the auxiliary verb *do*, never in the present form ending with *-s* or the past form with *-ed*.

Naima:	She went to Toronto.
Fatima:	Did she *go* (not *went*) to Montreal, too?

c. *Wh*-word Questions

When did you work for Union Bank?

Wh-word questions ask for information and begin with the words *where, when, why, what, who, whom, whose, which,* and *how.* In most *wh*-word questions, the word order after the *wh*-word is the same as that of yes-no questions.

AUXILIARY VERB	SUBJECT	MAIN VERB	
When	did	he	work	for Union Bank?
Why	is	he	leaving	that job?
How	long will	he	work	for us?

In questions where the *wh*-word is part of the subject, use statement word order, that is, the subject before the verb. Do not use *do, does,* or *did.*

SUBJECT	VERB	
Who	checked	his references?
Which department	needs	him?

d.   Short Answers

John: Is the woman winning the chess game?
Anna: Yes, she *is.*

Short answers usually include only the first auxiliary verb, and they can be affirmative or negative. In negative short answers, the auxiliary and *not* can be contracted.

John: Are they playing chess?
Anna: Yes, they *are.*
John: Is the man enjoying the game?
Anna: No, he *isn't (is + not).*

When the only verb is *be,* use that in the short answer. With verbs other than *be* that don't have an auxiliary, use *do, does,* or *did* in the short answer.

John: The man is a good chess player.
Anna: Is the woman a good chess player?
John: Yes, she *is.* She won the game.
Anna: Did she win the game easily?
John: Yes, she *did.*

When a yes-no question is used to start a conversation, a short answer alone often means that the speaker wants to end the conversation or change the topic.

    John: Do you play chess?
    Anna: Yes, I do.

When a speaker is willing to continue a conversation, more than a short answer is given.

    John: Do you play chess?
    Anna: No, I don't. I'd like to learn, though.

e.   Tag Questions

You remember Anita Choi, *don't you*?

A tag question can turn a statement into a yes-no question. Affirmative statements usually have negative tag questions, and negative statements usually have affirmative tag questions. The verb in the tag question is the first auxiliary verb, the verb *be*, or the auxiliary *do*.

Anita *is* working for an advertising agency,	*isn't* she?
She *has* worked there for several years,	*hasn't* she?
She's a manager now,	*isn't* she?
She *hasn't* been a manager for long,	*has* she?

With verbs that have no auxiliaries (except *be*), use *do*, *does*, or *did* in tag questions.

Anita worked on an ad campaign for you,	*didn't* she?
She still writes ads,	*doesn't* she?

Most tag questions have yes-no question intonation, which rises at the end, when the speaker is unsure of the answer. However, a tag question can end with statement intonation, which falls at the end, when the speaker expects the listener to agree with the statement.

You don't know what she earns, do you?

She's done very well for herself, hasn't she?

PRESENT TIME

4.3 Imperatives and Suggestions

> *Start* the car.

Use the simple form of the verb when you give directions or instructions.

> *Stop* at the red light.
> Then *turn* left and *drive* to the corner.

For negative imperatives, use *do not* or *don't* before the simple form of the verb.

> *Don't* turn right.
> *Don't* hit that police car!

Use *please* to make an imperative more polite.

> *Please* show me your license.
> Sign here, *please*.

A very polite request usually begins with a modal such as *would* or *could*.

> *Could* you please sign here?
> *Would* you mind unlocking the trunk?

Many polite requests are in the form of questions.

> Why don't you sit down?
> Would you like to take off your coat?

Suggestions and imperatives can be for the listener alone, for the listener and the speaker, or for the speaker alone. Compare these examples.

FOR THE LISTENER	FOR THE LISTENER AND SPEAKER	FOR THE SPEAKER
Hurry!	Let's hurry!	
Don't be late.	Let's not be late.	Let me carry it.

4.4 Simple Present

a. The Verb *Be* in the Simple Present

He is ready for dinner.

The verb *be* has three forms in the simple present. These forms are usually contracted in spoken and informal written English.

| I | am | early. | I'm | early. |

You	are		You're	
We	are	} on time.	We're	} on time.
They	are		They're	

He	is		He's	
She	is	} here at last.	She's	} here at last.
It	is		It's	

You can make negatives in two ways with the verb *be*.

1. Put *not* after *am*, *are*, or *is* or after the contracted forms of those verbs with personal pronouns.

    Kim: Are you late?
    Lee: No, *I'm not*.

2. Add *-n't* to the verbs *is* and *are* but not to *am*.

| I'm | not hungry. | I am not | hungry. |

You're		You aren't	
We're	} not hungry.	We aren't	} hungry.
They're		They aren't	

He's		He isn't	
She's	} not ready.	She isn't	} ready.
It's		It isn't	

b. Forms of the Simple Present

After dinner, she *relaxes* on the sofa.

Use the *-s* form with third person singular subjects in the simple present tense. Use the simple form with all other subjects.

I			He		
You	} need a nap.		She	} *needs* a nap.
We			It		
They					

Use the following rules to spell the -s form correctly.

1. For most verbs, add -s to the simple form.

    I drink coffee.   He *drinks* tea.
    I read books.   He *reads* newspapers.

2. Add -es to verbs that end in o, s, z, sh, x, and ch (unless the ch is pronounced with the sound of k).

    I go to work early.   She *goes* to work late.
    I watch the news.   She *watches* the opera.

3. Omit a final -y and add -ies unless the letter a, e, i, o, or u comes before the -y.

    I hurry to work.   He *hurries* home.
    I buy the food.   He *buys* the furniture.

4. For the verb be, use the irregular form is. For the verb have, use the irregular form has.

    I am a good skier.   She *is* a good tennis player.
    I have good skis.   She *has* a good racket.

c. The Simple Present as Unspecified Time

    Eugene *is* a city in Oregon.

The simple present usually doesn't refer to a particular time. Use the simple present for facts and general statements that include the present and are true at any time.

    This road *goes* to Eugene.
    Eugene *is* a city in Oregon.
    My cousin *lives* in Eugene.
    He *owns* a truck.
    He *likes* Oregon.
    He even *enjoys* the climate.

In the preceeding examples, the facts are true at any time. Because the simple present is sometimes used for an unspecified time, it sometimes contrasts with the present continuous tense. The simple present refers to a relatively long or permanent period, whereas the present continuous refers to a relatively short or temporary period.

SIMPLE PRESENT UNSPECIFIED TIME	PRESENT CONTINUOUS SPECIFIED TIME
He *lives* in Oregon.	He *is living* in Eugene, but he plans to move soon.
He *works* for a moving company.	He *is working* ten-hour days this summer.

d. The Simple Present with Repeated Events

Athletes *get up* early.

Some verbs, such as *leave,* describe events that can be repeated.

Most students *leave* school at three.
Athletes *leave* after practice.

Use the simple present with these verbs to describe actions that are scheduled, habitual, or repeated.

Most people *sleep* eight hours a night.
Athletes *sleep* longer.
Most people *get up* late on weekends.
Athletes *get up* early on weekends.

When the simple present is used to describe habitual or repeated actions, frequency expressions, such as *always, often, usually,* or *every day,* are used to tell how often the event occurs.

Athletes *usually* go to bed early.

e. The Simple Present with Future Meaning

What time *does* the team *arrive* next Sunday?

The simple present can be used for future events that are scheduled or expected.

The team *arrives* at nine-thirty in the evening tomorrow.
The game *begins* at two in the afternoon next Sunday.
The parade *is* before the game.

When events are not scheduled or expected, use the *will* or *going to* future tense.

Our team *will win* (not *wins*) on Sunday.
It *will* probably *rain* (not *rains*) this weekend.

When a future tense (*will* or *going to*) is used in the main clause of a sentence, the verb in the dependent clause uses the simple present to express future meaning.

MAIN CLAUSE	DEPENDENT CLAUSE
The band *will play*	before the game *begins.*
She*'ll work*	while he *studies.*

f. **The Simple Present as the Narrative Present**

Jackson *hits* a home run!

The present continuous tense is usually used to describe events that are happening at the moment of speaking. However, in a few very special cases, the simple present is used to describe events that are happening at the moment of speaking. These special cases are events that have a known structure or set of rules, such as games, ceremonies, or experiments. In narrating a game, for example, sports announcers will use the simple present, but they change to the present continuous to describe events that are not part of the game. Note the verbs in the following description of part of a baseball game:

Jackson *hits* a line drive to left field. Gomez catches it on one bounce and *throws* it to Bergman. Bergman *tags* Jackson, and Jackson *is* out! Wait! Wait! It seems that Jackson is unhappy with the decision. Jackson *is shouting* and *waving* his arms at the umpire. Bergman *is walking* toward them.

g. **Time Expressions Used with the Simple Present**

Does she *always* go to bed so late?

The following words are called adverbs of frequency. They are often used with the simple present.

frequently	usually	sometimes	seldom
always	often	rarely	never

Adverbs of frequency come before the verb in the simple present tense. However, when the verb is *be (is, am, are)*, they follow it.

She *usually* gets up at nine.
She is *often* late for work.

Longer time expressions that describe repeated actions usually come at the beginning or the end of the sentence.

She rides the train *every morning*.
She buys a pass *every month*.
Once in a while, she misses the train.
From time to time, she drives her car.

4.5 Present Continuous

A little boy *is eating* an ice cream cone.

a. Forms of the Present Continuous

In the present continuous tense, the auxiliary verb *be (am, is, are)* is used with the *-ing* form of the main verb. The full forms and the contractions with *be* are as follows:

FULL FORMS	CONTRACTIONS
I am	I'm
you are	you're
we are	we're
they are	they're
he is	he's
she is	she's
it is	it's

These forms are used in sentences like the following:

They're eating cake.
He's enjoying it tremendously.

b. Present Continuous with Present Time

He *is cooking* dinner now.

The present continuous tense focuses on the moment of speaking. It is used to show that an action is not finished at the moment of speaking.

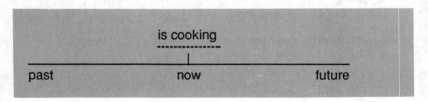

c.   Present Continuous with Future Intention

I *am leaving* tomorrow.

Use the present continuous to describe an intention or plan. The event is in the future, but the speaker's intention is in the present.

We *are leaving* for Mexico tomorrow at five in the afternoon.
My husband *is taking* two suitcases.

The present continuous is often used this way with travel verbs such as *go, come, arrive, leave,* and *land.*

Nancy: Where are you *going* for your vacation?
Judy: We *are going* to Mexico City.

The phrases *going to* and *going to go to* usually have the same meaning when showing present intention.

I'm *going to* Acapulco. (I'm *going to go to* Acapulco.)

Do not use the present continuous tense for future time unless there is present intention.

CORRECT   We *are stopping* in Texas.
                       We *are arriving* early in the morning.

INCORRECT   *It *is raining* in Mexico City tomorrow.
                       *A bus *is waiting* at seven o'clock tonight.

d.   Verbs Usually Not Used in Continuous Tenses

Certain verbs are usually not used in the continuous tenses. Some of these are verbs of preference *(like),* verbs of knowing *(understand),* linking verbs *(seem),* and verbs that refer to a mental state or to a permanent condition.

Note the following examples with verbs of preference:

He *wants* (not *is wanting*) a job in France.
He *likes* (not *is liking*) Europe.

The following verbs of preference are usually not used in the present continuous tense.

agree	distrust	like
appreciate	doubt	love
care	feel (believe)	need
detest	hate	prefer
disagree	hope	want
dislike	imagine	wish

Note the following examples with verbs of knowing:

I *know* (not *am knowing*) that man.
I *believe* (not *am believing*) he is an actor.

The following verbs of knowing are usually not used in the present continuous tense.

believe	know	remember
forget	recognize	suppose
imagine	recollect	think (believe)

Note the following examples with linking verbs:

He *is* (not *is being*) tall.
His wife *seems* (not *is seeming*) happy.
They *look* (not *are looking*) nice.

However, sometimes linking verbs are used in the present continuous tense if the sentence refers to a temporary state.

PERMANENT STATE	TEMPORARY STATE
She always *looks* sick.	She *is looking* sick today.
He *is* a foolish person.	He *is being* foolish right now.

Verbs that describe relatively permanent states do not usually occur in the present continuous tense.

She *owns* (not *is owning*) a Mercedes-Benz.
That car *costs* (not *is costing*) a lot.

The following verbs describe relatively permanent states rather than events or actions. They are not usually used in the present continuous tense.

appear	deserve	own
be	equal	possess
belong to	fit	require
concern	have (possess)	resemble
consist of	involve	seem
contain	look (appear)	sound
cost	matter	tend
depend on	owe	

Some verbs of perception are usually not used in the present continuous tense. These verbs, such as *hear, taste, smell, see,* and *feel,* describe actions that people do not consciously control. Other similar verbs, such as *look at, listen to,* and *touch,* describe actions that can be controlled. Verbs describing actions that can be controlled can be used in the present continuous.

CONTROL	NO CONTROL
I *am looking* at the parade.	I *see* (not *am seeing*) a clown.
I *am listening* to my friend.	I *hear* (not *am hearing*) music.
I *am touching* the traffic light.	I *feel* (not *am feeling*) a hand in my pocket.

e.   Time Expressions Used with the Present Continuous

Time expressions like *now, right now,* and *at this moment* are used in sentences like these.

> It's snowing *now.*
> *At this moment,* traffic is moving normally.

Other time expressions often used with the present continuous are:

at this time	this week/year/semester
for the time being	
for a short time	
currently	
temporarily	

They are used in sentences like the following:

> They're working for their father *temporarily.*

4.6   Simple Present versus Present Continuous

With most verbs, the present continuous shows that an action is in progress at the moment of speaking.

The simple present is often used to show that an action or event

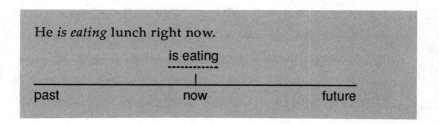

The simple present is often used to show that an action or event is repeated or habitual.

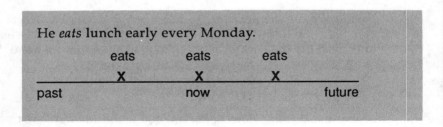

With some verbs, such as *live* and *work,* the simple present seems to refer to a longer period of time than the present continuous. The present continuous refers to a temporary period when used with these verbs.

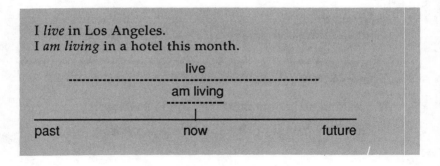

FUTURE TIME

4.7 Future with *Will*

a. Forms and Uses of *Will*

The wedding *will start* at three o'clock in the afternoon.

Use *will* for a future event or action. *Will* has the same form with all subjects.

There *will be* a cake at the reception.
I *will* probably *eat* a lot of cake.

Will sometimes suggests a promise.

Don't worry. I *will behave* myself.

The negative form of *will* is *will not* or its contraction, *won't*.

The reception *will not be* at the church.
It *won't last* long.

The use of *won't* sometimes suggests the idea of refusal.

My mother *won't drive* to the wedding. (She refuses to drive.)

b.   Time Expressions with *Will*

The parents will meet again *soon*.

These are some time expressions that are used with *will*.

at this time tomorrow	soon
next Monday/month/year	the day after tomorrow
on August 15	tomorrow
sometime	

They are used in sentences like the following:

They'll meet in New York *the day after tomorrow*.

4.8   Future with *Going To*

He's *going to* play tennis in a few minutes.

Use the following form for the *going to* future tense:

BE	+	GOING TO	+	MAIN VERB	
We	are	going to		go	on vacation.
I	am	going to		learn	how to ski.

Both *will* and *going to* are used for future actions and events. However, English speakers usually use the *going to* future when there is some present evidence that a future action or event will occur.

He has skis on top of his car. He's *going to* go skiing.
He's wearing a coat. He's *going to* leave soon.
His wife is pregnant. She *isn't going to* go skiing.

In most sentences with subjects that are not human, either *will* or *going to* can be used.

It *is* probably *going to* rain.
It *will* probably rain.

In questions, the *going to* future is used to ask about plans and intentions.

Where *are* you *going to* go tonight?
When *are* you *going to* come back?

The time expressions used with the *will* future can also be used with the *going to* future (see section 4.7b).

4.9 Future Continuous

a. Forms and Uses of the Future Continuous

David *will be bringing* a friend with him.

The future continuous is used for an action or event that will take place at a definite time in the future. The future continuous is formed in the following way:

	FUTURE MARKER +	BE +	-ING FORM	
Chris	will	be	leaving	the party early.
Gloria	is going to	be	staying	with me overnight.

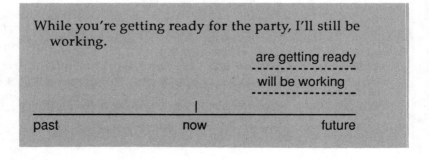

While you're getting ready for the party, I'll still be working.

are getting ready
- - - - - - - - - - - - - - - -
will be working
- - - - - - - - - - - - - - - -

past   now   future

When two actions will take place at the same time in the future, the future continuous can be used. It is often used this way in sentences with *when* or *while* clauses.

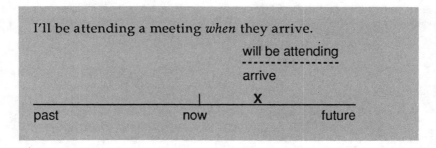

The future marker *will* is used only once in a sentence, even though both events refer to future time.

> I'll be working while you *are getting* (not *will be getting*) dressed.

Verbs that are not used in the present continuous are not used in the future continuous, either.

> You *will recognize* (not *will be recognizing*) him from the picture.
> He *will want* (not *will be wanting*) five dollars.

b.   Time Expressions Used with the Future Continuous

> The officials will be meeting *for another hour*.

Any time expression that can be used with the *will* or *going to* future can also be used with the future continuous. In addition, expressions that show the duration of an event or state are often used.

> for another hour/week/month
> until six o'clock/Monday/1998

4.10   Future Perfect

a.   Uses of the Future Perfect

> He *will have finished* the housework by noon.

The future perfect is used to describe an action that the speaker thinks will be completed before a specific future time.

The future perfect can also be used to talk about an event that may have happened.

> She usually eats lunch at twelve noon.
> It's one o'clock now.
> She *will have eaten* by now.

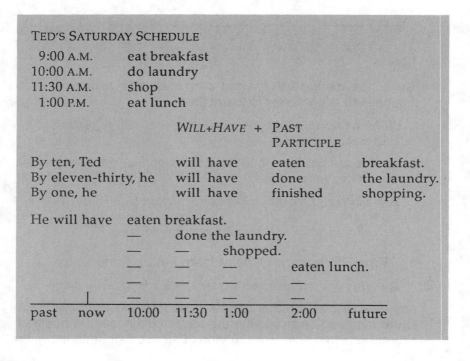

TED'S SATURDAY SCHEDULE

9:00 A.M.	eat breakfast
10:00 A.M.	do laundry
11:30 A.M.	shop
1:00 P.M.	eat lunch

	WILL+HAVE +	PAST PARTICIPLE	
By ten, Ted	will have	eaten	breakfast.
By eleven-thirty, he	will have	done	the laundry.
By one, he	will have	finished	shopping.

He will have	eaten breakfast.			
—	done the laundry.			
—	—	shopped.		
—	—	—	eaten lunch.	
—	—	—	—	

| past | now | 10:00 | 11:30 | 1:00 | 2:00 | future |

b. Time Expressions Used with the Future Perfect

> She will have eaten *by now*.

Prepositional phrases beginning with *by* and *before* are frequently used with the future perfect.

> by now (at or before the present moment)
> by noon (at or before noon)
> by Saturday (on or before Saturday)
> before evening/midnight/Sunday morning

These phrases are used in sentences like the following:

She will have written the report by six o'clock.

4.11   Contrasting the Future, Future Continuous, and Future Perfect

As the charts show, the following sentences have different meanings.

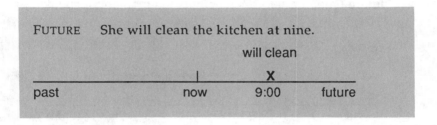

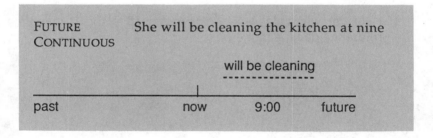

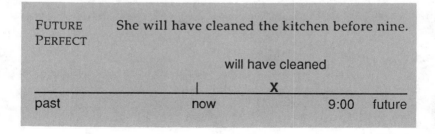

4.12   Past Future Tenses

I left work early because I *was going to* take a driving test.

The expressions *was going to* and *were going to* are used with actions that were, in the past, expected to occur.

I *was going to* borrow my cousin's car.
My cousin and his wife *were going to* drive me to the test.

Notice the different reference points when using *going to* for expressing future time. When *is/am/are going to* is used to show future time, the reference point is the moment of speaking.

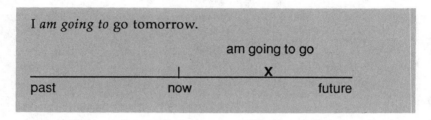

However, when *was/were going to* is used to show future time, the reference point is in the past.

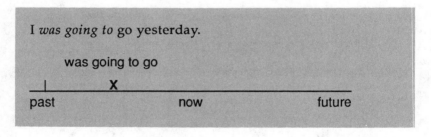

Sentences with *would* can also show future time with a reference point in the past.

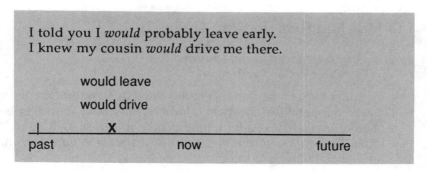

In contrast, sentences with *will* have a reference point in the present.

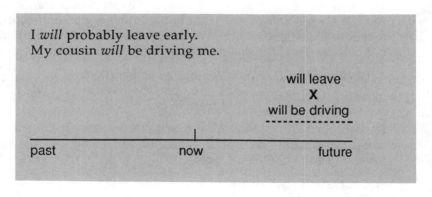

PAST TIME

4.13 The Past Form and Past Time

They *were* in Spain last summer.
I wish I *were* in Spain now.

The past form of the verb is usually used to show that an event or action happened in the past. However, the past form has other uses in English. It is a form that always shows some kind of "distance." When the verb forms express *distance in time,* they have the usual meaning of the past form—that is, past time.

They *were* in Spain.
They *went* last summer.

The past form is also sometimes used to expresses *distance from the speaker.* When people want to be formal or polite, they often stand or sit far apart. In the same way, it is possible to be formal or polite by using the distant, or past, form of the verb.

POLITE	*Will* you open the window.
MORE POLITE	*Would* you open the window. (*Would* is the past form of *will.*)

Another kind of distance from a speaker is indirect speech. By using the distant past form, speakers can show that they are repeating someone else's words.

Debbie:	I *see* our plane.
Tom:	What did she say?
Jill:	She *said* that she *saw* our plane.

For more examples of indirect speech, see section 6.5.

A final kind of distance is distance from reality. The past form sometimes shows that an event is imaginary.

My parents don't live in Spain.
They wish they *lived* there.
They aren't happy in Kansas.
If they *were* in Spain now, they *would* be happy.

In these sentences, the time is not past. The verb is in the past form because the event is not real.

4.14 Simple Past

a. *Was* and *Were*

It *was* a wonderful trip.

In the simple past, *be* has two forms, *was* and *were*.

I/He/She *was* in Puerto Rico last week.
We/You/They *were* there for a week.

In negative statements, *not* follows *was* or *were*. The contractions *wasn't* and *weren't* can also be used.

He *was not* in San Juan on Friday.
She *wasn't* there, either.
We *were not* in an expensive hotel.
They *weren't* near the beach.

Do not use the auxiliary verb *did* with *was* and *were* in negative statements, questions, or short answers.

Judy: The hotel was beautiful.
Nancy: *Was* it expensive?
Judy: No, it *wasn't*.
Nancy: It was near a beach, *wasn't* it?
Judy: Yes, it *was*.

b. Regular Past Tense Verbs

She *watched* television last night.

Use the simple past for events or states that are completed or finished before the moment of speaking.

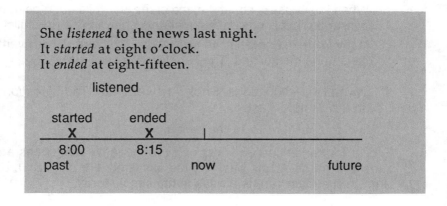

c.   Simple Past, Spelling

She *emptied* the wastepaper baskets.

The simple past is the *-ed* form of the verb. To make the *-ed* form for regular verbs, do the following:

1. Add *-ed* to the simple form of most verbs.	walk jump	walked jumped
2. Add *-d* to the simple form of verbs that end in *-e*.	arrive agree type	arrived agreed typed
3. For verbs that end in *-y* follow one of these procedures:	stay annoy	stayed annoyed
a. When the letter before the *y* is a vowel (a, e, i, o, u), simply add *-d*.	study try	studied tried
b. When the letter before the *-y* is not a vowel, change the *y* to *i* and add *-ed*.	perMIT ocCUR plan stop	permitted occurred planned stopped
4. When verbs end in one vowel and one consonant, repeat the consonant if the stress is at the end of the word or if the verb has only one syllable.	VISit TRAVel	visited traveled

When the stress is not at the end of the word, do not repeat the consonant. (This rule does not always apply in British English.)

Many verbs in English have an irregular past form. These verbs have to be memorized. They are listed in section 6.2.

d.   Negatives, Questions, Short Answers, and Tag Questions in the Simple Past

He *didn't put* money in the parking meter.

Except for sentences with *was* or *were,* negative sentences and questions in the simple past use the auxiliary verb *did.* When *did* is used, the main verb is always in the simple form.

She *parked* between the painted lines.
She *didn't park* between the painted lines.
Did he *close* the window?

In short answers and tag questions, only the auxiliary verb *did* is used.

She parked close to the curb, *didn't* she?
No, she *didn't*.

e. Simple Past in Indirect Speech

He *said* that our plane *was* late.

The past tense is often used after *said, told, asked, knew, thought,* and other such verbs (see section 6.5).

Announcer:	Flight 208 has been delayed by thirty minutes.
Kenji:	What did he say?
Yoko:	He *said* that our plane *was* delayed.

The use of the past form in indirect speech does not necessarily mean that the events have been completed or that they occurred in the past.

Kenji:	I like the food on this airline.
Yoko:	I *knew* you *liked* it. That's why I suggested this airline.

f. Time Expressions Used with the Simple Past

He arrived in Washington *two days ago.*

The words *ago* and *last* are often used with verbs in the simple past. They indicate that the action is completed. They are used in sentences like the following:

He arrived in Washington *two days ago.*
He went to Europe *three years ago.*
He called his family *five minutes ago.*

She arrived in Washington *last summer.*
She left for New York *last week.*
She bought a car *last June.*

Yesterday and *the day before yesterday* are also used in sentences like these.

4.15 Past Continuous

a. Forms and Uses of the Past Continuous

When Bob called Jenny, she *was washing* her hair.

The past continuous is formed with *was* or *were* and the *-ing* form of the verb.

When Bob called Eugene and Doris, they *were eating*.

Use the past continuous for an event that was in progress at a particular time in the past.

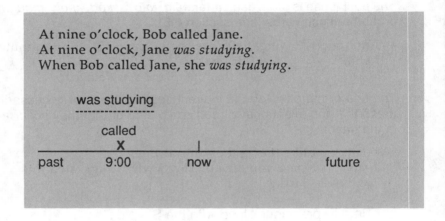

The past continuous can also be used when two events are in progress at the same time.

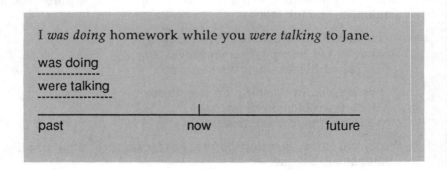

The past continuous is often used in sentences that have clauses beginning with *when* and *while*. (See section 8.12 for the use of these clauses.)

Both the simple past tense and the past continuous tense can be used for events in the past that are finished. However, when a specific time is mentioned, sentences with the simple past and the past continuous have slightly different meanings.

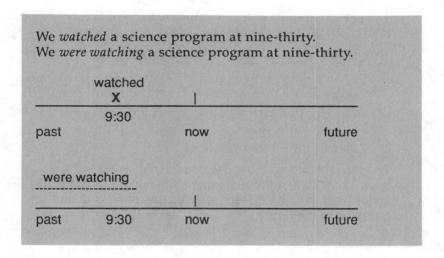

b. Time Expressions Used with the Past Continuous

She was working in Washington *at that time*.

The past continuous can be used for events that took place for a limited time. It also refers to an action or event that was in progress at a time in the past. Here are some expressions often used to show limited time, or actions or events in progress.

at that time   temporarily
that day/week/month   for a short time

They are used in sentences like the second and third ones that follow.

Gary and I worked together a few years ago.

I was living in Washington *that year*.
I was staying in a friend's house *temporarily*.

4.16 Present Perfect

a. Form of the Present Perfect

Mrs. Rose *has visited* fifty-three countries so far.

The present perfect tense is formed with *have* or *has* or their contracted forms, plus the past participle (*-ed/-en* form).

FULL FORM	CONTRACTED FORM
She *has been* to many places.	She*'s been* to many places.
We *have visited* many cities.	We*'ve visited* many cities.

He is used like *she. You* and *they* are used like *we*.

b. Uses of the Present Perfect

The present perfect is used to describe an event in the past whose effect is still felt at the moment of speaking. It is also used for an action that has been repeated in the past and that could be repeated in the future.

Mr. Rose *has eaten* some strange foods on his trips.

```
            has eaten
            X X X X X X X|
_____
past                     now              future
```

When a verb describes a state, use the present perfect to show that the state began in the past and still exists at the moment of speaking.

Mr. Rose *has wanted* to travel all his life.

```
has wanted
------------------------------------
                        |
_____
past                    now              future
```

When an action occurred at an indefinite time in the past (that is, when the time is not known or not important), the present perfect is used.

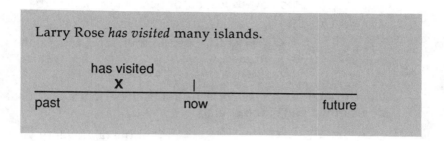

Larry Rose *has visited* many islands.

In questions, the present perfect is often used when the exact time is unstated or unknown. When a past time is stated, the present perfect is usually not used.

CORRECT   Has he *visited* Tibet?
                 Has he *been* to China?

INCORRECT   *Has he visited India last year?
                 *Has he gone to Japan in 1984?

Questions beginning with *how much, how many,* or *how often* frequently use the present perfect.

How many times *has* he *traveled* to Asia this year?
How often *has* he *been* to China?

The present perfect is used to report events in the recent past, particularly with the word *just*.

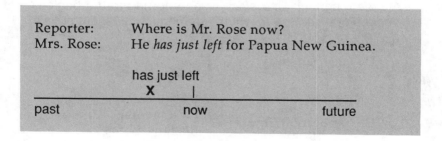

Reporter: Where is Mr. Rose now?
Mrs. Rose: He *has just left* for Papua New Guinea.

c. Time Expressions Used with the Present Perfect

With the present perfect tense, time expressions may come in different positions in the sentence. In statements, adverbs of frequency and the adverb *just* occur before the main verb.

Mr. Rose has $\begin{Bmatrix} \text{just} \\ \text{never} \\ \text{often} \\ \text{already} \end{Bmatrix}$ been to the Marquesas Islands.

When the time expression is a prepositional phrase, it usually comes at the end of the sentence.

He has taken lots of pictures $\begin{cases} \text{in the last twenty years.} \\ \text{since 1955.} \\ \text{so far (until now).} \end{cases}$

The adverbs *still, never,* and *ever* are often used in sentences with the present perfect. In most sentences, *still* comes before *have* or *has,* and *never* and *ever* come before the main verb.

He *still* hasn't used his first-aid kit.
He hasn't *ever* been hurt.

The time expressions *already* and *yet* are also used with the present perfect. *Already* usually occurs in affirmative sentences; *yet* usually occurs in negative sentences and questions. Moreover, *already* is most often placed after *have* and *has; yet* most often occurs at the end of the sentence.

Larry Rose has *already* sailed around the world.
He hasn't had a serious accident *yet.*

Time expressions with *since* and *for* are frequently used with the present perfect. Use *since* when referring to the beginning of a period of time. Use *for* when referring to the length of time.

He has been away $\begin{cases} \text{since July 2.} \\ \text{since last March.} \\ \text{since noon.} \end{cases}$

He has been in Europe $\begin{cases} \text{for ten days} \\ \text{for a month.} \\ \text{for three hours.} \\ \text{for a long time.} \end{cases}$

The time expressions *ago* and *from ... to ...* are not used with the present perfect. These expressions are usually used with the simple past.

CORRECT   He *went* to the Marshall Islands three years ago.
They *visited* the Cook Islands from March to April.

INCORRECT   *He has gone to the Marshall Islands three years ago.
*They have visited the Cook Islands from March to April.

4.17   Present Perfect Versus Simple Past

Henry *used to be* a waiter, but he *has been* a teacher since 1975.

Look at the following information about Henry Gonzalez:

EMPLOYMENT HISTORY

1979-1981   Waiter, Harvey's Steak House, Lawrence, Kansas (part-time)

1981-1985   English teacher, Edina High School, Edina, Minnesota

1985-present   Instructor in English, Greenfield Community College, Greenfield, Massachusetts

Use the simple past to describe events or states that are finished.

Henry Gonzalez *was* a waiter in 1979. He is not a waiter now.
He *lived* in Lawrence, Kansas, for two years. He does not live there now.
He *taught* high school in Edina before he came to Greenfield.

Use the present perfect to describe events or states that are not finished.

Henry *has taught* English since 1981. He still does.
He *has lived* in Massachusetts since 1985. He lives in
Greenfield.
He *has* always *lived* in the United States.

The simple past is often used when the time of the event is stated in the sentence and the time does not include the moment of speaking.

Henry *taught* high school from 1981 to 1985.
He *left* Edina in 1985.

Use the present perfect when the time of the event is indefinite.

Henry *has lived* in Kansas and Minnesota.
He *has traveled* a lot.

The simple past is used for time expressions that indicate an interval or break between the state or action and the present.

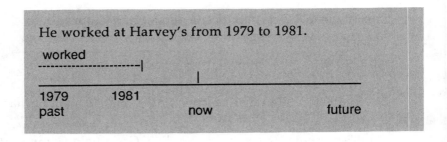

Time expressions that indicate no interval or break in the state or action are used with the present perfect.

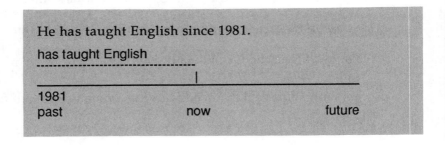

4.18   Present Perfect Continuous

a.   Forms and Uses of the Present Perfect Continuous

The man in the lobby *has been waiting* since one-twenty.

Use the present perfect continuous to tell about an action or state that began in the past and is still in progress. Use this tense when you want to emphasize the period of time. The period of time is usually stated when the present perfect continuous is used.

HAVE + *BEEN* + PRESENT PARTICIPLE	TIME
The clerks *have been filing*	since twelve.
A client *has been sitting* in the lobby	for an hour.
The secretary *has been typing*	all this time.

With verbs that describe actions or states that can take place over a long period of time, the present perfect and the present perfect continuous can have very similar meanings.

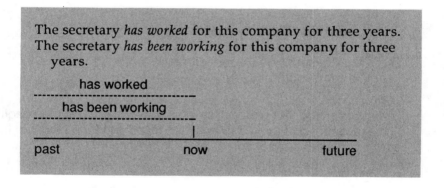

However, with some verbs there can be a difference in meaning between the present perfect and the present perfect continuous. The continuous forms of these verbs are used for actions or states that are not completed at the moment of reference. The present perfect is used for actions or states that are completed but still relevant to the situation at the moment of reference.

Mrs. Moore:	Where are the insurance forms?
Mr. Schuhmacher:	Ms. Gomez *has* already *filed* them.

Mrs. Moore: How do you know?
Mr. Schuhmacher: Ms. Gomez *has been filing* insurance forms all morning.

I *have read* the report. I finished it before lunch.
I *have been reading* the report. I'll finish it this afternoon.

Questions about an action in progress that began in the past are usually in the present perfect continuous.

How long *has* the office manager *been talking* on the phone?
How long *have* the secretaries *been typing*?

However, with verbs not usually used in continuous tenses (see section 4.5d), the present perfect can be used to show a state that still exists.

How long *has* he *been* angry?
How long *have* you *known* about this problem?

The present perfect continuous can be used with actions that were completed in the very recent past.

I *have* just *been* talking to a computer expert.
He *has been telling* me about word processors.

b. Time Expressions Used with the Present Perfect Continuous

Phrases beginning with *since* and *for* are often used with the present perfect continuous. Use *since* when mentioning the beginning of a period of time. Use *for* when referring to the length of the period of time (see section 8.3).

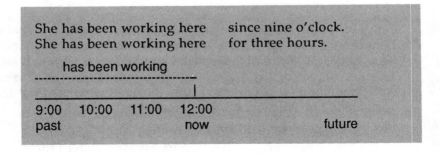

She has been working here   since nine o'clock.
She has been working here   for three hours.

has been working

|
9:00   10:00   11:00   12:00
past   now   future

4.19   Past Perfect

a.   Form and Uses of the Past Perfect

> By the time the guards got there, someone *had stolen* two paintings.

The past perfect is formed with *had* plus the past participle (the *-ed/-en* form).

> They *had seen* the paintings on Saturday.
> They'*d seen* them before they left.

Use the past perfect tense for a past action completed before another action in the past.

> When the guards *arrived,* the thieves *had* already *left.*
>
> had left   arrived
>   X   X |
> _____
> past   now   future

Notice that the two actions did not occur at the same time. When both actions occur at the same time or almost the same time, the verbs are in the simple past or the past continuous according to the following patterns.

> When the guards *arrived,* the thieves *were leaving.*
>
> arrived
>   X
> were leaving
> -----------------
> |
> _____
> past   now   future

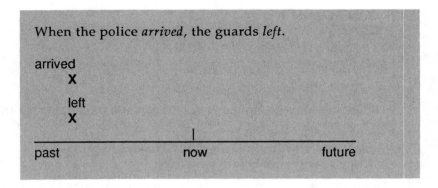

When the police *arrived*, the guards *left*.

arrived
X

left
X

past   now   future

The past perfect can be used for an event that happened a short time before another reported past event. In such cases, use the word *just*.

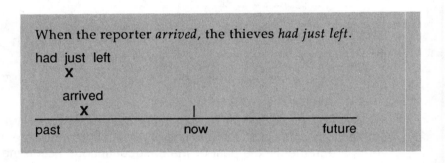

When the reporter *arrived*, the thieves *had just left*.

had just left
X

arrived
X

past   now   future

The past perfect is also used for reported or indirect speech (see section 6.5).

Guard:	They *have taken* a Picasso!
Police Officer:	What did she say?
Reporter:	She said that they *had taken* a Picasso.

b. Time Expressions Used with the Past Perfect

The past perfect is usually used with a time expression unless the time was mentioned in a previous sentence.

NOT CLEAR	A thief had robbed three museums.
CLEAR	Before anyone reported a robbery, a thief had robbed three museums.

Time expressions beginning with *by* and *before* are often used with the past perfect. *By* in this sense means "at (that time) or before."

By that time
By December ⎱ the same thieves had robbed three art
By then ⎰ galleries.

They had taken the paintings ⎰ before the reporter arrived.
⎱ before midnight.

The past perfect is often used in sentences with a phrase or clause beginning with words such as *when, until, before, after,* and *as soon as* (see section 8.12).

The guard had never discovered a robbery *before* this one.
The reporter had never reported an art theft *until* this one.

The time expressions *already* and *yet* can be used with the past perfect. Both expressions can come before the main verb. *Yet* can also be used at the end of the sentence.

By seven in the morning, the police had *already* searched the museum.
At that time, the police had not *yet* found any fingerprints.
They said that they had not called the director *yet*.

4.20 Past Perfect Continuous

Dennis was tired because he *had been traveling* for two weeks.

The past perfect continuous is formed with *had* followed by *been* and the present participle (*-ing* form of the verb). Use the past perfect continuous for an event that continued up to some other event or time in the past.

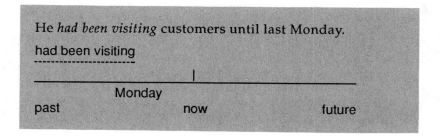

He *had been visiting* customers until last Monday.

had been visiting
- -

                                    |
_____
            Monday
past   now   future

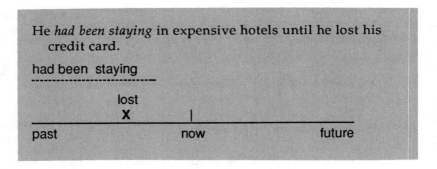

He *had been staying* in expensive hotels until he lost his credit card.

The past perfect continuous is often used in the main clauses of sentences that have adverbial clauses beginning with *when, while,* or *before* (see section 8.11).

He had been eating *alone* { before I arrived. / when I arrived. / until I arrived. }

POSSIBLE OR IMAGINARY EVENTS

4.21 Past and Imaginary Events

He can't dance. I wish he *could*.

In English, the verb forms used for imaginary or unreal events are different from the forms used for true events.

TRUE   Look, it's *snowing*.
IMAGINARY   I wish it *were* sunny.

In English you can use a more "distant" or more "past" form of the verb to show that an event is imaginary or untrue. The distant form is not the same for all tenses.

TIME	REAL EVENTS	IMAGINARY EVENTS
PRESENT	It is cloudy.	I wish it *were* sunny.
	He can't dance.	I wish he *could* dance.
PAST	I was sick yesterday.	I wish I *had been* well.
	I was reading a boring book.	I wish I *had been* reading another book.

TIME	REAL EVENTS	IMAGINARY EVENTS
PAST	I have finally finished that book.	I wish I *had finished* it sooner.
	I could play the piano as a teen-ager.	I wish I *had started* earlier.
FUTURE	They will use the large table.	I wish they *would use* the other one.
	We are going to finish late.	I wish we *were going to* finish earlier.

Note that with imaginary events, *were* is often used with singular subjects. (I wish it *were* sunny.)

4.22   Verb Tenses after *Wish* and *Hope*

The verbs *wish* and *hope* both mean approximately "want," but *hope* implies a desire that the speaker expects to be fulfilled.

I hope that your friend is home. (I expect he is.)
I hope that he likes this present. (I expect he will.)

Wish is used to express a desire less likely to be fulfilled.

I wish that I didn't have to work. (I have to work.)
I wish that I were rich. (I'm not rich.)

Wish is also used to indicate that a state or event is imaginary.

It's raining and my umbrella has a hole.
I wish it didn't have a hole.

When speaking of a possible future event, *will* or the present tense is used after *hope; would* or the past tense is used after *wish*.

I hope that your friend *will* offer us dinner.
I wish that we *would* get there soon.
I hope that he *comes* soon.
I wish I *had* a better car.

When speaking of a past event, use the past tense after *hope* and the past perfect tense after *wish*.

I hope that he *remembered* his invitation.
I wish that we *had brought* our raincoats.

In formal English, *were* is used after *wish,* even with singular subjects.

Your friend is late. I wish he *were* home.
I'm getting wet. I wish I *were* indoors.

4.23 Verb Tenses after *If*

If you *come* on Sunday, we *can play* baseball.

Sentences with *if* usually have two clauses. The *if* clause is a condition, and the main clause is a result.

CONDITION	RESULT
If it is raining in Norfolk,	the baseball field is getting wet.

In conditional clauses, the simple present tense is used for "timeless" conditions.

CONDITION	RESULT
If I *throw* the ball,	you catch it.
If you *catch* the ball,	touch that base.

The first sentence above means, "Whenever I throw the ball, you should catch it."

For past conditions and results that were real, the simple past can be used for both the condition and the result.

CONDITION	RESULT
If I *mentioned* baseball,	my father *started* talking about his favorite players.

Some conditional sentences make predictions. If the condition and result are probable, the simple present is used in the condition and a present modal plus a simple form of the verb is used in the result.

CONDITION	RESULT
If you *catch* the ball,	he *will be* out.
If he *drops* the ball,	you *can run*.

If the condition and result are not probable (and are more "distant"), the past form is used in the condition and a past modal plus a simple form of the verb is used in the result. The past forms in these sentences show that the events are not expected; they do not mean past time.

CONDITION   RESULT

If you *caught* the ball,   she *would be* out.
If he *dropped* the ball,   you *could run.*

If the condition is unreal or imaginary, the result is also unreal or imaginary. Past forms are used in conditional sentences to show unreal or imaginary conditions and results. *Were* is used with unreal conditions, even with singular subjects. In the following examples, the speaker is not fifteen years old and does not live in Chicago:

CONDITION   RESULT

If I *were* fifteen years old,   I *could run* faster.
If we *lived* in Chicago,   I *would take* you to see the
                                   Cubs.

If an unreal or imaginary situation in the past is described, the following tenses are often used: *had* plus the past participle in the condtion and a past modal plus *have* plus the past participle in the result.

CONDITION   RESULT

If you *had hit* the ball,   we *could have scored* another
                                   run.
If I *had thrown* the ball,   the runner *might have run* to
                                   second base.
If he hadn't dropped the ball,   we would have won the
                                   game.

The following examples summarize the conditional sentences described:

1. Real or probable events

    If I *throw* the ball, *catch* it.
    If you *throw* me the ball, I'*ll catch* it.

2. Unreal or imaginary events

    If I *threw* the ball, he *would catch* it.
    If I *were* fifteen years old, I *could run* faster.

3. Past time with real or probable events

    If I *mentioned* baseball, he *talked* about his favorite players.

4. Past time with unreal or imaginary events
   If I *had thrown* the ball to Sarah, she *would have caught* it.

PASSIVE VERBS

4.24 Verb Tenses

English verbs are understood in relation to three times: the present, the past, and the future. The continuous tenses refer to actions or states at these times. The perfect tenses refer to actions or states occuring before these times. Here are some examples.

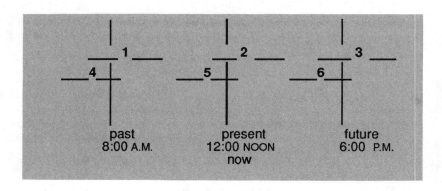

1 He was eating at eight o'clock.
2 He is eating now.
3 He will be eating at six o'clock.
4 He had eaten before eight o'clock.
5 He has eaten already.
6 He will have eaten before six o'clock.

4.25 Active Versus Passive Verbs

Her jewelry *was taken.*
Someone *took* it while she was sleeping.

In active sentences, the subject of the sentence is the doer of the action. In passive sentences, the subject is not the person doing the action, but rather the one who receives the action. Passive sentences often tell the result of an action.

ACTIVE

Mohammed *paid* the salesperson.

PASSIVE

Mohammed *was paid* for twenty hours of work.

ACTIVE

He *is writing* a letter.

PASSIVE

The letter *is being written* on company stationery.

Passive verb tenses have special forms. The main verb is always in the past participle (*-ed/-en*) form. Some form of the verb *be (be, am, is, are, was, were, being, been)* comes before the main verb. It is important to know if a sentence is active or passive because active and passive sentences have different meanings. The following sentences show a few examples of this.

ACTIVE

The duck *has eaten*.

PASSIVE

The duck *was eaten*.

She *has paid* $100 for a chair.

She *was paid* $100 for a chair.

4.26 Passive Present

The belt *is made* of leather.

The passive present is used when the result of an action is more important than the person who did the action. If you state the doer of the action, it is usually better to use the active voice.

ACTIVE	The secretary *opens* the mail before nine o'clock.
PASSIVE	The mail *is opened* before nine o'clock.
ACTIVE	The company *pays* all employees on Friday.
PASSIVE	All employees *are paid* on Friday.
ACTIVE	The company *sends* my check directly to the bank.
PASSIVE	My check *is sent* directly to the bank.

In cases where the doer of the action is stated in a passive sentence, the word *by* is used.

Her mail is usually opened *by* her secretary.
Memos are delivered *by* the mail clerk.

The passive is used to tell the source of a product or the material that a product is made of.

A lot of coffee *is grown* in Brazil.
This belt *is made* of leather.

The passive is often used in scientific writing.

The solution *is placed* in a sterile container.
Then it *is heated* to 40°C.
It *is* quickly *cooled*.

The passive is also used in very formal writing.

Employees *are encouraged* to take short coffee breaks.
Smoking *is prohibited* in unmarked areas.

Be careful to use the auxiliary verb *be* with the passive present.

CORRECT	Employees *are* not *allowed* to eat at their desks.
INCORRECT	*Employees not allowed to eat at their desks.

The passive present continuous uses *am, is,* or *are* followed by *being* and the present participle.

The letters *are being typed* now.
The report *is being written* at this moment.

Like the active present continuous, the passive present continuous is used for actions in progress at the moment of speaking.

4.27 Passive Past

The house *was built* in 1841.

To form the passive past tense, use *was* or *were* followed by the past participle.

I *was robbed*.
We *were* both *robbed*.

Newspaper reports of crimes often use the passive voice because the criminal is not known.

The Crocker Bank *was robbed* last night.
Three men *were shot* in a downtown bar last night.

When the time of an action is more important than the doer, the passive is often used.

This church *was built* in 1604.
Part of it *was destroyed* during the war.

In general, the passive past is used when a speaker or writer wants to place more emphasis on the result of an action than on the performer of the action.

An old diary *was found* in the old house.
It *was discovered* by the new owner.

4.28 Other Passive Tenses

Four dozen pies *have* already *been made*.

In active sentences, the subject is the doer of the action; in passive sentences, the subject is the receiver of the action.

One baker (doer) *will make* ten dozen pies a day.
Ten dozen pies (receiver) *will be made* this afternoon.

Active and passive sentences have similarities as well as differences. The following chart shows how active and passive sentences in the most common tenses are related.

	ACTIVE / PASSIVE	TENSE	USE
1.	The baker *makes* pies for restaurants. / These pies *are made* for restaurants.	Simple present	General statements and repeated actions
2.	He *is making* an apple pie now. / It *is being made* according to a secret recipe.	Present continuous	Present actions and relatively short (temporary) events
3.	He *made* a peach pie this morning. / A peach pie *was made* this morning.	Past	Completed past actions or events
4.	He *was making* a cherry pie when I arrived. / A cherry pie *was being made* when I arrived.	Past continuous	Event in progress at some time in the past
5.	He *has made* two lemon pies already. / Two lemon pies *have been made* already.	Present perfect	Past event with present effect or at indefinite time
6.	He *had made* the pumpkin pies earlier. / The pumpkin pies *had been made* earlier.	Past perfect	Past event before another past event
7.	He *will make* two blueberry pies this afternoon. / Two blueberry pies *will be made* this afternoon.	Future	Future action
8.	He *must make* a strawberry pie next. / A strawberry pie *must be made* next.	Modal tenses	Possibility, necessity, or obligation
9.	He *will have made* them by five o'clock. / They *will have been made* by five o'clock.	Future Perfect	Event ended before a specific future time

4.29 Passive Expressions with *Get*

Did anyone *get* killed?

In informal speech and writing, *get* may sometimes be used in place of *be* in a passive sentence. It is usually not used in formal writing.

Tony: A clerk *got* shot during the fight.
Kim: Did anyone *get* killed?
Tony: No, but several police officers *got* badly injured.

The passive *get* is used to describe actions rather than states. Moreover, it is not usually used with words like *known, built,* or *made.*

CORRECT   The criminal *is known* to the police.
INCORRECT *The criminal gets known to the police.

CORRECT   The church *was built* in 1604.
INCORRECT *The church got built in 1604.

CORRECT   The rug *was made* in China.
INCORRECT *The rug got made in China.

4.30 Negatives, Questions, Short Answers, and Tag Questions in the Passive Voice

All passive sentences have auxiliary verbs. Negatives, questions, short answers, and tag questions are formed according to the rules in section 4.2. In negative sentences, place *not* or *-n't* after the first auxiliary, both in main clauses and in tags. In questions, place the first auxiliary before the subject.

Customer: The pies *aren't* made here, are they?
Clerk: Yes, they are. They're made here.
Customer: You have fresh bread, too, *don't* you? Is it baked fresh every day?
Clerk: Yes, it is.
Customer: Where *is* the bread baked?
Clerk: It's baked here.

In affirmative and negative short answers and tag questions, use the first auxiliary.

Customer: Is the bread being baked now?
Clerk: Yes, it *is*.
Customer: It can be delivered by five o'clock, *can't* it?
Clerk: Yes, it *can*.

Chapter 5
Modals and Semimodals

THE GRAMMAR OF MODALS

5.1 Describing Modals and Semimodals

Everyone *should* learn about computers.

Modals are auxiliary verbs. In American English, the modals are the following.

can	may	shall	will	must
could	might	should	would	ought to

Modals have only one form. They do not occur with the suffixes *-s, -ing, -ed,* or *-en.* In contrast, most verbs, such as *take* and *speak,* occur with suffixes.

I *must* take three computer courses.
I am taking one now.
My teacher *should* speak faster.
He speaks very slowly.

A modal is always the first verb in a verb phrase, but in formal English a verb phrase cannot have two modals.

CORRECT	You *should have seen* the TV program about computers.
INCORRECT	*You will can see it on Sunday.
CORRECT	I *might buy* a computer.
INCORRECT	*I might should buy a microcomputer.

The simple form of the verb always follows the modal in a verb phrase.

	MODAL	SIMPLE FORM	
He	might	become	a computer programmer.
You	must	be very	interested in computers.

Only the modal *ought to* is composed of two words. However, it is still followed by the simple form of the verb.

CORRECT	You *ought to* read some books about computers.
INCORRECT	*You ought read computer magazines, too.
CORRECT	I *might* do that.
INCORRECT	*I might to learn something.
CORRECT	I *should* look in the library.
INCORRECT	*I should to go tonight.

Other English expressions called semimodals have meanings similar to those of modals.

MEANING	MODAL	SEMIMODAL
ability	can	be able to
future time	will	be going to
past habit	would	used to
obligation	should	be supposed to
	must	have to
		had better

Semimodals are sometimes used when modals cannot be used. For example, semimodals can sometimes be used after a verb and can follow the word *to*. Modals, however, can never follow a verb nor the word *to*. To talk about ability, for example, it is sometimes necessary to use the semimodal *be able to* instead of the modal *can*.

CORRECT	She wants to *be able to* write computer programs.
INCORRECT	*She wants to can write computer programs.
CORRECT	She might *be able to* study programming at night.
INCORRECT	*She might can study programming at night.

5.2 Negatives, Contractions, Questions, and Short Answers with Modals and Semimodals

a. Negatives with Modals

You *shouldn't* smoke here.

In negative sentences with modals, *not* follows the modal.

You may smoke in the back of the airplane.
You may *not* smoke in the front.

You must fasten your seat belt now.
You must *not* walk around.

Most of the modals form contractions with *not*. For example, *should not* can be contracted to *shouldn't*. Some of the modals, however, are usually not contracted in American English. A line indicates those cases in the following chart.

MODAL + NOT
CONTRACTED FORM

That man *cannot* find the correct gate for his flight.
He *can't* speak much English.

He *could not* understand me.
He *couldn't* tell me his problem.

He *may not* find the plane.
———

He *might not* arrive in Caracas on time.
———

He *must not* lose his ticket.
He *mustn't* leave it on the seat.

I *shall not* forget him.
———

He *should not* be afraid to ask for help.
He *shouldn't* be ashamed.

He *will not* be so helpless the next time.
He *won't be* embarrassed.

He *would not* like it if we offered to help him in Caracas.
He *wouldn't* be happy at all.

In American English, the negative *ought not to* is rarely used. It is too formal for most situations. Most speakers of American English use *should not* or *shouldn't* instead of *ought not to*. In the same way, *shall not* is formal and rare. Most people prefer to use *won't*.

AFFIRMATIVE	We *ought to*/*should* help him.
NEGATIVE	We *shouldn't* leave him.
AFFIRMATIVE	I *shall* speak to the flight attendant.
NEGATIVE	I *won't* write a letter to the airline.

b. Questions with Modals

In yes-no questions, the modal comes before the subject. In short answers, the modal is usually used without the main verb.

Koh:	*Will* we *arrive* on time?
Masayo:	No, we *won't*.
Koh:	*Can* you *see* Caracas yet?
Masayo:	Yes, I *can*.

Might and *ought to* are rarely used in questions because in questions these modals sound too formal for most situations. In negative questions, the contracted negative forms are used, except in very formal English.

CORRECT	*Can't* we help that man?
FORMAL	Can we not help that man?
CORRECT	*Shouldn't* the flight attendant speak Spanish?
FORMAL	Should the flight attendant not speak Spanish?

With the semimodals *used to, had better,* and *have to,* the auxiliary verbs *do, does,* and *did* are used in questions, negative statements, short answers, and tag questions. With the semimodals beginning with *be (be able to, be used to, be supposed to),* these auxiliary verbs are not necessary.

5.3   Time and Form

Modals have only one form. However, in certain sentences, some of the modals are used as past or "distant" forms of other modals. Semimodals may also be used as past forms of modals. These forms do not always mean past time.

MODAL	PAST FORM
can	could, was able to (semimodal)
may	might
must	had to (semimodal)
ought to	----
shall	should
will	would

Past forms of modals are used in indirect speech. In indirect speech, the forms *would* and *might* are used as past forms of *will* and *may. Had to* is sometimes used as the past of *must.*

DIRECT SPEECH
   INDIRECT SPEECH

The victim said, "I *will* call the police."
   A bystander said she *would* call an ambulance.

The driver asked, *"May* I sit down?"
   The driver asked the police officer if he *might* sit in the car.

The driver said, "I *must* call my wife."
The driver said that he *had to* call her right away.

The past forms *could, should, would,* and *might* are also used to make a request or question more polite.

POLITE   *Will* you lend me a dollar?
MORE POLITE   *Would* you lend me a dollar?
POLITE   *Can* you help me?
MORE POLITE   *Could* you help me?

Past modal forms are used with imaginary or improbable events.

I will give you a dollar.
I *would* give you more, but I'm broke, too.
I hope you can find a place to eat.
I wish we *could* eat at home.

Modals usually refer to present or future time. However, sometimes the past modal forms refer to past time.

PRESENT   Your baby can talk now.
PAST   My baby *could* talk last month.
PRESENT   Your baby won't take a nap.
PAST   She *wouldn't* take one yesterday, either.

But the usual way to show past time with a modal is with the pattern modal + *have* + past participle. The following sentences express possiblility in two tenses.

PRESENT OR FUTURE   She *may* bring her baby later.
PAST   She *may have left* home earlier.
PRESENT OR FUTURE   We *might* take a picture.
PAST   She *might have taken* one already.

5.4 Passive Sentences with Modals

The door *can be opened* from the inside.

In active sentences, the subject of the sentence is the doer of the action. In passive sentences, the subject is the receiver of the action (see section 4.25). Modals can occur in both active and passive sentences.

ACTIVE
PASSIVE

A thief *can open* a door easily.
  A window *can* also *be opened* easily.

Someone *could steal* the silver.
  That teapot *could be stolen*.

We *should have insured* the rugs.
  The coins *should have been insured,* too.

Passive verb phrases with modals have the following forms.

	MODAL +	*BE* +	PAST PARTICIPLE	
The lock	can	be	reached	easily.
The silver	could	be	sold	quickly.

	MODAL +	*HAVE BEEN* +	PAST PARTICIPLE
The rugs	should	have been	insured.
The TV	could	have been	stolen.

5.5 Sequence of Tenses

If my cousins *had called,* I *could have met* them at the airport.

Modals often occur in sentences with more than one clause. In most cases, the modal occurs in the independent clause (the clause that can stand alone as a sentence).

DEPENDENT CLAUSE	INDEPENDENT CLAUSE
When they get home,	we *can* have dinner.
If they come early,	we *should* take them to Central Park.

A modal following a dependent clause with a verb in the past should also be in the past form.

DEPENDENT CLAUSE	INDEPENDENT CLAUSE
If they *were* staying longer,	I *would* (not *will*) take them to Boston.
If they *had* come last week,	I *might* (not *may*) have taken them to Cape Cod.

When the first verb in the dependent clause is in a present form (the simple form or the *-s* form), any of the modals can be used in the independent clause.

If they *visit* next year, they *may* stay with me.
If they *come* in the summer, I *might* take them to the beach.

THE MEANINGS OF MODALS
AND SEMIMODALS

5.6 *Can* **and** *Be Able To*

a. Possibility with *Can* and *Be Able To*

Can you make a triangle?

Be able to means "have the power to" do something. *Can* has several different meanings. Some of these meanings are similar. The basic meaning of *can* is "be possible."

Tom: Here are three sticks. *Can* you make a
             triangle?
Dick: Yes, I *can.* Here it is.

Tom: Here are two sticks. *Can* you make a
             square?
Dick: No, I *can't.* It isn't possible to make a
             square with two sticks.
Tom: Yes, it is. You *can* make a square if you
             break the sticks in half.

The negative forms *cannot* (written as one word) and *can't* (written with one *n)* mean "it is not possible." *Cannot* is not used in negative questions; *can't* is used instead.

Steve: Open the door, please.
Joan: I *can't.* (It is not possible.)
Steve: Why *can't* you?
Joan: Because it's locked.
Steve: Try to unlock it. Someone's knocking.
Joan: It *can't* be our dinner guests. (It's not possible that
              it's our dinner guests.) It's too early.

With the meaning of possibility, *can* refers to either the present or the future.

> There are a hammer and a screwdriver in this tool kit. We *can* break the lock with the screwdriver. You *can* call the locksmith tomorrow.

b.   Ability with *Can* and *Be Able To*

> Louise *can* play the piano.

Sometimes *can* means "be able to" or "know how to."

> Louise *is able to* play the piano.
> In fact, she *can* play very well.
> Dennis *can* play the piano, too.
> He *can't* play as well as Louise *can*.

When a verb refers to a future ability, use *will be able to*.

> CORRECT   My piano lessons will begin next week.
> I *will be able to* play simple songs by the end of the year.

> INCORRECT   *I can play simple songs by the end of the year.

c.   Requests with *Can*

> *Can* you type this?

Sometimes *can* is used to make a request.

> Mr. Amir: *Can* you type this report for me?
> Ms. White: Of course. I'd be happy to.

Sometimes the request is a request for permission. Many people prefer *may* for requesting permission, but *can* is frequently used. *May* is often used to ask for individual permission, and *can* is used to ask about general rules.

> Mr. Lee: *Can* children under seventeen attend this movie?
> Ms. Jones: Yes, they *can*.
> Mr. Lee: *May* I have one adult and one children's ticket?

5.7 *Could* **and** *Could Have*

a. Possibility with *Could*

She *could* take a nap.

Use *could* to show that an opportunity exists in the present or the future. The action or event is probable; nothing prevents it.

Maria:	There's chicken and hamburger in the refrigerator.
Yoko:	We *could* make fried chicken.
Maria:	What can we do after lunch?
Yoko:	The library is open. We *could* study.
Maria:	I have ten dollars. We *could* go to a movie.

In some sentences, *could* has a meaning very similar to *might*. In these sentences, both *could* and *might* mean "it is possible."

Maria:	Where is Janet?
Yoko:	She *could* (*might*) be at the movies, or she *could* (*might*) be at home.

Negative sentences with *could not* or *couldn't* often mean "it is not possible."

She *couldn't* be at the movies. She doesn't have any money.
She *couldn't* be at home. I just called there.

Sometimes *could* is used with *be* and the present participle (the *-ing* form of the verb) to express a present or future possibility.

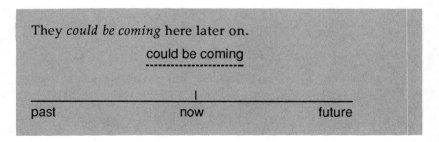

Could is sometimes used in conditional sentences (see section 4.23). In the second sentence below, *could* is used for a less probable (more "distant") event.

If the teacher comes early, we can ask him some questions.
If we ask enough questions, he *could* forget to give the test.

b. Imaginary Situations with *Could*

We *could* live forever.

Sometimes *could* is used for sentences that describe an imaginary situation or a situation that will probably not occur.

Imagine that U.S. income tax rates were cut in half.
We *could* save more money.
We *could* travel more.
We *could* give more to charity.

In the following sentences, the imaginary situation is stated in an *if* clause (see section 4.23):

If taxes were lower, we *could* buy a new car.
If we had a new car, we *could* drive across the country.

c. Polite Requests with *Could*

Could I ask you a favor?

Use *could* to make polite requests. A request beginning with *could* is slightly more formal and polite than one beginning with *can*.

POLITE   Can you lend me your car?
                  Can you come early and help me with
                      dinner?

MORE POLITE   *Could* you lend me your car?
                  Could you come early and help me with
                      dinner?

d. *Could* in Indirect Speech

He said he *could* open the jar.

In indirect speech (section 6.5), *could* is usually used instead of *can* after the past tense of verbs such as *tell, say,* or *ask*.

DIRECT SPEECH
    INDIRECT SPEECH

"Can you open this jar?" she asked.
    She asked if he *could* open the jar.

He said, "I *can* probably open it."
    He said that he *could* probably open it.

e. Past Ability with *Could*

I *couldn't* escape from the fire.

Could means "was/were able to" when it refers to the past.

There was a bad fire last night.
I *couldn't* put it out. (I was not able to put it out.)
I *could* hear a fire engine coming. (I was able to hear a fire
    engine coming.)
Because of the smoke, I *couldn't* go down the stairs. (I was
    not able to go down the stairs.)

When it refers to possibility, *could* alone is not used for past time.
Could have is used instead.

PRESENT POSSIBILITY	You *could* report the fire now.
	(It is possible to report the fire now.)
PAST POSSIBILITY	You *could have* reported the fire last night.
	(It was possible to report the fire last night.)

f. Past Time with *Could Have*

She *could have* fallen from the ladder while she was
    painting.

Could have followed by a past participle is often used to show past
possibility or past opportunity.

She painted the ceiling from a ladder.
She *could have broken* a leg.
She *could have hurt* her back.

I got paid last night.
I *could have gone* to a movie, but I didn't.
I *could have eaten* out, but I didn't.

If clauses with *could have* sometimes refer to imaginary situations in the past.

> If she *could have* afforded to pay a painter, she wouldn't have painted her house herself.
> If I *could have* gotten a reservation at Alfredo's, I would have eaten out.

5.8   *Will, Won't,* **and** *Will Have*

a.   Future Events

> We'*ll watch* him work.

Will and *won't* followed by the simple form of the verb are often used to refer to future events.

> This afternoon, I *will introduce* you to Sam, a stunt man.
> We'*ll watch* him work.
> You *won't see* this very often.

Will have or *won't have* with the past participle make up the future perfect tense. It is used to talk about a future event or action that will be finished before another future event or action.

> Before you leave, you *will have seen* some amazing stunts.

b.   Present Attitudes

> He *won't go* into a lion's cage no matter how much you pay him.

Will and *won't* can be used to describe what someone is willing or unwilling to do. Notice that the following sentences do not refer to a particular event but to a present attitude.

> For some movie directors, Sam *will drive* a car off a cliff.
> He *will sometimes jump* from a moving train.
> But he *won't go* into a lion's cage. (He refuses to go into a lion's cage.)
> And he *won't work* on Sundays. (He refuses to work on Sundays.)

Sentences with *won't* sometimes have different meanings from negative *going to* sentences.

He *won't work* with the director Jonas Dale.
(He refuses to work with the director Jonas Dale.)
He *isn't going to work* with the director Jonas Dale.
(He is going to work with another director, and he has no
particular feelings about working with Jonas Dale.)

To express the meaning "be willing to" in the past, use *would* or *was/were willing to*.

When Sam was young, he *was willing to work* with lions.
He *would work* with tigers and elephants, too.
Then a lion attacked him.
He *wouldn't work* with lions again.

c.   *Will* with Polite Requests

Will you help me?

Will can be used to make polite requests and to agree to them.

Peter: I will be on vacation next week. *Will* you
           feed my cat?
Kathy: Sure. I'*ll feed* her on my way to work.

d.   *Will* and *Won't* with Promises and Refusals

We *will stay* at your house while you're away.

The phrases *I will/I'll* and *we will/we'll* can be used to offer to do something. When they do, they have the meaning, "I promise."

I'll water the plants. (I promise to water the plants.)
I'll bring in your mail. (I promise to bring in your mail.)
We won't forget. (We promise not to forget.)

5.9   *Would, Would Have,* **and** *Used To*

a.   *Would* with Imaginary Situations

What *would* you do?

Would has several different uses. One of the most important uses is for imaginary situations.

I'm bored with this picnic.
I wish that a plane *would land* in this field.
I wish the pilot *would take* me for a ride.

Sentences with *if* clauses sometimes describe conditions that are imaginary (see section 4.23). In these sentences, *would* can be used to describe actions and events that will probably not occur.

If a plane landed in this field, I *would take* a picture of it.
I *would sell* the picture to the newspapers.

b. *Would Have* with Imaginary Situations in the Past

Without the lifeboats, more people *would have* died.

Would have is often used to describe imaginary situations in the past. Compare the following real and imaginary situations.

REAL SITUATION

In 1912, the White Star liner *Titanic* hit an iceberg and sank. About 1,500 people died.

IMAGINARY SITUATION

If the *Titanic* had been traveling farther south, it *would* not *have* hit an iceberg.
If it had carried more lifeboats, fewer people *would have* died.
If the ship had been smaller, there *would have* been fewer passengers.

c. Past Habit with *Would* and *Used To*

I *used to* be very careless.

With certain verbs, the expression *used to* indicates that an action was repeated in the past. *Used to* can express the idea in the past that *usually* expresses in the present.

My father *usually* feeds his dogs in the morning. (present habit)
When I was young, I *used to* help him. (past habit)

Would has a meaning similar to that of *used to*, but the two expressions are not always used in the same way. In the following sentences, both *used to* and *would* refer to past habitual actions.

When I was young, I *used to* take care of the dogs.
I *would* give them water every morning and evening.
But I *used to* daydream a lot.
My father *would* scold me when I forgot to turn off the water.

Would is only used to describe repeated actions. It cannot be used to express a situation or condition that existed in the past. Therefore, it cannot be used with verbs that describe states, such as *have* and *live*. In these cases, only *used to* is possible.

CORRECT	I *used to* be very careless.
INCORRECT	I would be very careless.
CORRECT	I *used to* own two dogs when I was young.
INCORRECT	I would own two dogs when I was young.

Sometimes a condition that existed in the past is compared with a current condition. Since it is a condition, *used to* is used, not *would*.

CORRECT	I'm not as careless as I *used to* be.
INCORRECT	*I'm not as careless as I would be.
CORRECT	My father has fewer dogs now than he *used to* have.
INCORRECT	*My father has fewer dogs now than he would have.

Used to is used in short answers, but *would* is not (when it expresses past habit).

Andrea:	Do you have dogs?
Phillipe:	No, but I *used to* (not *would*).

To make questions and negatives with *used to*, use the auxiliary verb *did*. The following questions are informal:

Did you *use to* mow the lawn when you were young?
Didn't you *use to* deliver newspapers?

d.   *Would* As The Past Form of *Will*

Houdini *would do* very dangerous tricks.

One of the meanings of *will* is "be willing to" (see Section 5.8). *Would* is sometimes used with the meaning "was/were willing to."

PRESENT	Doug Henning is a famous magician. He *will* sometimes do some very dangerous tricks. He *will* escape from a locked trunk that is under water.

PAST   Houdini was a famous magician.
            He *would* risk his life doing very dangerous tricks.
            He *would* escape from a locked trunk that was
            under water.

In a negative sentence, *wouldn't* means "wasn't/weren't willing to"
or "refused to."

PRESENT   Henning *won't* perform very often.
            He *won't* tell his secrets.

PAST   Houdini *wouldn't* retire.
            He *wouldn't* tell anyone the secret of his tricks.

In indirect speech, *would* is usually used instead of *will* after verbs
in the past tense such as *said, asked,* or *told.*

He said, "I *will* perform a new trick." (direct speech)
He said he *would* perform a new trick. (indirect speech)

e.   Polite Requests with *Would*

Would you please hand me those scissors.

Would can be used to make polite requests. A request beginning
with *would* is slightly more formal or polite than a request beginning with *will.*

POLITE   *Will* you hold this rope.
                Will you put the rope here.

MORE POLITE   *Would* you hold this rope.
                Would you put the rope here.

5.10   Expressions with *Would*

a.   *Would Like*

They*'d like* some help.

Would like is used to talk about what a person wants.

Klaus: We're lost. We*'d like* a map.
Pat: What kind of map *would* you *like*?
Klaus: We*'d like* a small map of the city.

Sometimes *would like* is followed by *to* and the simple form of the verb.

> I'd like *to go* now.
> We'd like *to arrive* before dark.
> I wouldn't like *to get* lost again in this storm.

Would like can also be followed by a noun phrase.

> I'd like *some coffee*. (I want some coffee.)
> Would you like *cream*? (Do you want cream?)

Would like does not have the same meaning as *do like*. Do not confuse these two expressions.

> CORRECT   *Would* you *like* some help?
> INCORRECT   *Do you like some help?

In affirmative sentences, *would* can be contracted to *'d*. This contraction is usually not used in negative sentences.

I'd		I	
You'd		You	
He'd	like to go.	He	wouldn't like to get lost.
She'd		She	
We'd		We	
They'd		They	

The past form of *would like* is *would have liked*.

> I'm sorry we're leaving.
> I *would have liked* some coffee.
> I *would have liked* a cigarette, too.

b. *Would Mind*

> *Would* you *mind* if I drove?

Would mind is used to ask for agreement.

> The weather is terrible.
> *Would* you *mind* if we went home? (Let's go home, please.)
> *Would* you *mind* not going to the party? (Let's not go to the party, please.)

Sometimes *would mind* is used to make polite requests.

The car is stuck again.
Would you *mind* handing me the shovel? (Please hand me the shovel.)
Would you *mind* brushing the snow the other way? (Please stop brushing snow at me.)

The phrase *would mind* is followed by a present participle (the -*ing* form), a clause with *if,* or a noun phrase.

Would you mind *driving*?
Would you mind *if I took a nap*?
Would you mind a *short delay*?

Would mind is not usually used in affirmative statements, but it can be used in negative statements to express a preference.

I *wouldn't mind* stopping for a cup of coffee. (I would like to stop for a cup of coffee.)
I *wouldn't mind* if we turned back. (I would like to turn back.)

c. *Would Rather*

I should do my homework, but I'*d rather* read a book.

Use *would rather* to talk about preferences. In affirmative statements, *would rather* can be contracted to -'*d rather.*

Tony: I'm really hungry.
Judy: *Would* you *rather* eat at home or at a restaurant?
Tony: I'*d rather* eat in a restaurant.
Judy: *Would* you *rather* have Chinese food or Italian?

There are several differences between *would rather* and *would like. Would like* is usually used when choices are not limited. *Would rather* is used when a limited number of choices is being discussed.

Would you *like* to go to a restaurant?
Would you *rather* eat at home or at a restaurant? (limited choices)
Would you *like* to go to China Garden?
Would you *rather* go to China Garden or the Peking Restaurant?

Would rather is not followed by *to*.

CORRECT   I'*d rather* have Chinese food.
INCORRECT   *I'd rather to have Chinese food.

CORRECT   I'*d rather* eat at China Garden.
INCORRECT   *I'd rather to eat at China Garden.

The negative of *would rather* is *would rather not* or the contracted form *'d rather not*.

I'*d rather not* have pizza.

5.11 *May*

a. Permission with *May*

May I smoke in your office?

May is often used to ask permission.

May I come in? (Do I have your permission to come in?)

May is used to give permission, and *may not* is used to deny it. In American English, there is no contraction for *may not*. Both *can* and *may* are used in informal English, but only *may* is used in formal English when asking for or giving permission.

INFORMAL   *Can* I talk to you for a minute?

FORMAL   *May* I talk to you for a minute?
               May I speak with you now?

b. Possibility with *May* and *May Have*

I *may* give a party.

May and *may have* are sometimes used to suggest that something is or was possible. In the following sentences, the meaning of *may* is similar to the meaning of *could* and *might* :

I *may* (*might*) give a party.
I *may* (*could*) cook chicken.

May have is used to talk about possible events in the past.

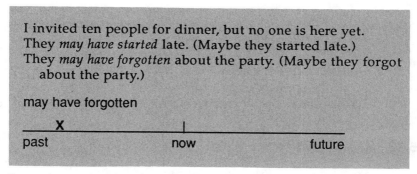

I invited ten people for dinner, but no one is here yet.
They *may have started* late. (Maybe they started late.)
They *may have forgotten* about the party. (Maybe they forgot
  about the party.)

may have forgotten

Sometimes *may* is used with *be* and the *ing* form of the verb to refer to an activity that is possible at the moment of speaking.

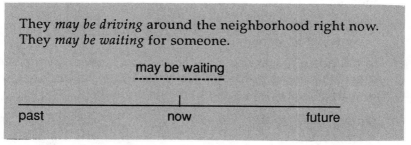

They *may be driving* around the neighborhood right now.
They *may be waiting* for someone.

may be waiting

This form can also refer to a future time.

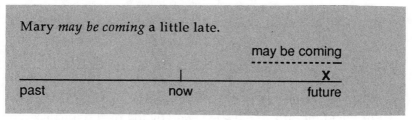

Mary *may be coming* a little late.

may be coming

May be and *maybe* both mean "possibly," but they are used differently. *Maybe* is an adverb; it is written as one word; it usually comes before the subject and the verb. *May be* is a verb phrase; it is written as two words; it usually comes after the subject.

Maybe they called while we were out.
They *may be* at home now.

To ask questions about possibilities, speakers of American English do not usually use *may* or *may have*. They usually use such expressions as *do you think* or *do you suppose*.

STATEMENTS OF POSSIBILITY
They *may* come later.
They *may* be lost.

QUESTIONS OF POSSIBILITY
Do you think they'll come at all?
Do you suppose they'll find us?

5.12 *Might* **and** *Might Have*

He *might* be on the wrong trail.

Might is sometimes used to talk about possibilities or "good guesses."

He *might* be lost.
We *might* be wrong, too.

To talk about present or future time, *might* followed by the simple form of the verb is used. *Might* followed by *be* and the *-ing* form of the verb can also be used for present or future possibility.

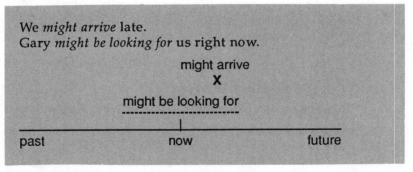

We *might arrive* late.
Gary *might be looking for* us right now.

For past time, *might have* followed by the past participle is used.

We *might have turned* at the wrong place.
We *might have missed* the trail.

In most sentences about possibilities, the modals *may, might,* and *could* have almost the same meaning. You can use any of these modals in the following sentences:

We *may/might/could* be walking north.
We *may/might/could* be going west.
We *may/might/could* have gone in a circle.

b.   Questions and Negatives

Kim: Do you think we're lost?
Lee: Yes, I do. We might be late for dinner.

To ask questions about possibilities, speakers of American English usually do not use *might* or *might have*. Other expressions, such as *do you think* and *do you suppose,* are used.

STATEMENTS OF POSSIBILITY

It *might* rain.
We *might* be lost.

QUESTIONS OF POSSIBILITY

Do you think it will rain?
Do you suppose we're lost?

The negative forms *might not* and *might not have* are usually not contracted.

We *might not* find a telephone.
I *might not have* brought any matches.

5.13   *Shall*

Shall we go to a movie tonight?

Shall is usually used in questions with *I* or *we* as the subject. Questions beginning with the words *shall we* are often suggestions.

Shall we have dinner first? (Let's have dinner first.)
Shall we take the bus? (Let's take the bus.)

Sometimes questions beginning with the words *shall I* are similar to questions beginning with *do you think*.

Shall I wear the blue dress or the red one? (Do you think I
should wear the blue dress or the red one?)
Shall I bring a flashlight? (Do you think I should bring a
flashlight?)

A less common use of *shall* is to show the speaker's intention.
This use of *shall* is limited to formal speech and writing in
American English.

We *shall* not tolerate this kind of movie in our city.
We *shall* demonstrate until this theater is closed.

5.14   *Should, Should Have,* **and** *Ought To*

a.   Advice and Suggestions with *Should, Should Have,*
and *Ought To*

You *should* pay attention to sales.

Should is often used in sentences that give advice or suggestions. *Ought to* is also used to give advice. These words suggest
that it is a good idea to do something but that there is a choice.

You look sick.
You *should* see a doctor.
You *ought to* call Dr. Sharma right now.
You *should* go to bed.
You *ought to* rest.

In negative sentences, speakers of American English use *should
not* or *shouldn't*. The negative forms *ought not to* and *oughtn't to*
are rarely used.

You *shouldn't* go to work tomorrow.
We *shouldn't* stand in the cold.

Should is used to ask for advice or opinions. Questions with *ought
to* are formal and rare.

Should I go to the clinic?
Should I take vitamin C?

Some questions with *should* are really suggestions.

Shouldn't you take a taxi home? (You should take a taxi
home.)
Should you be smoking with that cough? (You shouldn't be
smoking.)

Sometimes *should* and *ought to* are used for suggestions. Both
imply that a better situation is possible. The following sentences
are general statements. The time is unspecified.

REAL SITUATION	POSSIBLE BETTER SITUATION
Some parties are boring.	People *should* enjoy parties.
	People *ought to* have fun.
Most people don't dance.	They *should* dance at parties.
	They *ought to* learn to dance.
Many people drink too much.	They *shouldn't* drink so much.

Should have is used for suggestions about the past. When *should
have* is used, a desirable event did not take place; a better
situation was possible.

REAL SITUATION
POSSIBLE BETTER SITUATION

Donna drove her car through a red light.
  She *should have* stopped. (She didn't.)
A truck driver was lighting a cigarette.
  He *should have been* watching the road. (He wasn't.)
He didn't see Donna.
  He *should have* stopped. (He didn't.)

b. Expectation with *Should* and *Ought To*

The guests *should* be here soon.

Sometimes *should* and *ought to* are used to show what the
speaker expects to happen. In the following sentences, the action
is expected. *Should* and *ought to* have almost the same meaning.

I invited the guests for six o'clock.
It's almost six now.
They *should* be here soon.

The chicken has been cooking for an hour.
It *ought to* be done by now.

When an action is certain, use *will* rather than *should* or *ought to*.

Mary's train arrives at 6:15.
She *will* be a little late.

5.15 *Had Better* **and** *Be Supposed To*

a. Advice with *Had Better*

She'd *better not* walk home alone.

The expression *had better* (*-'d better*) is used for giving advice. When used for present and future time, sentences with *should* and *had better* have almost the same meaning, but *had better* is stronger. The difference is that *had better* suggests consequences of an action.

You look sick.
You *should* go home. (It's a good idea to go home.)
You *had better* go home now. (You might get worse if you don't go home.)
You *should* be in bed. (It's a good idea to go to bed.)
You*'d better* take some aspirin. (The pain will continue if you don't take some aspirin.)

b. Expectation with *Be Supposed to*

You*'re supposed to* eat with chopsticks.

The verb *be supposed to* is used to show expectation. It has a slightly different meaning from that of *should*. When speakers use *should*, they often mean that an action or event is expected because it is desirable. When speakers use *be supposed to*, they usually mean that an action is expected because it is customary.

This dessert is tasteless.
You *should* find a new recipe.

You*'re supposed to* eat with chopsticks in this restaurant.
They don't even give you a fork.

c. Expectation in the Past with *Should Have* and *Was/Were Supposed to*

Phil *was supposed to* call.

Should have is used to report an action that did not occur but that was expected.

> Phil said he would call.
> He *should have* called by now.

Was/were supposed to is used to show than an action was expected. The action may or may not have occurred.

> Phil *was supposed to* talk to Anita.
> I wonder if he did.
> He *was supposed to* get her class notes.
> I hope he did.

5.16 *Must, Have to,* and *Have Got to*

a. Necessity and Obligation with *Must, Have to,* and *Have Got to*

> We *must* keep the dairy clean.

Both *have to* and *have got to* show that something is an obligation. *Have to* is more formal that *have got to.* The words *have* and *has* can be contracted with the pronoun in the construction *have got to* but not in the construction *have to.*

> You *have to* do everything correctly in the dairy.
> We'*ve got to* be careful about germs.

The modal *must* is used to show that something is necessary.

> You *must* milk the cows twice a day.

In affirmative sentences, there is very little difference in meaning among *must, have to,* and *have got to.* In the following sentences, any one of them can be used.

> Everyone *must/has to/has got to* wear a mask in this room.
> The equipment *must/has to/has got to* be washed every day.
> You *must/have to/have got to* wash your hands before you
> start.

In questions about necessity and obligation, *have to* is usually used. Questions with *must* are very formal.

> *Do* you *have to* wash the equipment every day?
> *Must* we wear masks? (formal)

b. Prohibition with *Must Not* and Lack of Necessity with *Don't/Doesn't Have to*

You *must not* smoke in here.

The negative forms of *must* and *have to* are as follows:

AFFIRMATIVE You *must* smoke outside.
You *have to* go outside.
We *have got to* put up a sign.

NEGATIVE You *must not* smoke in here.
You *don't have to* go far.
We *don't have to* put up a sign.

Notice that the negative form of *have got to* is not used. Use *don't/doesn't have to* instead.

Although *must* and *have to* have similar meanings in affirmative sentences, they have different meanings in negative sentences. Use *must not* or *mustn't* to show that something is prohibited (not allowed).

You *must not* smoke near the gas tank. It is not allowed because it is too dangerous.
You *must not* work without a mask.

Use *don't have to* or *doesn't have to* to show that something is not necessary.

You *don't have to* clean the barn. Someone else will.
We *don't have to* milk by hand here. We have machines.

c. Questions with *Have to* and Requests with *Must*

Do you *have to* take a written test?

Have to (not *must*) is usually used in questions about obligation or necessity. The auxiliary verb *do (does, did)* is used in questions with *have to*.

Does she *have to* take a written test?
Does the fee *have to* be paid at the same time?

In some cases, questions with *must* and *have to* are really requests.

Must you smoke in here? (Please don't smoke in here.)
Do you *have to* sing now? (Please don't sing now.)

d.   Assumptions with *Must* and *Have To*

She *must* be a police officer.

In some sentences, *must* and *have to* indicate that something is probably true; that is, because of the facts or the situation, the speaker makes an assumption.

It's thirty degrees today.
That river *has to* be freezing. (I assume that the river is very cold.)
A man just jumped into the river.
He *must* be crazy. (I assume that the man is crazy, given his actions.)
No, look! There's a little girl yelling for help.
He *must* be trying to help her.

The negative form *must not* is used when the speaker is making a negative assumption.

The girl is screaming.
She *must not* be able to swim. (I assume that she cannot swim.)
She is looking the other way.
She *must not* see him. (I think that she doesn't see him.)

The negative form of *have to* has a different meaning. It is not used when the speaker is making a negative assumption. The negative of *have to* means that an action isn't necessary.

She *doesn't have to* worry now.
She sees him.
They *don't have to* call an ambulance.
She is safe.

5.17   Uses of the Modals and Semimodals

a.   Requests, Requests for Permission and Suggestions

May I come in?

Most of the modals can be used to make requests. A request is like a command, but it is more polite. Requests are often in question form, but the speaker does not expect an answer. Usually, a request with a modal is more polite than a request without a modal. Requests with the modals *could* and *would* are more polite than requests with *can* and *will*.

REQUESTS

Mail this letter, please.
Please open the window.

POLITE REQUESTS

Will you please mail this letter.
Can you open the window, please.

VERY POLITE REQUESTS

Would you mail this letter, please.
Could you please open the window.
Might I see you after class?

Notice that *please* can go before the main verb or at the end of the sentence.

Some requests are requests for permission. *Can, could, may,* and *might* are used in these requests.

POLITE

Can I talk to you?
May I come in?

VERY POLITE OR FORMAL

Could I talk to you?

Some speakers consider *may* more formal and correct than *can* in asking if something is permitted. However, in common practice, *may* is often used to ask for individual permission, and *can* is used to ask about general rules.

INDIVIDUAL PERMISSION

May I ask you a question?
May I see a menu?

GENERAL RULES

Can students park in this lot?
Can we still get breakfast in the cafeteria at ten o'clock?

The modals *can, could, may, might, shall,* and *should* are all used to make suggestions. These suggestions are sometimes in the form of statements and sometimes in the form of questions.

INFORMAL

Let's go now.
Get the car.
Tell him to park in the garage.

FORMAL OR POLITE

Shall we go now?
Can you get the car now?
He *may* want to park in the garage.
Should we go now?
Could you get the car now?
He *might* want to park in the garage.

b.   Possibility and Probability

It *might* rain.

Nobody knows the future, but people often guess about it. Modals and semimodals express people's certainty or uncertainty about the future.

CERTAIN

It *will* rain.
It *is going to* rain.
I didn't water the plant all week.
It *must* be dry by now.

LESS CERTAIN

It *may* rain.
It *might* rain.
I didn't water the plant today.
It *could* be dry by now.

Many of the modals are used to guess about events. Speakers show how certain they are about these events by their choice of modal.

MORE CERTAIN

Maria:	My ring is not here.
Yoko:	It *must* be in the kitchen.
Yoko:	You*'ll* probably find it on the sink.

LESS CERTAIN

It *should* be on the windowsill.
It *may* be on the floor.
It *might* be in the bathroom.
You *could have* put it in your pocket.

c. Necessity and Advisability

The baby *should* have a nap.

Some events and actions are more necessary than others. Some modals and semimodals show how important an event or action is. For example, a baby needs many things, but some things are more important than others.

NECESSARY

You *must* feed the baby.
You *have to* keep her warm.
You *have got to* keep her safe.

ADVISABLE

You *should* hold the baby often.
You *ought to* play with her.
You *are supposed to* change her diapers.
You *had better* watch her carefully.

The expressions *should have* and *ought to have* are used when something advisable was not done.

The baby is crying.
She *should have* taken a nap, but she didn't.
She's crying.
You *ought to have* fed her earlier.

When the consequences of not doing the action are considered, *had better* can be used.

You *had better* move that milk, or the baby will spill it.

d. Preferences

I should do my homework, but I *would rather* read a book.

Several expressions with *would* are used to state or ask about a preference. These expressions are followed by different forms of the verb.

Would you like *to read* a novel?
Would you mind *reading* my essay?
Would you rather *read* some poetry?

In addition to the differences in the verbs that follow these expressions, there are differences in meaning. *Would like* and *would mind* are often used in yes-no questions. *Would rather* is used to ask about or state a choice.

Would you *like* to read this?
Would you *mind* sitting on the couch?
Would you *rather* read poetry or short stories?
Would you *rather* sit on the chair or on the couch?

e.   Hypothetical Situations

I can't understand this question.
I wish I *could*.

The modals *would* and *could* are often used in sentences about hypothetical (imaginary) situations.

CORRECT	I wish that I *could* pass this test.
	I *would* be very happy to get a score of 500.
INCORRECT	*I wish that I pass this test.
	*I am very happy if I get a score of 500.

When a suggestion or prediction is being made, *should* and *ought to* can be used for hypothetical situations.

If you want to pass the test, you *should* study more.
If you work hard, you *ought to* pass.

f.   Past Habit

I *used to* collect butterflies.

The expressions *used to* and *would* describe something that was customary in the past. *Used to* only refers to past time, so it is not necessary to use a time expression, such as *last year,* to show the past meaning. Because *would* can be used for past, present, and future time, it is necessary to use a time expression with *would* to show that past time is meant.

UNCLEAR   I *would* collect small animals.

CLEAR   When I was young, I *would* collect butterflies.
              I *used to* put them in an album and keep them
              in my room.

Chapter 6

Special Kinds of Verbs

6.1 Some Properties of Verbs

a. Regular and Irregular Verbs

Some features of English verbs can be described with general statements. The past forms of regular verbs, for example, are always formed in the same way. To make the past form and the past participle form of a regular verb, add -d, -ed, or -ied to the simple form of the verb.

SIMPLE FORM	I *walk.*
PAST	I *walked.*
PAST PARTICIPLE	I have *walked.*

With irregular verbs, the past form and past participle form are often quite different from the simple form.

SIMPLE FORM	I *eat.*
PAST	I *ate.*
PAST PARTICIPLE	I have *eaten.*

b. Phrasal Verbs

Not all English verbs are single words. Some verbs consist of two or three words. These two- and three-word verbs are sometimes called phrasal verbs. The meanings of phrasal verbs are usually different from the combined meanings of the words they are made of. For example, the meaning of *call on* is not the combination of *call* and *on*. *To call on* can mean "to visit." The special meanings of phrasal verbs must be learned.

Some phrasal verbs are separable; that is, when the verb has an object, the two parts of the verb can separate.

We *broke up* the fight.
We *broke* it *up* fast.

Other phrasal verbs are inseparable; the object always comes after all parts of the phrasal verb.

CORRECT	*Turn into* that garage over there. That will be close enough to the theater.
INCORRECT	*Turn that garage *into*.
CORRECT	I *called on* Joe last week. He'll have the goods here by Friday.
INCORRECT	*I called Joe *on* last week.

c. Verb Complements

Many times a verb requires a particular word, phrase, or structure to complete its meaning. Whatever is used to complete the meaning of a verb is called a verb complement.

SUBJECT	VERB	VERB COMPLEMENT
The magician	lifted	his hat.
He	tried	to do a trick.
I	enjoy	watching magic tricks.

Not all verbs can be completed with all kinds of complements. The use of different complements with different verbs is discussed in section 6.4.

6.2 Irregular Verbs

> I *caught* you.

Irregular verbs are different from regular verbs in several ways. A regular verb has a past form that is made by adding -d, -ed, or –ied to the simple form. The past participle of regular verbs is the same as the past form.

REGULAR VERBS

SIMPLE FORM	I must fix that fence.
PAST	I *fixed* it yesterday.
PAST PARTICIPLE	I have *fixed* it three times this week.

For most irregular verbs, the past participle is different from the past form. Many irregular past participles end in -n or -en.

IRREGULAR VERBS

SIMPLE FORM	Don't *break* that branch.
PAST	I *broke* one last week.
PAST PARTICIPLE	We have *broken* the hammer.

When learning the forms of irregular verbs, it is useful to recognize that many verbs have similar patterns of sound and spelling. Irregular verbs can be put into four groups as follows:

		SIMPLE FORM	PAST	PAST PARTICIPLE
1.	All forms the same:	hit	hit	hit
2.	Different first form:	catch	caught	caught

		SIMPLE FORM	PAST	PAST PARTICIPLE
3.	Different second or third form:	run	ran	run
4.	All forms different:	drink	drank	drunk

a. All Forms the Same

I always *cut* myself with this knife. (simple form)
I *cut* myself yesterday. (past)
I've just *cut* myself again. (past participle)

The irregular verbs with no change at all end in either *d-* or *-t.* The following verbs all have the same simple form, past form, and past participle.

bet	hit	shed
bid	hurt	shut
burst	let	slit
cast	put	split
cost	quit	spread
cut	rid	wet
fit	set	

b. Different First Form

Luis: You *feed* the cat today, will you?
Maria: I *fed* him yesterday.
Luis: You haven't *fed* him very often.

These irregular verbs have one simple form and another past and past participle form.

Maria: Find the dog's collar. (simple form)
Luis: I *found* it yesterday. (past)
Maria: I thought I had *found* it. (past participle)

For some verbs, the vowel in the past and past participle forms is different from the vowel in the simple form.

SIMPLE FORM	PAST	PAST PARTICIPLE
cling	clung	clung
dig	dug	dug
hang	hung	hung
sling	slung	slung
spin	spun	spun
stick	stuck	stuck
sting	stung	stung
strike	struck	struck
swing	swung	swung
wring	wrung	wrung
bleed	bled	bled
breed	bred	bred
feed	fed	fed
lead	led	led
meet	met	met
read	read (pronounced like *red*)	read (pronounced like *red*)
speed	sped	sped
bring	brought	brought
buy	bought	bought
catch	caught	caught
fight	fought	fought
seek	sought	sought
teach	taught	taught
think	thought	thought
bind	bound	bound
find	found	found
grind	ground	ground
wind	wound	wound

For some of these verbs there is a vowel change as well as a -*t* or -*d* ending in the past and past participle forms.

SIMPLE FORM	PAST	PAST PARTICIPLE
creep	crept	crept
feel	felt	felt
flee	fled	fled
keep	kept	kept
kneel	knelt	knelt

SIMPLE FORM	PAST	PAST PARTICIPLE
leave	left	left
mean	meant	meant
sleep	slept	slept
sweep	swept	swept
weep	wept	wept
bend	bent	bent
lend	lent	lent
send	sent	sent
spend	spent	spent
build	built	built
lay	laid	laid
pay	paid	paid
say	said	said

The verbs *dream* and *leap* have regular *(-ed)* past and past participle forms. However, they also have older past and past participle forms as follows:

SIMPLE FORM	PAST	PAST PARTICIPLE
dream	dreamt	dreamt
leap	leapt	leapt

You might hear these in formal speech or read them in literature.

c. Different Second or Third Form

There are only a few verbs in English that have one form for the simple form and the past participle and a different form for the past. Two common ones are *run* and *come*.

Don't *run*. (simple form)
You *ran* too fast. (past)
You shouldn't have *run*. (past participle)

Don't *come* in. (simple form)
Who just *came* in? (past)
You shouldn't have *come*. (past participle)

Only one common verb has a different third form.

Will the Yankees *beat* the Red Sox?
They *beat* them last week.
They've *beaten* them three times this year.

d. All Forms Different

> I can't *sing* anymore.
> I *sang* too much yesterday.
> I have *sung* too much today.

Verbs with all three forms different usually have a past participle ending in *-n* or *-en*. For the following verbs, the past participle is formed by adding *-n* to the irregular past form, sometimes after omitting a final *-e*.

> Did you *speak* to your teacher about the piano? (simple form)
> I *spoke* to her yesterday. (past)
> She has already *spoken* to the piano tuner. (past participle)

Here are some of the verbs that follow this pattern:

SIMPLE FORM	PAST	PAST PARTICIPLE
break	broke	broken
choose	chose	chosen
freeze	froze	frozen
steal	stole	stolen
speak	spoke	spoken
weave	wove	woven
bear	bore	borne (or *born*)
swear	swore	sworn
tear	tore	torn
wear	wore	worn

For some verbs, the past participle is made by adding *-n* or *-en* to the simple form. However, the vowel in the past form is usually different.

> Don't *throw* that. (simple form)
> He *threw* the plate. (past)
> You have *thrown* two of them. (past participle)

Here are more verbs that are formed on this pattern:

SIMPLE FORM	PAST	PAST PARTICIPLE
blow	blew	blown
draw	drew	drawn
grow	grew	grown

SIMPLE FORM	PAST	PAST PARTICIPLE
know	knew	known
throw	threw	thrown
sew	sewed	sewn
show	showed	shown (or *showed*)
forbid	forbade (or *forbad*)	forbidden
forgive	forgave	forgiven
give	gave	given

Some irregular verbs have different vowels for all the forms. For some of these verbs, the past participle ends in *-n* or *-en*.

SIMPLE FORM	PAST	PAST PARTICIPLE
begin	began	begun
drink	drank	drunk
ring	rang	rung
shrink	shrank	shrunk
sing	sang	sung
sink	sank	sunk
spring	sprang	sprung
stink	stank	stunk
swim	swam	swum
drive	drove	driven
ride	rode	ridden
rise	rose	risen
write	wrote	written

The following list gives the simple, the past, and the past participle forms of many common irregular verbs:

SIMPLE FORM	PAST	PAST PARTICIPLE
awake	awoke (or *awakened*)	awoken (or *awoke, awakened*)
be (*am, is, are*)	was/were	been
beat	beat	beaten
become	became	become
begin	began	begun

SIMPLE FORM	PAST	PAST PARTICIPLE
bend	bent	bent
bet	bet	bet
bid	bid	bid
bind	bound	bound
bite	bit	bitten
bleed	bled	bled
blow	blew	blown
break	broke	broken
breed	bred	bred
bring	brought	brought
broadcast	broadcast	broadcast
build	built	built
burst	burst	burst
buy	bought	bought
catch	caught	caught
choose	chose	chosen
cling	clung	clung
come	came	come
cost	cost	cost
creep	crept	crept
cut	cut	cut
deal	dealt	dealt
dig	dug	dug
dive	dived	dived
	or (dove)	
do	did	done
draw	drew	drawn
drink	drank	drunk
eat	ate	eaten
fall	fell	fallen
feed	fed	fed
feel	felt	felt
fight	fought	fought
find	found	found
fit	fit	fit
flee	fled	fled
fly	flew	flown

SIMPLE FORM	PAST	PAST PARTICIPLE
forbid	forbade (or *forbad*)	forbidden
forget	forgot	forgotten
forgive	forgave	forgiven
freeze	froze	frozen
get	got	gotten
give	gave	given
go	went	gone
grind	ground	ground
grow	grew	grown
hang	hanged	hanged (people)
hang	hung	hung (things)
have	had	had
hear	heard	heard
hide	hid	hidden
hit	hit	hit
hold	held	held
hurt	hurt	hurt
keep	kept	kept
know	knew	known
lay	laid	laid
lead	led	led
leave	left	left
lend	lent	lent
let	let	let
lie	lay	lain (recline)
lie	lied	lied (tell an untruth)
light	lit	lit
lose	lost	lost
make	made	made
mean	meant	meant
meet	met	met
pay	paid	paid
prove	proved	proven

SIMPLE FORM	PAST	PAST PARTICIPLE
put	put	put
quit	quit	quit
read	read (pronounced like *red)*	read (pronounced like *red*)
rid	rid	rid
ride	rode	ridden
ring	rang	rung
rise	rose	risen
run	ran	run
say	said (pronounce like *led)*	said (pronounced like *led*)
see	saw	seen
seek	sought	sought
sell	sold	sold
send	sent	sent
set	set	set
sew	sewed	sewn
shake	shook	shaken
shine	shone	shone (give light)
shine	shined	shined (polish)
shoot	shot	shot
show	showed	shown
shrink	shrank	shrunk
shut	shut	shut
sing	sang	sung
sink	sank	sunk
sit	sat	sat
sleep	slept	slept
slide	slid	slid
slit	slit	slit
speak	spoke	spoken
spend	spent	spent
spin	spun	spun
split	split	split
spread	spread	spread

SIMPLE FORM	PAST	PAST PARTICIPLE
spring	sprang	sprung
stand	stood	stood
steal	stole	stolen
stick	stuck	stuck
sting	stung	stung
stink	stank	stunk
strike	struck	struck
string	strung	strung
strive	strove	striven
swear	swore	sworn
sweep	swept	swept
swell	swelled	swollen
swim	swam	swum
swing	swung	swung
take	took	taken
teach	taught	taught
tear	tore	torn
tell	told	told
think	thought	thought
throw	threw	thrown
understand	understood	understood
wake	woke	woken
wear	wore	worn
weave	wove	woven
weep	wept	wept
win	won	won
wind	wound	wound
wring	wrung	wrung
write	wrote	written

6.3 Phrasal Verbs

The man fainted; he *passed out* in the street.

a. Particles

Some verbs in English consist of more than one word. These verbs are called phrasal verbs. Sometimes they are called two-word verbs or three-word verbs.

He *passed out* in the street. (He fainted in the street.)
He didn't *feel up to* walking for a while. (He didn't feel well enough to walk for a while.)

Phrasal verbs consist of verbs, such as *pass,* and particles, such as *out.* The particles are usually the following words:

about	at	in	out
across	away	into	over
along	back	of	through
against	down	off	up
around	for	on	with

Some phrasal verbs are considered idioms because the meaning of the verb and particle together is different from the meanings of the verb and particle separately.

She couldn't *put up with* her son's behavior anymore.
He wasn't *living up to* her expectations.

b. Separable and Inseparable Phrasal Verbs

Hand it *in* now.

Some phrasal verbs have objects.

SUBJECT	PHRASAL VERB	OBJECT
You	handed in	your paper late.

With phrasal verbs that are separable, the object can come before or after the particle (except when the object is a pronoun).

SUBJECT	VERB + PARTICLE	OBJECT	
You	handed in	your paper	late.

SUBJECT	VERB	OBJECT	PARTICLE	
You	handed	your paper	in	late.

When a phrasal verb is separable and the object is a pronoun, such as *it* or *him,* the pronoun must come before the particle.

CORRECT   You handed it in late.

INCORRECT   *You handed in it late.

When a phrasal verb is inseparable, the object follows the particle, even when the object is a pronoun.

CORRECT   What has become of *my term paper*?
           What has become of *it* ?

INCORRECT *What has become *it* of?

There are many phrasal verbs in English. The following rules are helpful for remembering which ones are separable and which ones are inseparable.

1.   Phrasal verbs consisting of two one-syllable words are generally separable unless they end in *-for*, *-with*, or *-on*.

SEPARABLE

He *gave out* the tests at nine.
He *gave* the tests *out* at nine.
We *turned in* the tests at five.
We *turned* the tests *in* at five.

INSEPARABLE

The teacher wouldn't *stand for* any noise.
After the test, we *headed for* the cafeteria.
I couldn't *deal with* that last question.

2.   Two-word phrasal verbs that end in *away, down, off, out, over,* and *up* are usually separable.

I couldn't *figure out* the question.
I couldn't *figure* the question *out*.

Could we *talk over* the test?
Could we *talk* the test *over*?

3.   Most three-word phrasal verbs are inseparable.

I should *read up on* Chinese history over vacation.
I can't *put up with* another wasted summer.

4.   Two-word phrasal verbs that end in *about, across, against,* and *into* are usually inseparable.

Roberto: Did you *hear about* the airline strike?
Maria: Yes, I did. I *ran across* an article about it in the newspaper.

c.   Summary of Separable and Inseparable Phrasal Verbs

1.   Usually separable

a. Two-word verbs consisting of two one-syllable words, except those ending in *for* or *with*.

b. Two-word verbs ending in *away, down, off, out, over,* or *up.*

2. Usually inseparable

a. Three-word verbs.

b. Two-word verbs ending in *about, across, against,* or *into.*

6.4 Verb Complements: Objects

a. Intransitive Verbs

The lights dimmed.

The verb is the most important part of a sentence. Some verbs are not followed by objects. These verbs are called intransitive verbs.

	SUBJECT	INTRANSITIVE VERB
Then	the rabbit	vanished.
	the magician	disappeared.
	his assistant	waited.

Intransitive verbs are often followed by adverbials, such as prepositional phrases.

SUBJECT	INTRANSITIVE VERB	ADVERBIAL
The magician	disappeared	before our eyes.
His assistant	waited	on the stage.

Some other common intransitive verbs follow:

complain	fall	rain	sleep
die	lie	sit	yawn

A direct object is not used after an intransitive verb.

INCORRECT   *The magician disappeared the rabbit.
*His assistant waited something.

b. Transitive Verbs with One and Two Objects

The magician *removed* a *rabbit* from the hat.

Verbs that can be followed by objects are called transitive verbs. Some transitive verbs can be followed by only one noun, but other transitive verbs need other kinds of phrases and clauses to complete the meaning of the verb.

SUBJECT	TRANSITIVE VERB	INDIRECT OBJECT	DIRECT OBJECT	PREPOSITIONAL PHRASE
The magician	lifted		the hat.	
He	offered	a woman	the hat.	
She	put		it	on the table.

The indirect object usually answers questions beginning with *who* or *whom,* and the direct object usually answers questions beginning with *what.* When the indirect object comes after the direct object, it is part of a prepositional phrase beginning with *for* or *to.*

SUBJECT	TRANSITIVE VERB	DIRECT OBJECT	INDIRECT OBJECT
He	gave	the rabbit	to his assistant.
His assistant	moved	the table	for him.

When the indirect object comes before the direct object, the prepositions *to* and *for* are not used.

CORRECT	The man handed *his assistant* a rabbit.
	The assistant made *the magician* a blindfold.
INCORRECT	*The man handed to his assistant a rabbit.
	*The assistant made for the magician a blindfold.

Not all verbs with two objects can have the indirect object both before and after the direct object. With the following verbs, the indirect object can occur either before or after the direct object:

VERB	INDIRECT OBJECT	DIRECT OBJECT
Bring	*us*	the coins.
Send	*them*	the note.

VERB	DIRECT OBJECT	*To* + INDIRECT OBJECT
Bring	the coins	*to us.*
Send	the note	*to them.*

Other verbs that follow this sentence pattern are the following:

give lend sell take
hand offer show

	VERB	INDIRECT OBJECT	DIRECT OBJECT
She	will bake	us	something.

	VERB	DIRECT OBJECT	FOR + INDIRECT OBJECT
She	will bake	something	for us.

Other verbs that follow this sentence pattern are the following:

bring buy draw get make
build cook find knit take

Verbs of communication often have indirect objects. There are only a few of these verbs that can have the indirect object both before and after the direct object.

He will { teach / tell / write } *me* the answers.

He will { teach / tell / write } the answers *to me.*

For most verbs of communication, the indirect object must be part of a prepositional phrase after the direct object.

CORRECT She admitted the mistake *to her mother.*
INCORRECT *She admitted her mother the mistake.

Other verbs that follow this sentence pattern are the following:

announce describe confess report
communicate explain mention

Say and *tell* are the most common verbs of communication. With both *say* and *tell*, the indirect object can follow *to.* However, with *tell* but not *say,* the indirect object can come after the verb.

CORRECT	She told the news to her mother.
	She said many things to her sister.
	She told her mother the news.
INCORRECT	*She said her sister many things.

6.5 Direct and Indirect Speech

a. Differences between Direct and Indirect Speech

Verbs of communication introduce both direct, quoted speech, and indirect, reported speech. In direct speech, the exact words of a speaker are repeated. In indirect speech, the meaning of what has been said is reported, but the exact words are not used. Quotation marks are used for direct speech, but not for indirect speech.

| DIRECT SPEECH | Barbara's mother said, "You're too young to get married." |
| INDIRECT SPEECH | Barbara's mother said that Barbara was too young to get married. |

In direct speech, the pronouns and time expressions correspond to the point of view of the person who first said the sentence. In indirect speech, the pronouns and time expressions correspond to the point of view of the person who is reporting what was said.

| DIRECT SPEECH | Her uncle said, "*You* can't get married *now*." |
| INDIRECT SPEECH | Her uncle said that *she* couldn't get married *at that time*. |

Commas are used to separate the quotation from the rest of the sentence in direct speech. Commas are not used to set off indirect speech.

| DIRECT SPEECH | Her uncle said to her, "You'll be sorry later." |
| INDIRECT SPEECH | Her uncle said that she'd be sorry later. |

In direct speech, there is no introductory word such as *that* or *whether*. In indirect speech, there is usually an introductory word. Statements are usually introduced with *that*. Questions are introduced with *if, whether,* and other *wh*-words.

Her cousin asked, "Will you keep your job?"
Her cousin asked *if* she would keep her job.

She replied, "I plan to get a new job."
She replied *that* she planned to get a new job.

In direct speech, questions are quoted exactly. In indirect speech, statement word order is used for both statements and questions. *If* and *whether* introduce questions in indirect speech.

DIRECT SPEECH   Her cousin asked, "Will you keep your job?"
                     Her sister asked, "Have you met his family?"

INDIRECT SPEECH   Her cousin asked if *she would keep* her job.
                     Her sister asked whether *she had met* his family.

In direct speech, imperatives are quoted exactly. Imperatives are introduced by *to* in indirect speech. Negative imperatives are introduced by *not to* in indirect speech.

DIRECT SPEECH
INDIRECT SPEECH

Her mother told her, "Wait until you're older."
Her mother told her *to* wait until she was older.

Her uncle said, "Don't get married so soon."
Her uncle said *not to* get married so soon.

b. Sequence of Tenses in Indirect Speech

Her father said that she *was* too young.

In sentences with indirect speech, if the main verb (such as *said, told,* or *asked)* is in the past, the verb in the noun clause will usually be a past form introduced by *that.*

DIRECT SPEECH
INDIRECT SPEECH

"I *want* to get married."
She *said* that she *wanted* to get married.

"I *am planning* the wedding."
She *said* that she *was planning* the wedding.

"I *have invited* everyone."
She *said* that she *had invited* everyone.

"I *will talk* to the minister."
She *said* that she *would talk* to the minister.

However, when indirect speech reports something that has just been said, the verb in the noun clause is sometimes in the present form. In cases where the reported sentence deals with a general statement, the verb also stays in the present form.

DIRECT SPEECH
  INDIRECT SPEECH

"The wedding is on Sunday."
She just said that the wedding is on Sunday.

"Young people sometimes make mistakes."
Her father said that sometimes young people make mistakes.

6.6 Verbs with *That* Complements

a. Verbs of Communication

She *said* that there was a dead body in the bedroom.

Sometimes the meaning of a verb is completed with a clause beginning with *that.* Quite often, *that* clauses occur with verbs of communication.

He *told* us that Elvira was dead.
The maid *said* that she had been murdered.

With some verbs, like *tell,* it is necessary to name the listener. With other verbs, like *say,* it is not necessary to name the listener.

The gardener told *the police* that he had seen a man.

CORRECT   He *said* that the man was very tall.
INCORRECT   *He told that the man was very tall.

With verbs like *tell,* the noun or pronoun that names the listener does not come after the word *to. To* cannot be used before the indirect object.

CORRECT   The maid told *the police* that she was afraid.
INCORRECT   *She told to them that the man had hit her.

The following verbs are like *tell* because the listener must be mentioned and *to* is not used before the indirect object:

advise	inform	promise
assure	notify	remind
convince	persuade	warn

In the following sentences 1 is the verb, 2 is the indirect object, and 3 is the *that*-clause:

$$\overset{1}{\text{The maid}}\ \overset{}{\text{told}}\ \overset{2}{\text{the police}}\ \overset{3}{\text{that Elvira had been alone.}}$$

$$\overset{1}{\text{She}}\ \text{didn't convince}\ \overset{2}{\text{them}}\ \overset{3}{\text{that she was telling the truth.}}$$

With verbs such as *say,* the listener does not have to be named. However, when the listener is named, the word *to* is necessary.

CORRECT   The gardener explained *to the police* that he saw a man arrive.

INCORRECT   *He explained them that he didn't know the time.

The following verbs are like *say* because the listener does not have to be mentioned. If the listener is mentioned, *to* is used before that word (the indirect object).

admit	explain	report
announce	hint	shout
boast	indicate	state
complain	mention	suggest
confess	proclaim	swear
declare	remark	whisper

In these sentences 1 is the verb, 2 is *to* + the indirect object, and 3 is the *that*-clause:

$$\overset{1}{\text{The butler}}\ \overset{}{\text{admitted}}\ \overset{2}{\text{to the police}}\ \overset{3}{\text{that he had seen a man.}}$$

$$\overset{1}{\text{He}}\ \text{didn't mention}\ \overset{2}{\text{to them}}\ \overset{3}{\text{that he knew the man.}}$$

$$\overset{1}{\text{He}}\ \text{swore}\ \overset{3}{\text{that the man left early.}}$$

The verbs *speak* and *talk* cannot be used to introduce *that*-clauses.

INCORRECT   *He spoke to the police that he loved Elvira.
             *He talked to them that he had been reading.

b. Verbs of Mental Activity

I *believe* that the butler knows something.

Verbs of mental activity, such as *think,* are often followed by *that-*clauses.

	VERB	THAT-CLAUSE
The police	believed	*that* the butler had seen something.
They	decided	*that* he wasn't telling the truth.

After verbs of mental activity, the word *that* can be omitted without changing the meaning of the sentence.

The police learned	*that*	Elvira had gone to the hairdresser.
The police learned		Elvira had gone to the hairdresser.

Some common verbs of mental activity are the following:

assume	dream	indicate	regret
believe	feel	know	remember
calculate	find out	learn	reveal
conclude	forget	notice	think
consider	guess	pretend	understand
decide	hear	prove	
discover	hope	realize	
doubt	imagine	recall	

6.7 Verbs with Infinitive Complements

We want *to buy* a new house.

An infinitive or infinitive phrase can sometimes complete the meaning of a verb. The infinitive is always *to* plus the simple form of a verb. The infinitive can never have an suffix, such as *-s,* and can never be in the past form.

CORRECT   We wanted *to buy* a house last year.
INCORRECT   *We wanted to bought a house last year.

Infinitive phrases can be the object of the sentence. In addition, the infinitive itself can have an object.

OBJECT OF SENTENCE		
	OBJECT OF INFINITIVE	
We want	to buy	a new house.

Verbs of mental activity are often followed by infinitive phrases that refer to unfulfilled actions; that is, actions that have not occurred.

VERB	INFINITIVE PHRASE
We	hope	to find a four-bedroom house.
We	plan	to have a large family.

Some verbs of mental activity that often occur in this sentence pattern are the following:

agree	decide	intend	prefer
arrange	expect	learn	pretend
choose	forget	like	refuse
consent	hope	plan	want

Many verbs, especially verbs of compelling, ordering, and advising, are often followed by a noun or pronoun and an infinitive phrase. In the following sentences, 1 is the verb, 2 is the noun or pronoun, and 3 is the infinitive phrase:

                1   2   3
The salesperson advised us to buy an old house.

       1   2   3
He encouraged us to look at a lot of houses.

Some verbs that occur in this sentence pattern are the following:

advise	convince	get	request
allow	dare	instruct	require
cause	direct	invite	teach
caution	encourage	order	tell
challenge	expect	permit	urge
command	forbid	persuade	warn
compel	force	remind	

In negative infinitives, *not* comes before the infinitive.

The salesperson advised us *not* to buy this house.
He warned us *not* to buy a house near the freeway.

In some sentences, *for* also comes before the infinitive phrase.

Our families would prefer *for* us to buy a house near theirs.
They are waiting *for* us to decide.

Some verbs can be followed by a *wh*-word, such as *when, who, where,* or *why,* followed by an infinitive phrase.

	VERB	*WH*-WORD	INFINITIVE PHRASE
I	don't know	when	to move.
I	can't decide	where	to live.

In some sentences, the verb is followed by a noun or pronoun, a *wh*-word, and an infinitive phrase.

	VERB	NOUN OR PRONOUN	*WH*-WORD	INFINITIVE PHRASE
He	told	the woman	how	to get a loan.
He	showed	her	where	to get the forms.

There are many other verbs that can be followed by infinitives and infinitive phrases.

In some cases, a verb can be followed by the simple form of the verb alone, that is, without *to*.

I helped them *do* it.

These verbs are discussed in section 6.10.

6.8 Verbs with Gerund Complements

I dislike *cleaning* the house.

The meanings of some verbs can be completed with gerund phrases. A gerund phrase begins with a gerund, a verb in the *-ing* form.

SUBJECT	VERB	GERUND PHRASE
I	love	cleaning the house.
My sister	dislikes	washing dishes.

Gerund phrases can be objects of sentences. In addition, a gerund itself can have an object.

SUBJECT	VERB	OBJECT OF SENTENCE	
		OBJECT OF GERUND	
My sister	enjoys	drying	the dishes.
She	hates	folding	clothes.

Gerund phrases can also have subjects.

SUBJECT	VERB	OBJECT OF SENTENCE
		SUBJECT OF GERUND

I	appreciate	her helping me.
Mother	encourages	our doing the housework.

The subject of a gerund can be a noun phrase, such as *my sister,* a possessive noun (phrase), such as *Joan's,* or a possessive adjective, such as *our.*

	SUBJECT OF GERUND	GERUND
Mother counted on	my sister	cleaning the house.
She appreciates	Joan's	helping me.
She encourages	our	working together.

Gerunds and gerund phrases often follow phrasal verbs and prepositi ons.

	GERUND PHRASE
We decided against	cleaning the refrigerator.
We forgot about	washing the frying pan.
I brushed up on	making doughnuts.
I look forward to	eating them.
I stopped Joan from	eating the cookies.

Infinitives cannot be used after phrasal verbs and prepositions.

INCORRECT   *I stopped her from to eat the cookies.

In negative gerund phrases, *not* comes before the gerund.

She understood our *not* working in the morning.
She appreciated Joan's *not* eating the cookies.

6.9   Verbs with Infinitive or Gerund Complements

I love *to go* to the circus.
She loves *going* there, too.

Some verbs may be followed by either infinitive phrases or gerund phrases.

> I like *to go* to the circus.   I like *going* to zoos, too.
> I prefer *to watch* the animals.   I prefer *watching* the lions.

Some common verbs that can be followed by either infinitive or gerund phrases are the following:

begin	hate	love	prefer	start
continue	like	neglect	propose	try

In some cases, sentences with gerund complements have meanings different from sentences with infinitive complements. Infinitive complements often refer to an unfulfilled event; that is, an event that has not happened yet. Gerund complements often refer to fulfilled events; that is, events that have already happened.

> He will remember *to meet us* outside the circus tent at noon.
>   (The meeting has not happened yet.)
> He will always remember *going to the circus* as a child.
>   (Going to the circus has happened.)
> I forgot *to invite Charlie.*
>   (The forgetting happened first, so the inviting didn't occur.)
> I forgot about *your inviting Susan.*
>   (The inviting occurred.)

6.10 Verbs with Bare Infinitive Complements

a. *Make, Have,* and *Let*

> Ms. Mendoza *made* her son *clean* his room.

In some sentences, the verbs *make* and *have* have a causative meaning; that is, one person causes another person to do something.

SUBJECT	VERB	DOER	ACTION	OBJECT
Ms. Mendoza	makes	her son	clean	his room every day.
She	has	him	vacuum	the rug.
She	makes	him	hang up	his clothes.

Not all verbs that have a causative meaning are followed by the simple form. The verbs *get* and *force* are followed by infinitives.

DOER	*TO* + ACTION	OBJECT	
She forced	Jimmy	to store	his old books.
She got	him	to put	them	away.

The verbs *let* and *allow* have similar meanings.

Ms. Mendoza *let* Jimmy call his friend.
Ms. Mendoza *allowed* Jimmy to call his friend.

However, the verb *let* follows the same sentence pattern as the verbs *make* and *have* with no *to* before the action.

	DOER	ACTION	OBJECT
Ms. Mendoza let	Jimmy	keep	his old football.
She didn't let	him	throw away	his text books.

The verb *allow* follows the same sentence pattern as *get* and *force*.

	DOER	*TO* + ACTION	OBJECT
She allowed	him	to keep	his football jersey.
She didn't allow	him	to throw away	his old pictures.

b.   Verbs of Perception and Their Complements

I *watched* him *clean up* his room.

Like causative verbs, verbs of perception such as *see, notice,* and *hear* are often followed by a noun phrase and a simple verb.

SUBJECT	VERB	DOER	ACTION	OBJECT
I	watched	Jimmy	clean up	his room.
We	listened to	his mother	complain.	
I	heard	Jimmy	vacuum	the rug.

Most verbs of perception can also be followed by a noun phrase and a gerund phrase.

	DOER	GERUND PHRASE
I watched	Jimmy	cleaning up his room.
We listened to	his mother	complaining.

6.11 Summary of Verbs and Their Complements

The following lists indicate which verbs can be followed by which complements. Some individual verbs will not be correct for all dialects and all speakers.

1. Verb + Infinitive

   He cannot *afford* to do it.

afford	continue	hope	prepare	think
agree	dare	intend	pretend	treaten
appear	decide	know	promise	try
arrange	demand	learn	propose	volunteer
ask	deserve	like	refuse	wait
attempt	desire	love	remember	want
bear	determine	manage	resolve	wish
beg	expect	mean	seem	
begin	fail	need	(can't)stand	
bother	forget	neglect	start	
care	get	offer	stop	
choose	go	plan	struggle	
claim	hate	pledge	swear	
consent	hesitate	prefer	tend	

2. Verb + Noun Phrase + Infinitive

   He *urged* me to do it.

advise	compel	forbid	notify	send
allow	convince	force	order	teach
appoint	count on	get	permit	tell
ask	dare	hire	persuade	tempt
beg	direct	induce	prepare	train
cause	drive	inform	promise	trust
caution	enable	instruct	remind	urge
challenge	encourage	invite	request	want
choose	expect	lead	require	warn
command	find	need	risk	

3. Verb + Gerund

   She wouldn't *acknowledge* doing that.

acknowledge	defend	go on	object to	resent
admit	delay	hate	omit	resist
advise	deny	(can't)help	postpone	resume
anticipate	detest	imagine	practice	risk
appreciate	discuss	insist on	prefer	(can't)
avoid	dislike	keep on	put off	stand
begin	dread	like	quit	stop
bother	endure	love	recall	suggest
cease	enjoy	mention	recognize	tolerate
consider	feel like	mind	recommend	try
continue	finish	miss	regret	under-
count on	forget	notice	remember	stand

4.   Verb + Noun Phrase or Possessive Adjective + Gerund

He can't *imagine* Jack('s) doing that.

acknowledge	discuss	imagine	object to	resent
anticipate	dread	insist on	permit	resist
appreciate	endure	investigate	postpone	risk
challenge	encourage	like	refer	tolerate
count on	enjoy	love	recall	under-
defend	excuse	mention	recognize	stand
delay	forbid	mind	recommend	
detest	forget	miss	regret	
dislike	hate	notice	remember	

5.   Verb + *That* Clause

He couldn't *admit* that it had happened.

acknowledge	declare	imagine	pretend	resent
admit	deny	insist	proclaim	resolve
announce	discover	judge	promise	say
appreciate	expect	know	propose	see
assume	explain	learn	prove	state
believe	feel	like	recall	suggest
boast	find	mean	recognize	suppose
care	forget	mention	regret	swear
claim	guess	mind	remark	teach
complain	hate	notice	remember	think
confess	hear	object	report	under-
consider	hint	plan	request	stand
decide	hope	pledge	require	urge
				whisper

6. Verb + Noun Phrase + *That* -Clause

This is to *advise* you that your flight has been canceled.

advise	convince	notify	promise	warn
assure	inform	persuade	remind	

7. Verb + Noun Phrase + Simple Form of Verb

She wouldn't *let* them do it.

have	help	listen	to see
hear	let	make	watch

6.12 *Make* and *Do*

She *did* the housework and *made* her family happy.

The verbs *make* and *do* have similar meanings. However, *make* and *do* cannot replace each other. *Make* often means "create or produce something," as in these sentences:

Bernadette will *make* a nice cake.
She *made* a nice fire.
Before she *makes* dinner, she *makes* an effort to relax.

Make is often used in the following sentence pattern.

MAKE		NOUN PHRASE	ADJECTIVE
The cake	made	her children	happy.
The fire	made	the room	comfortable.
The dinner	made	everyone	sleepy.

Do is used for actions, especially routine tasks.

Bernadette *did* the housework.
She *did* the laundry first.
She *did* the ironing and the cleaning in the afternoon.

However, *make* is used with food and meals.

She *made* dinner.

Some nouns, such as *discovery,* are related to verbs *(discover).* With these nouns, use *make* and not *do.*

They *discovered* a new star.
They *made* an important discovery.
They *announced* it yesterday.
They *made* an announcement.
I *phoned* my editor.
I *made* a quick phone call.

Compare the following words and phrases used with *make* and *do*.

MAKE

an agreement	a discovery	a profit
an announcement	an effort	progress
an attempt	an error	a promise
a bargain	a mistake	a search
a bed	money	a speech
a change	noise	a start
a decision	an offer	a statement
dinner	a phone call	a left turn

DO

one's best	the gardening	justice
business	good	the laundry
the cleaning	harm	reseach
the dishes	homework	work
one's duty	the housework	
an exercise	the ironing	

Chapter 7

Adjectives and Adjectivals

7.1   Defining Adjectives and Adjectivals

The *short blue* coat is *nice*.

Adjectives are words that describe nouns or add something to their meaning.

ADJECTIVE	NOUN		ADJECTIVE	NOUN
My older	sister	told me about a	good	sale.

Phrases and clauses called **adjectivals** can be used in the same way as adjectives. Anything used as an adjective is called an adjectival. Many adjectivals answer the questions *which one(s)* and *what kind(s)*.

Let's avoid that *rude* salesperson. (adjective)
The salesperson *in the boys' department* annoyed me last
   week. (adjectival phrase)
The salesperson *who was rude to me* isn't here today.
   (adjectival clause)

7.2   Determiners

That coat is on sale, but *those* coats aren't.

The first word in a noun phrase is usually a determiner. The following are the four main kinds of determiners:

1.   **Articles**: a, an, the (see section 2.6-9)
2.   **Demonstratives**: this, that, these, those (see section 2.5)
3.   **Possessive Adjectives**: my, your, his, her, its, our, their (see section 2.10)
4.   **Wh–Words**: whose, which, what (see section 3.7)

The *wh*-determiners are used in questions; like other determiners, they come before adjectives.

DETERMINER	ADJECTIVE	NOUN	
Whose		car	is this?
Which		car	is yours?
That	yellow	car	is mine.
Which	yellow	car	do you mean?

The *wh*-determiners can also be used to introduce dependent clauses (see sections 2.19-20). The different meanings of *whose, which,* and *what* are given in section 3.7.

7.3 Adjectivals That Come before Nouns

a. Adjectives

The faucet leaks. Do you know a *good* plumber?

In noun phrases, adjectives usually come after the determiner and before the noun.

	DETERMINER	ADJECTIVE	NOUN
Do you know	an	inexpensive	plumber?
I know	a	good	plumber.
I can't afford		expensive	plumbers.

Sometimes no determiner is used before plural nouns. However, the determiner cannot be omitted before a singular count noun, even when there is an adjective.

CORRECT	Do you know *an* inexpensive plumber? I know *a* good plumber.
INCORRECT	*Do you know inexpensive plumber? *I know good plumber.

b. Nouns as Adjectivals

The *kitchen* sink doesn't work.

Nouns can be used as adjectivals. For example, *kitchen* and *copper* are nouns, but they are used as adjectivals in these sentences (see section 2.14).

The *kitchen* sink doesn't work.
The *copper* pipes are very old.

When nouns are used as adjectivals, they are always used in the singular form. Units of measurement used before nouns are also always in the singular form.

CORRECT	We need a *three-inch* piece of pipe. I bought a *two-foot* board for that hole.
INCORRECT	*We need a three-inches piece of pipe. *I bought a two-feet board for that hole.

However, when units of measurement follow nouns, they can be plural.

	NOUN	MEASUREMENT ADJECTIVAL
We need	a piece of pipe	*three inches* long.
I bought	a board	*two feet* long for that hole.

Adjectivals that are proper names begin with capital letters.

The publishing company is *French.*
They publish *Shakespearean* plays.
They also publish *English* and *Spanish* textbooks.

c.   Verbs as Adjectivals

The *working* hours are long.

Verbs can also be used as adjectivals. The present participle (the *-ing* form of the verb) is often used this way (see section 7.11).

I work for a *publishing* company.
The *working* hours are long.
It's an *interesting* business.

The past participle (the *-ed /-en* form of the verb) can also be used as an adjectival.

The *married* employees don't like to travel.
Some *retired* employees work part-time.

There is a difference in meaning between the present participle and past participle when they are used as adjectivals (see section 7.11).

The movie was not interesting. What a *boring* movie!
Some *bored* teen-agers finally left.

d.   Adjectivals Not Used before Nouns

One of the managers is *asleep* at his desk.

Some adjectivals are not usually used before nouns. Prepositional phrases usually follow the nouns they modify when they are used as adjectivals.

The man *in the gray suit* is the president.
The woman *next to him* is the vice president.

There are also some one-word adjectives that are not used before nouns. Most of them begin with the letter *a*. They are used after linking verbs (see section 7.9). *Asleep* and *sleeping* have similar meanings; however, *asleep* can only be used after the verb.

CORRECT One of the managers is *asleep* at his desk.
The staff is laughing at the *sleeping* man.

INCORRECT *The staff is laughing at the asleep man.

Some of the opposites of these special adjectives that begin with *a* cannot be used before a noun, either.

CORRECT The man 'was *unashamed* when he awoke.

INCORRECT *The unashamed man finally awoke.

The following adjectives do not usually occur before nouns:

ablaze	alike/unalike	ashamed/unashamed
afloat	alive	asleep/awake
afraid/unafraid	alone	astride
aghast	apart/together	aware/unaware
ahead/behind		

7.4 Quantifiers and Numbers

How *much* money did you take?

Certain words, such as *all, a lot, much, many,* and *some,* tell "how much" or "how many." These words are called quantifiers. Quantifiers come before other adjectives in the noun phrase.

Susan: Did you buy *any* large balloons for the party?
Anna: I bought *some* small ones yesterday. I couldn't find any big ones.

Quantifiers can also be used as pronouns (see section 3.6).

a. *Many, Much, Lots of, A lot of*

I spent *a lot of* money.

Many, much, lots of, and *a lot of* are used for large quantities. *A lot of* and *lots of* can be used with either countable or uncountable nouns; they can be used in affirmative or negative statements or questions. *Lots of* is considered informal and is used mostly in spoken English.

Susan: Did you buy *lots of* presents in Europe?
Anna: Yes, we visited *a lot of* stores. But we didn't have *a lot of* time to shop.

b. *Few, a Few, Little, a Little, Several*

I need *a few* books.

For small quantities, *few, a few, little, a little,* and *several* are used. *Few, a few,* and *several* are used with plural nouns.

Leslie spent *a few* hours in the library.
She checked out *several* books.

Little and *a little* are used before uncountable nouns, such as *time.*

She spent *a little* time reading magazines.

The expressions *few* and *a few* have different meanings. *A few* has a positive meaning, but *few* has a negative meaning.

POSITIVE MEANING   I'll be ready soon. I want to check out *a few* books. (*a few* = "some")

NEGATIVE MEANING   Library security is good. *Few* books are stolen. (*few* = "not many")

The expressions *little* and *a little* also have different meanings. *A little* has a positive meaning, but *little* has a negative meaning.

The comparative and superlative forms of *few/a few* are *fewer* and *fewest.* The comparative and superlative forms of *little/a little* are *less* and *the least.*

I'll have *a little* free time on Monday.
I'll have *less* time on Tuesday.
I'll have *the least* time on Wednesday. Don't come then.

I can usually talk to *a few* students on Monday.
I can talk to *fewer* students on Tuesday because my schedule is busier.
The class with *the fewest* students meets on Thursday.

Many is used with plural countable nouns. *Much* is used with uncountable nouns.

We didn't visit *many* places in Europe. (countable)
We didn't have *much* time. (uncountable)

Although *much* and *many* can always be used in questions and negative statements, there are times when these words are awkward or incorrect in affirmative sentences. In affirmative sentences, it is always safe to use *a lot of*, or, informally, *lots of*.

CORRECT	We spent *a lot of* money in France.
INCORRECT	*We spent much money in France.
AWKWARD	We visited *many* places.
BETTER	We visited *lots of* places.

The comparative form of *much* and *many* is *more.* The superlative form is *the most.* Both forms are used with countable as well as uncountable nouns.

I spent *more* money in Germany than in France.
However, we bought *the most* souvenirs in Italy.

c.   Summary: Quantifiers

	COUNTABLE
AFFIRMATIVE	We visited *a lot of/lots of* places.
	We saw *a few* museums.
NEGATIVE	I didn't see *many* tourists.
	I saw *few* Americans.
QUESTION	Did you visit *many* art galleries?
	Did you see *a few* shows?
COMPARATIVE	Does Germany have *more* castles than France?
	Does it have *fewer* large cities?
SUPERLATIVE	What country had *the most* tourists?
	Which had *the fewest*?

	UNCOUNTABLE
AFFIRMATIVE	We spent *a lot of/lots of* money.
	We spent *a little* money foolishly.
NEGATIVE	We didn't have *much* time in Italy.
	We spent *little* time there.
QUESTION	Did you have *much* time in France?
	Did you spend *a little* time in Paris?

COMPARATIVE   Did you spend *more* money in France or in Spain?

SUPERLATIVE   Where did you spend *the most* money?
Where did you spend *the least*?

d.   *Some* and *Any*

Is there *any* food in the house?

The quantifiers *some* and *any* are used when it is not important to state how large a quantity is. These words are used with both countable and uncountable nouns.

Craig: Is there *any* milk?
Ian: No, but there are *some* cans of orange juice.

Some is usually used in affirmative statements; *any* is usually used in negative statements.

Craig: Are there *any* crackers in the cupboard?
Ian: I don't see *any* soda crackers. Here are *some* graham crackers.

Both *some* and *any* are used in questions. *Any* is usually used when the speaker does not know what answer to expect. However, when the speaker expects a yes answer, *some* is sometimes used.

Craig: I don't know what we have. Do we have *any* bread?
Ian: Yes, we do. You like tuna, don't you? Would you like *some* tuna salad sandwiches for lunch?

e.   *No* As a Quantifier

There are *no* factories in town.

The word *no* can be used as a quantifier to mean "not any." *No* can be used before singular, plural, and uncountable nouns.

There is *no* hotel in town. (singular)
There are *no* bars there. (plural)
Fortunately, there is *no* air pollution. (uncountable)

f.   *Either, Neither,* and *Both*

Both knives are dull.

The word *either* is used for a choice between two items.

I have two knives. You can use *either* one.

Neither means "not either." *Neither* is not used with another negative word because *neither* is already negative.

CORRECT	*Neither* knife is sharp.
	I can't use *either* one.
INCORRECT	*I can't use neither one.

Both, meaning "the two," is used before plural count nouns of two items. *Either* and *neither* are used before singular count nouns of two items.

There are two knives and a screwdriver in the drawer.
Both knives are sharp.
I can use *either* one.
Neither knife needs to be sharpened.

g. *All, Each,* and *Every*

Each singer will perform a solo.

Each and *every* have a meaning that is similar to the meaning of *all.* However, *all* is used before plural nouns, whereas *each* and *every* are used before singular nouns.

All the singers are here.
Each singer will perform a solo.
Every performer is donating his or her services.

All refers to a group; *each* and *every* refer to individuals. Note that *each* is usually not used in negative sentences.

CORRECT	Not every concert is this good.
INCORRECT	*Not each concert is this good.

h. Numbers and Related Words

Of the *two* songs, I liked the *first* one better.

There are two kinds of numbers. Numbers such as *one, two,* and *three* (1, 2, and 3) are called cardinal numbers. Numbers such as *first, second,* and *third* (1st, 2nd, and 3rd) are called ordinal numbers (see section 11.1 for lists). *Next* and *last* are used like ordinal numbers.

Here are four circles.
The *first* circle is the largest.
The *next* circle is smaller.
It is the *second* circle.
The *last* circle is the smallest.
It is the *fourth* circle.

When both cardinal and ordinal numbers are used in the same phrase, the ordinal number comes first.

The *first two* circles are black.

i. *Another, the Other, the Others, Some Other*

The *other* ties are made of silk.

The other and *another* have meanings related to *the* and *an*. *The other* can be used with countable nouns to mean "the only one(s) left."

There are five ties.
Four ties are plain.
The other tie (the only tie left) is
   striped.
One tie is black.
The other ties (all but one) are gray.

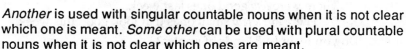

Another is used with singular countable nouns when it is not clear which one is meant. *Some other* can be used with plural countable nouns when it is not clear which ones are meant.

Here are five ties.
One tie costs $25.

Another one costs $45. (The speaker does not say which one.)
Do you want to see *some other* ties? (The speaker does not say which ones.)

j.   Summary: Quantifiers Used As Adjectives

QUESTIONS
   NEGATIVE STATEMENTS
      AFFIRMATIVE STATEMENTS

SINGULAR

Is *either* pineapple ripe?
   Neither one is ripe.
   I won't buy *either* one.
      Give me *either* one of those mangos, instead.

Is *every/each* chicken here fresh?
--------(no negative)
      Every/each chicken is dated.

PLURAL

How *many* tomatoes are left?
   There aren't *many* good ones left.
      There are *a lot of* spoiled ones.

Are there *any* onions?
Would you like *some* onions?
   There aren't *any* green onions.
      We have *some* yellow onions.

Do you need *a few* eggplants?
   There were *few* good ones last week.
      There are *a few* small ones that look good this week.

Do you want *both* kinds of apples?
   No, I really can't use *both* kinds.
      Perhaps next week I'll buy *both* kinds for a change.

Why are there *no* papayas?
   No papayas came in today.

UNCOUNTABLE

How *much* spinach do you have?
   There's not *much* today.
      I had *a lot of* spinach yesterday.
Do you have *any* corn?
   There isn't *any* corn yet.
      I expect *some* white corn next week.
Could we get *a little* parsley?
   There's *little* parsley left.
      I have *a little* parsley at home.
Why is there *no* garlic?
   My supplier had *no* garlic this week.

7.5   Positive, Comparative, and Superlative Degrees of Adjectives

It has *the most exciting* roller coaster ride in the world.

The comparative and superlative forms of adjectives are used for showing differences. The comparative form is used to compare two people, things, places, or groups; the superlative form is used to compare more than two.

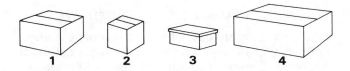

Here are four boxes.
Box 1 is *larger* than box 2.
Box 4 is *the largest*.

The comparative and superlative forms differ according to the number of syllables an adjective has. Add *-er* and *-est* to most one-syllable adjectives. If the adjective ends in a single vowel plus a consonant, the consonant (except for *y* and *w*) is usually doubled.

POSITIVE	COMPARATIVE	SUPERLATIVE
big	bigger	the biggest
cheap	cheaper	the cheapest
new	newer	the newest
old	older	the oldest

Some two-syllable adjectives also form the comparative and superlative forms by adding *-er* and *-est*. When the adjective ends in a consonant and *y,* change the *y* to *i* and add *-er* and *-est*.

POSITIVE	COMPARATIVE	SUPERLATIVE
dir-ty	dirtier	the dirtiest
ea-sy	easier	the easiest
hap-py	happier	the happiest
noi-sy	noisier	the noisiest
pret-ty	prettier	the prettiest
sun-ny	sunnier	the sunniest

When two-syllable adjectives end in -*le*, add only -*r* and -*st*.

POSITIVE	COMPARATIVE	SUPERLATIVE
hum-ble	humbler	the humblest
no-ble	nobler	the noblest
sim-ple	simpler	the simplest
sub-tle	subtler	the subtlest

Two-syllable adjectives that do not end in -*y* or -*le* usually form the comparative and superlative with *more* and *most* when they end in -*ed*, -*ful*, -*ing*, -*ish*, -*less*, -*ous*.

POSITIVE	COMPARATIVE	SUPERLATIVE
care-less	more careless	the most careless
child-ish	more childish	the most childish
fam-ous	more famous	the most famous
need-ed	more needed	the most needed
tir-ing	more tiring	the most tiring
use-ful	more useful	the most useful

Two-syllable adjectives ending in -*er*, -*le*, -*ow*, or -*some* can form the comparative and superlative either with -*er* and -*est* or with *more* and *most*.

POSITIVE	COMPARATIVE	SUPERLATIVE
clever	cleverer	the cleverest
	more clever	the most clever
handsome	handsomer	the handsomest
	more handsome	the most handsome
narrow	narrower	the narrowest
	more narrow	the most narrow
noble	nobler	the noblest
	more noble	the most noble
shallow	shallower	the shallowest
	more shallow	the most shallow
tender	tenderer	the tenderest
	more tender	the most tender

Never use both *more* and -*er* or *most* and -*est* when making comparisons.

CORRECT   This room is narrow, but that one is *narrower*.
             The couch is the *handsomest* one in the store.

INCORRECT   *That room is more prettier.
             *The couch is the most handsomest one
             in the store.

Spelling rules for adding *-er* and *-est* to adjectives are given in section 11.12.

Comparatives and superlatives of adjectives of three or more syllables are formed with *more* and *most*.

POSITIVE	COMPARATIVE	SUPERLATIVE
beau-ti-ful	more beautiful	the most beautiful
ex-cit-ing	more exciting	the most exciting
ex-pen-sive	more expensive	the most expensive

This apartment is *expensive*.
The one in Manhattan is *more expensive*.
The most expensive apartments are in Manhattan.

Some comparative and superlative forms are irregular.

POSITIVE	COMPARATIVE	SUPERLATIVE
bad	worse	the worst
far	farther/further	the farthest/furthest
good	better	the best
little	less	the least
much/many	more	the most

In some cases, *less* and *the least* are used to form the comparative and superlative degrees of adjectives instead of *more* and *the most*. *Less* is the opposite of *more*, and *the least* is the opposite of *the most*.

POSITIVE	COMPARATIVE	SUPERLATIVE
expensive	less expensive	the least expensive
terrible	less terrible	the least terrible

I'm short of money.
You'd better order something *less* expensive than steak.
What's *the least* expensive dinner?

7.6 Making Comparisons with Adjectives

a. Comparatives

> She is almost *as old as* her husband.

There are many ways to make comparisons. One way is to use adjectives such as *alike, different, equal, inferior, similar,* and *superior.*

> She and her husband are *alike* in appearance.
> However, they are *different* in their personality.

There are several other ways to make comparisons. The pair of words *as . . . as* is often used with adjectives for comparisons.

> Anita is nineteen years old.
> Carlos is nineteen years old.
> He's *as old as* his wife.
> She's five feet nine inches tall.
> He's five feet eight inches tall.
> He's almost *as tall as* she is.
> He's not quite *as tall as* she is.

Another way to make comparisons is to use the comparative form of the adjective (see section 7.5) and the word *than.*

> He wears a size ten shoe.
> She wears a size nine shoe.
> His feet are *larger than* hers.

> She is a rock star.
> He is her manager.
> She's *more famous than* he is.
> He's *less famous than* his wife.

Both *different from* and *different than* are used for comparisons in informal speaking and writing. In formal writing, *different from* is preferred.

> Anita's last name is Morse.
> Carlos's last name is Gonzalez.
> Her last name is *different from* his last name.
> Her last name is *different from* his.

In making comparisons, it is often possible to omit part of a sentence.

She's very famous.
He's not *as famous as* she is.
He's not *as famous as* she.
He's not *as famous*.

When a comparison is made with *than,* it is important not to leave parts of the sentence out when the sentence can have more than one meaning.

He likes basketball better than his wife.

This sentence can mean either "He likes basketball better than he likes his wife" or "He likes basketball better than his wife does."

When comparing two nouns, the comparative form of the adjective is used; when comparing more than two nouns, the superlative form of the adjective is used (see section 7.5).

Paul can run *faster* than Dick can.
Paul is *the fastest* runner on his team.

b.   Superlatives

She is *the tallest* woman on her team.

When talking about relative differences, the comparative is used. It is often used when comparing two people or things.

Sandra is *shorter than* Angela, but she is not short.
Sandra is five feet nine inches tall; Angela is five feet
    eleven inches tall.

When talking about how one person or thing is different from others, the superlative is used. It is often used when comparing more than two people or things.

CORRECT   She is *the tallest* woman on her team.

INCORRECT   *She is the taller woman on her team.

The superlative refers to a specific person or thing. It is usually used with *the.*

She is *the* best player on her team.

c.   Double Comparisons

The more, the merrier.

Some sentences contain two comparatives.

The *older* I get, the *less* I sleep. (As I become older, I sleep less than when I was younger.)

In these double comparisons, it is sometimes possible to omit a great deal of information.

Dan: How many people shall we invite?
Nancy: The more, the merrier.

The phrase *the more, the merrier* in this context means, "The more people we invite, the merrier the party will be."

Dan: What kind of restaurant shall we go to?
Nancy: The cheaper, the better.

The cheaper, the better in this context means, "The cheaper the restaurant is, the better I'll like it." With double comparisons, the situation often indicates what has been omitted.

7.7   The Order of Adjectivals before Nouns

Sandy brought *two beautiful chocolate* cakes to the picnic.

There is a specific order in which adjectivals occur before a noun. For example, numbers come before adjectives that refer to age, and both these adjectivals come before adjectives that refer to materials.

NUMBER	AGE	MATERIAL
those three	old	metal chairs

The order of adjectives described in this section is not the only possible order, but it is always acceptable.

Determiners (see section 7.2) come before all other adjectivals.

DETERMINER	ADJECTIVE	NOUN
this	red	tablecloth
your	three	candles

Quantifiers and numbers come after determiners and before other adjectivals.

DETERMINER	QUANTIFIER	ADJECTIVE	NOUN
a	few	fresh	salads
the	four	cherry	pies

When a phrase has both an ordinal number, such as *first,* and a cardinal number, such as *two,* the ordinal number comes before the cardinal number.

DETERMINER	ORDINAL NUMBER	CARDINAL NUMBER	NOUN
the	first	ten	cars

Adjectives that refer to opinions or judgments, such as *beautiful, charming,* and *disgusting,* usually come before adjectives of size, shape, and condition.

My aunt was wearing an *ugly,* tattered old apron.
Her *cute* little boy was wearing a playsuit.

Adjectivals that refer to size, shape, and condition come before adjectivals that refer to age, color, or material.

Ask one of those *tall* young people to hand you the jars.
We'll use that *round* oak table for the food.
Don't use the *broken* old chair.

Adjectivals that refer to age come before adjectivals that refer to color or material.

Put the *old* red cotton tablecloth on the table.

Adjectivals that can also be used as nouns usually come after all other adjectivals.

This is the best red *cotton* tablecloth I have.
We use it for all our fancy *garden* parties.

Sometimes two or more adjectivals of the same kind are used before a noun. When adjectivals refer to the same quality, such as color, they can be joined by *and.* When there are more than two adjectivals of the same kind, they are separated by commas, and the word *and* is used before the last adjectival.

Let's use a *red* and *white* tablecloth for this table.
We can use the *red, white,* and *blue* napkins.

When adjectives refer to different qualities, they are not separated by commas or by *and.*

We'll use the *old green metal* chairs.

The following chart shows the order of adjectivals before nouns. Adjectivals do not always appear in this order, but this order is always correct.

1 determiner
2 ordinal number
3 cardinal number/quantifier
4 adjectival of opinion
5 adjectival of size/shape/condition
6 adjectival of age/color
7 adjectival also used as noun
8 noun

1	2	3	4	5	6	7	8
the	first	two	beautiful	big	red	plastic	balls
those		three	kind	tall		British	men
my			ugly	long	blue	wool	scarf
our	last	few	wonderful			summer	days

7.8 Adjectivals after Nouns

a. Phrases

Stop that man *in the baseball cap* !

Prepositional phrases used as adjectivals follow the nouns they modify.

Help! A man *in a baseball cap* just took my purse!
He ran into that store *on the corner.*

Participial phrases often follow the nouns they modify. These phrases begin with present participles, such as *running,* or past participles, such as *driven.*

The robber, *running very fast,* pushed the woman down.
A car *driven by an off-duty police officer* stopped to help.

Some adjective phrases with *and* follow nouns.

The woman, *unhurt and angry,* began to chase the thief.

Phrases with *to* followed by the simple form of the verb are infinitive phrases. Some infinitive phrases are used as adjectivals.

The place *to go* now is the police station. (The place where
we should go is the police station.)
I didn't have the courage *to chase the thief.* (I was afraid, so I
didn't chase the thief.)

b.   Clauses

The man *who stole the purse* was very tall.

An adjective clause is a group of words that contains a subject and
a verb and is used as an adjectival. Adjective clauses are also
called relative clauses. They begin with *that* or a *wh*-word and follow the noun they modify (see section 7.10).

The woman *that he robbed* described him.

c.   Essential and Nonessential Adjective Phrases and Clauses

The thief, *who was very fast,* carried a gun.

Some adjectival phrases and clauses are essential to the meaning of the sentence. They are called essential (or restrictive) adjectivals. Essential adjectivals tell *which one(s),* and are not
separated from the rest of the sentence by commas (see section
7.10).

Most people *who see a crime* do nothing.

When an essential modifier is omitted, the sentence is often
strange or untrue.

Most people *who see a crime* do nothing.
Most people do nothing.

Prepositional phrases, participial phrases, and relative clauses
can all be essential modifiers.

The man *in the baseball cap* took the purse and ran.
A woman *wearing a blue suit* ran after him.
A man *who had been standing on the corner* quickly left.

Nonessential phrases and clauses do not tell *which one(s).* Nonessential (or nonrestrictive) adjectivals are separated from the
rest of the sentence by commas.

The police officer, *shouting a warning,* stopped the car.
The thief, *who had seen the officer,* ran into a store.

When nonessential adjectivals are omitted, the sentences are still clear.

> The police officer, *shouting a warning,* stopped the car.
> The police officer stopped the car.

> The thief, *who had seen the officer,* ran into a store.
> The thief ran into a store.

7.9 Adjectivals Used as Subject and Object Complements

> The trip was *wonderful,* but it made me *tired.*

Some adjectives follow the verb in the sentence. These are called subject complements because they modify the subject.

SUBJECT	VERB	SUBJECT COMPLEMENT
The trip	was	wonderful.
It	was also	very long.

Because they occur in the predicate, subject complements are also called predicate adjectives. Predicate adjectives can follow only linking verbs. In most cases, the verb *be* can be substituted for other linking verbs.

SUBJECT	LINKING VERB	PREDICATE	ADJECTIVE	
I	became		sick	yesterday.
I	felt		very bad	by ten.
I	seemed		better	by noon.

These are some common linking verbs.

appear	get	seem
be	grow	sound
become	look	smell
feel	remain	turn (become)

Adverbs cannot be substituted for adjectives after linking verbs.

> INCORRECT   *I felt very badly by ten.

Similarly, adjectives cannot be substituted for adverbs when the verb in the sentence is not a linking verb.

> CORRECT   I didn't study very *well* on Tuesday night.

Study is not a linking verb. Therefore, the adverb *well* is used.

INCORRECT   *I didn't study very good on Tuesday night.

There are a few adjectives, such as *afraid, alike, alone,* and *a-sleep,* that can be used only as predicate adjectives. (See section 7.3d)

CORRECT   I called a friend, but she was *asleep.*

INCORRECT   *I want to talk to my asleep friend.

Some predicate adjectives are measurement phrases. Compare these sentences.

	NOUN	+ VERB	+ ADJECTIVE
My	niece	is	two years old.
Her	doll	is	four feet tall.

	ADJECTIVE	+ NOUN
I have a	two-year-old	niece.
She has a	four-foot-tall	doll.

Participles are often used as predicate adjectives. With adjectives of emotion, the past participle (*bored, surprised,* etc.) and the present participle (*boring, surprising,* etc.) have different meanings. When the past participle is used, the subject of the sentence is the cause of emotion(see also section 7.11).

This movie bores me.
I am *bored* by this movie. (The "I" is the experiencer.)
This movie is *boring*. (The movie is the cause of the boredom.)

The book amused me.
I was *amused* by the book. (The "I" is the experiencer.)
The book was *amusing*. (The book was the cause of the amusement.)

Loud music annoys some people.
Some people are *annoyed* by loud music. (Some people experience the annoyance.)
Loud music is *annoying* to some people. (Loud music is the cause of the annoyance.)

Other adjectives of emotion that can be used as predicate adjectives are:

bewildered/bewildering   irritated/irritating
disturbed/disturbing   puzzled/puzzling

interested/interesting   surprised/surprising

7.10 Relative Clauses

We went on a hike *that I will always remember.*

A clause used as an adjectival is called a relative clause. A relative clause can be used to combine two sentences that refer to the same noun phrase.

I have a good friend.   *He* has climbed Mt. Everest.
I have a good friend *who* has climbed Mt. Everest.

We went on a hike.   *The hike* was very strenuous.
We went on a hike *that* was very strenuous.

Words such as *that, who,* and *which* introduce relative clauses. They are called relative pronouns. *Who* is used for people, and *which* is used for things. *That* can be used for either people or things.

The friend *that* I hiked with last week likes hikes *that* last all day.

a. Relative Pronouns as Subjects

In the preceding examples, the relative pronouns *who* and *that* replace the subjects of the sentences. These relative pronouns become the subjects. A second pronoun is not necessary.

	SUBJECT	VERB	
My friend likes hikes	that	last	all day.
He loved our last hike,	which	exhausted	me.
I won't hike with friends	who	climb	mountains.

The following sentences are incorrect:

*My friend likes hikes that they last all day.
*He loved our last hike, which it exhausted me.
*I won't hike with friends who they climb mountains.

b. Relative Pronouns as Objects

The mountain *that* we climbed was very steep.

Sometimes the relative pronoun replaces the direct object of a sentence.

The mountain was very steep.
We climbed *it.*
The mountain *that* we climbed was very steep.

Another group of hikers was very tired.
We met *them.*
The hikers *whom* we met were very tired.

When a relative pronoun replaces a direct object, another pronoun is not used as a direct object.

INCORRECT   *The mountain that we climbed *it* was
                very steep.

When *that* replaces a direct object, it can be omitted. When it is omitted, do not use another pronoun in the object position.

CORRECT   The mountain we climbed was very steep.

INCORRECT   *The mountain we climbed *it* was very steep.

The relative pronouns *who, which,* and *that* can replace both subjects and direct objects. However, in very formal writing, the relative pronoun *whom* is used instead of *who* to replace objects. *Whom*, like *who,* is for people only.

FORMAL   Some hikers, *whom* I won't name, leave trash
             on the trails.
INFORMAL   Some hikers, *who* I won't name, leave trash on
               the trails.

c.   Relative Pronouns as Objects of Prepositions

One hiker *who* I talked *to* had run out of water.

Relative pronouns come at the beginning of relative clauses even when they replace objects.

The mountain was very steep.   We climbed *it.*
The mountain *that* we climbed was very steep

When the relative pronoun is the object of a preposition, it is possible for the preposition to begin the relative clause.

We hiked to a lake.   We swam in the lake.
We hiked to a lake, *which* we swam *in*.
We hiked to a lake, *in which* we swam.

In formal writing, *whom* is used instead of *who* when the relative pronoun replaces a person as the object of a preposition.

FORMAL   Alan, *to whom* I gave the map, led the hike.
              Alan, *whom* I gave the map *to*, led the hike.

INFORMAL   Alan, *who* I gave the map *to*, led the hike.

Do not use a preposition or object of a preposition twice, and do not omit the preposition.

INCORRECT   *Alan, *to* whom I gave the map *to*, led the hike.
              *Alan, whom I gave the map, led the hike.

The relative pronouns *that* and *which* can also be used to replace the object of a preposition. However, the relative pronoun *that* is not used directly after a preposition. *Which* is used to refer to things; *that* is used to refer to people or things.

CORRECT   The parking lot *which* we started *from* was
                 very small.
              The parking lot *from which* we started was
                 very small.
              The parking lot *that* we started *from* was
                 very small.

INCORRECT   *The parking lot from that we started was
                 very small.

d. *Whose* as a Relative Pronoun

We met a hiker *whose* pack was torn.

The relative pronoun *whose* replaces possessives, such as *his* or *the hiker's*. *Whose* usually refers to people, but occasionally it can refer to animals or things.

We met a hiker.   *His* pack was torn.
We met a hiker *whose* pack was torn.

I heard a bird.   *Its* call was very unusual.
I heard a bird *whose* call was very unusual.

e. *When* and *Where* in Relative Clauses

The park *where* we met is near her home.

The words *when* and *where* can introduce relative clauses. Relative clauses that begin with *when* and *where* replace adverbials in sentences (see section 8.1).

A state park is near her home.   We met *there*.
The park *where* we met is near her home.

It was noon.   We arrived at the top *then*.
It was noon *when* we arrived at the top.

f. Essential Relative Clauses

The friends *who went with us* are good hikers.

Some relative clauses complete the meaning of a sentence. They are called essential (restrictive) relative clauses. Essential relative clauses tell *which one(s)*.

The hikers *who were going up the mountain* looked energetic.
The hikers *who were coming down the mountain* looked tired.

Essential relative clauses are not separated from the rest of the sentence by commas. Without the relative clauses, the preceding sentences do not seem to be related.

The hikers looked energetic.
The hikers looked tired.

g. Nonessential Relative Clauses

We stayed in Woodland, *which is in the mountains.*

If a relative clause is not necessary in order to tell which one(s), it is a nonesssential (nonrestrictive) relative clause. Nonessential relative clauses add further information to sentences.

We stayed in Woodland, *which is in the mountains.*
Alan and Marilyn, *who live in Woodland,* own a house there.

When the nonessential relative clauses are omitted, the sentences give less information, but they do not sound strange or untrue.

We stayed in Woodland.
Alan and Marilyn own a house there.

Nonessential relative clauses are different from essential relative clauses in several ways.

1. Commas are used around nonessential relative clauses but not around essential relative clauses.
2. The relative pronoun *that* is used in essential relative clauses but not in nonessential relative clauses.

Woodland, *which* has no hotels, is a quiet town.
Towns *that* have no hotels are very rare in that area.

3. Nonessential relative clauses can modify proper names, but essential relative clauses cannot.

We stayed in Woodland, which is in the mountains.

7.11 Participles

Those people *waiting at the post office* are becoming angry.

Participles are verb forms used as adjectives. Present participles end in *-ing*. A one-word participle can come before the noun.

PARTICIPLE   NOUN

The   annoying   music   is coming from next door.

A participial phrase can come after the noun.

NOUN   PARTICIPIAL PHRASE

The   music   *annoying the customers*   is from a radio.

Past participles are the *-ed/-en* form of the verb.

PARTICIPLE   NOUN

The   *interested*   employee   is listening to Mr. Green.

NOUN   PARTICIPIAL PHRASE

The   employee,   *interested in Mr. Green's story,*   is trying to give him his change.

With verbs that refer to emotions or feelings (such as *surprise, bore, amuse*), it is easy to confuse the meanings of the present participle and the past participle. If the present participle is used, the subject of the sentence is the cause of the emotion. If the past participle is used, the subject of the sentence is the experiencer of the emotion.

Mr. Green's story interests the employee.
The story is *interesting*. (The story is the cause of the interest.)
The employee is *interested*. (The employee is the experiencer of interest.)

a. Participial Phrases after Nouns

The following sentences with participial phrases have the same meanings as the sentences with relative clauses.

RELATIVE CLAUSE
    PARTICIPIAL PHRASE

The people *who are waiting in line* seem very impatient.
    The people *waiting in line* seem very impatient.
The car *that is parked outside* is illegally parked.
    The car *parked outside* is illegally parked.

The forms of *be* are not used before participial phrases.

INCORRECT   *The people are waiting in line seem very impatient.

The present and past forms of verbs are not used in place of participles in participial phrases.

CORRECT   There is a counter *separating* the employees from the customers.

INCORRECT   *There is a counter separates the employees from the customers.

b. Participial Phrases before Nouns

Shaking his head, the supervisor walked away.

Some participial phrases come before the nouns that they modify, often at the beginning of a sentence.

PARTICIPIAL PHRASE   NOUN

Talking to the other cashier,   Tony gave me the wrong change.
Scolded by his supervisor,   Tony apologized.

In these sentences, the participial phrase describes the subject of the sentence, Tony. (Tony was talking to the other cashier; Tony was scolded.) Participial phrases that do not describe the subject are usually incorrect. They are called dangling participles.

*Walking down the aisles, the vegetables looked wilted.
(This sounds as if the vegetables were walking down the aisles.)
*Leaving the store, employees were seen putting fresh vegetables out. (This sounds as if the employees were leaving the store.)

Dangling participles can be corrected by using the noun modified by the participial phrase as the subject.

Walking down the aisles, *I* noticed that the vegetables looked wilted.
Leaving the store, *I* saw the employees putting fresh vegetables out.

7.12 Adjectives That Have Complements

I'm *ready* to go camping.

Many adjectives are followed by complements, which are phrases and clauses that complete the meaning of the adjectives.

	ADJECTIVE	COMPLEMENT
She is	interested	in camping.
She is	aware	that I have never gone camping.

In some cases, a complement must be used after an adjective.

INCORRECT   *She is aware.

Some adjectives can be followed by more than one kind of complement.

	ADJECTIVE	COMPLEMENT
I am	afraid	to go camping.
		of sleeping outdoors.
		that bears may come near the camp.

Not all adjectives can be followed by all kinds of complements. The choice of complement depends on the adjective.

Prepositional phrases can follow most adjectives. However, only certain prepositions can be used after certain adjectives.

CORRECT   She isn't afraid *of* bears.

INCORRECT   *She isn't afraid about bears.

A list of adjectives and the prepositions that can follow them is given in section 9.9.

In some cases, the prepositional phrase consists of a preposition and a gerund phrase (see section 2.17).

	PREPOSITION	GERUND PHRASE
She was excited	about	having a vacation.

Not all adjectives can be followed by a preposition and a gerund phrase.

CORRECT	She's ready for a vacation.
	She's ready to take a vacation.

INCORRECT	*She's ready for taking a vacation.

Infinitive phrases can follow some adjectives. An infinitive is *to* plus the simple form of the verb.

	ADJECTIVE	INFINITIVE PHRASE
She's	glad	to take a long vacation.

In some cases, the complement of an adjective is a clause beginning with *that*.

	ADJECTIVE	*THAT*-CLAUSE
She's	certain	that she'll enjoy camping.

In sentences that begin with the introductory word *it* (see section 3.5), some adjectives can be followed by either a clause beginning with *that* or by an infinitive phrase.

It's apparent *that* he likes to go camping. (That he likes to go camping is apparent.)

It's very difficult *to camp out* in the winter. (To camp out in the winter is very difficult.)

Some adjectives that can occur in these sentence patterns are listed next:

IT	+	*BE*	+	ADJECTIVE	+	*THAT*-CLAUSE
It		is		apparent		that he enjoys camping.

bad	likely/unlikely	right
certain/uncertain	necessary	surprising
convenient	nice	wonderful
doubtful	obvious	wrong
good	possible/impossible	
interesting	probable/improbable	

IT	+	BE	+	ADJECTIVE	+	INFINITIVE PHRASE
It		is		difficult		to do it.

bad	interesting
convenient	necessary
easy	nice
foolish	possible/impossible
good	right
hard	suitable
honest/dishonest	wrong

COMPLEMENTS OF COMMON ADJECTIVES

ADJECTIVE	GERUND PHRASE	INFINITIVE PHRASE	THAT-CLAUSE
able		to do it	
accustomed	to doing it		
afraid	of doing it	to do it	that they can't do it
angry	about doing it		
ashamed	of doing it	to do it	that they can't do it
aware	of doing it		that they can do it
bad	at doing it		
capable	of doing it		
careful	about doing it	to do it	
certain	about doing it	to do it	that they can do it
clever	about doing it		
	at doing it		
committed	to doing it		
confident	of doing it		that they can do it
content	about doing it	to do it	that they can do it
dedicated	to doing it		
disappointed	about doing it		that they can't do it
	at doing it it		
doubtful	about doing it		that they can do it
experienced	at doing it		
expert	at doing it		
famous	for doing it		
foolish	for doing it	to do it	

ADJECTIVE	GERUND PHRASE	INFINITIVE PHRASE	THAT-CLAUSE
glad		to do it	that they can do it
good	at doing it	to do it	
happy	about doing it	to do it	that they can do it
honest	about doing it		
ignorant	about doing it		that they can do it
interested	in doing it		
nice	about doing it	to do it	
opposed	to doing it		
qualified	for doing it	to do it	
ready		to do it	
right	about doing it	to do it	that they can do it
serious	about doing it		that they can do it
successful	at doing it		
sure	of doing it	to do it	that they can do it
surprised	at doing it		that they can do it
wrong	about doing it	to do it	

7.13   Adjectives Used as Nouns

The young are very comfortable with computers.

Some adjectives that describe people can be used as nouns. These adjectives have the word *people* understood.

The young are very comfortable with computers. (Young people are very comfortable with computers.)
The rich are not the only ones who own computers. (Rich people are not the only ones who own computers.)

When adjectives are used as nouns, they make general statements about people and agree with plural verbs.

INCORRECT   *The young is very comfortable with computers.

Adjectives used as nouns usually follow the determiner *the*. However, they can also be used with possessives such as *my* or *your*. The poem by Emma Lazarus that is inscribed on a tablet in the base of the Statue of Liberty contains the words, "Give me *your* tired, *your* poor, . . ."

Not all adjectives that describe people can be used as nouns. Some common ones are:

blind	foolish	innocent	poor	strong
brave	guilty	lazy	rich	wise
elderly	healthy	old	sick	young

A few adjectives that do not describe people can be used as nouns. These adjectives describe abstract ideas.

She always tries to do *the impossible*.
He wants to explore *the unknown*.

Chapter 8

Adverbs and Adverbials

8.1 Defining Adverbs and Adverbials

The plane will arrive *soon*.

The word *adverb* refers to single words that modify verbs, adjectives, and adverbs. Sometimes phrases and clauses are used in the same way one-word adverbs are used. Any word, phrase, or clause that is used as an adverb is called an **adverbial**.

The plane will arrive *soon*. (word)
It will depart *in half an hour*. (phrase)
We can board *after we check in*. (clause)

A word, phrase, or clause that answers questions beginning with *how, when, where,* or *why* is usually an adverbial.

Where did the plane crash?
The accident occurred *in Colorado*.

When did it happen?
It happened *in 1982*.

Why did the plane crash?
It crashed *because the weather was bad*.

How long was the plane in the air?
It was in the air *for thirty minutes*.

How often do planes crash?
These things *seldom* happen.

How bad was the damage?
It was *quite* severe.

Some adverbs, called sentence adverbs, modify an entire sentence. Sentence adverbs sometimes express the speaker's feelings or opinions about what is said in the sentence.

Luckily, a few passengers were saved.
Unfortunately, most of the passengers were killed.
Clearly, the pilot should not have taken off.
She *probably* did not understand the danger.

a. Kinds of Adverbials

Adverbs answer the questions *how, when, where,* and *why*. Most adverbs modify or describe actions, states, or qualities. An adverb can modify a verb.

                    VERB   ADVERB
The plane from Chicago   arrived   late.

          ADVERB   VERB
It   seldom   arrives   late.

An adverb can modify an adjective.

                ADVERB   ADJECTIVE
A 747 is a   very   large   plane.

Adverbs such as *very* can modify other adverbs.

                ADVERB   ADVERB
A 727 can climb   very   quickly.

b.   Adverbials in Questions and Negative Statements

They haven't arrived *yet*.

With certain adverbs, a different form is usually used for negative sentences and questions than for affirmative statements.

AFFIRMATIVE STATEMENTS
    NEGATIVE STATEMENTS
        QUESTIONS

Three guests have *already* arrived.
    But many guests haven't come *yet*.
        Has your husband arrived *yet*?
The musicians are *still* waiting to play.
    But the pianist won't wait *anymore*.
        Is the bass player *still* here?
The guitar player left his music *somewhere*.
    He can't find it *anywhere*.
        Have you seen it *anywhere*?

Certain adverbs have a negative meaning even when the sentence does not have the word *no* or *not*.

I have *never* seen such a crowd. (*never* = "not ever")
We *rarely* invite so many people. (*rarely* = "not often")

When negative adverbs are used at the beginning of a sentence, the word order changes from statement order to question order.

The question order does not mean that these sentences are questions.

ADVERB	AUXILIARY VERB	SUBJECT	
Never	have	I	seen such a crowd!
Rarely	do	we	invite so many people.

8.2 *How Often:* **Adverbials of Frequency**

In Minnesota, it *always* snows in the winter.

Adverbs of frequency often occur with verbs in the simple present tense (see section 4.4), although they can also occur with verbs in other tenses. Adverbs of frequency come after the verb *be*. With other verbs, they usually come before the main verb.

It is *always* cold in Minnesota.
It *always* snows a lot there.
Have you *ever* visited Minnesota?

If there are two auxiliary verbs, the adverb of frequency comes after the first one.

Temperatures that low had *never* been recorded.

Here are some common adverbs of frequency. They are arranged in order of frequency from high to low.

It *always* snows in the winter.
It *usually* snows a lot in December.
It *frequently* snows in January.
It *often* snows in February and March.
It *sometimes/occasionally* snows in April.
It *seldom/hardly ever/rarely* snows in May.
It *never* snows in June or July.

Adverbs that tell the exact number of times *(once, twice, three times, four times, daily)* usually come near the end of a sentence (after the verb and its complements); but they can come at the beginning of a sentence, too.

My car didn't start *three mornings in a row.*
Despite the weather, some people go jogging *daily.*
Twice I went skiing when it was twenty below zero.

8.3 *When, For How Long:* **Adverbials of Time**

She was sales manager *for four years.*

Adverbials of time answer questions that begin with *when* or *how long.* Many adverbials of time relate a time or event to the moment of speaking. Imagine that today is February 16:

FEBRUARY						
SUN	MON	TUES	WED	THURS	FRI	SAT
			1	2	3	4
5	6	7	8	9	10	11
12	13	14	15	(16)	17	18
19	20	21	22	23	24	25
26	27	28				

It is February 16 *today.*
It will be Washington's Birthday in six days.
It was Valentine's Day *the day before yesterday.*
It was Lincoln's Birthday *four days ago.*
There will be no holidays *next week.*
Groundhog Day was *two weeks ago.*

Phrases such as *last Friday* or *last Sunday* can have more than one meaning. A speaker might use *last Sunday* to refer to February 12 or February 5. For this reason, speakers sometimes use phrases such as *this past Sunday* (February 12) or a *week ago Sunday* (February 5) in order to avoid confusion.

Time expressions for future events are often understood by their relation to the moment of speaking. Imagine that today is July 15:

JULY						
SUN	MON	TUES	WED	THURS	FRI	SAT
					1	2
3	4	5	6	7	8	9
10	11	12	13	14	(15)	16
17	18	19	20	21	22	23
24/31	25	26	27	28	29	30

It is July 15 *today*.

There will be a good baseball game on TV *tomorrow*. (July 16)

There will be lots of baseball games *this month*. (July)

There will be a good game between Chicago and New York *the day after tomorrow*. (July 17)

The Houston Astros played two games *this week*, one on July 11 and another on July 13.

Next week there will be two tennis tournaments. One begins on July 18.

A celebrity golf tournament will be held in California *the week after next*. It begins on July 24.

Some time expressions do not refer to a specific hour, day, or week. The time expressions *just, recently, lately*, and *a while ago* usually refer to past time. The following time expressions are arranged from most recent to most remote (past):

I *just* saw a good science-fiction movie.

I *recently* saw another movie by the same director.

There have been a lot of good movies *lately*.

The first science-fiction movie was made *quite a while ago*.

The time expressions *immediately, at once, soon*, and *later* usually refer to future time. Here they are arranged in order of increasing remoteness in the future.

Turn on your TV *immediately*.

If you turn it on *at once*, you'll see a news bulletin.

My favorite movie is going to be on Channel 3 *soon*.

There's another good movie *later*.

Many time adverbials emphasize a period of time. These adverbials are often prepositional phrases beginning with *since, for, until, in*, or *from* (see section 9.3).

I have been going to Japanese movies *for several years*.

I haven't seen an American film *since last year*.

The latest Kurasawa film will be at the Uptown Theater *until Wednesday*.

Still refers to a period of time that began in the past and has continued.

I have seen the movie *The Wizard of Oz* many times.

I *still* enjoy seeing it. (I enjoyed it before, and I enjoy it now.)

I *still* don't like the witch. (I didn't like the witch before, and I don't like her now.)

After negative words, *anymore* is used instead of *still*.

My brother doesn't like that movie *anymore*. (He liked it before, but he doesn't like it now.)

I don't like sad movies *anymore*. (I liked sad movies before, but I don't like them now.)

Both *already* and *yet* are used to refer to a period of time. *Already* is usually used in affirmative sentences, and *yet* in negative sentences.

Jack is going to Europe next summer.

He has *already* made hotel reservations. (sooner than expected)

He hasn't renewed his passport *yet*. (up until now)

In questions, *yet* is usually used. When *already* is used in questions, it expresses surprise.

Has Jack talked to a travel agent *yet?* (up until now)

Has he *already* packed his suitcase? He's not leaving for six months! (sooner than expected)

Time adverbials can occur in various positions in a sentence. When they are prepositional phrases, they often come at the end of sentences.

I worked on that jigsaw puzzle *on Saturday.*

I finished *at noon.*

When two time adverbials occur in a sentence, the smaller unit of time usually comes first.

I worked on another puzzle *one evening last week.*

Time adverbials can also come at the beginning of a sentence, particularly when there are other kinds of adverbials at the end of the sentence.

On Sunday, I started another puzzle *because I was bored.*

Prepositional phrases referring to time are described in section 9.3.

There are a few time adverbials that usually come either after the first auxiliary verb or before the main verb. These are *just, still,* and *already.*

> I am *still* working on that puzzle.
> I *just* bought it last week.
> I have *already* worked on it for six hours.

The negative forms *yet* and *anymore* usually come at the end of a sentence or after the verb complements.

> I haven't finished the top of the puzzle *yet.*
> I don't get much schoolwork done *anymore.*

Prepositions of time are discussed in section 9.3. Chapter 4 has eight sections which tell about how to use time expressions with different verb tenses. They are: 4.5e, 4.9b, 4.10b, 4.14f, 4.15b, 4.16c, 4.18b, and 4.19b.

8.4 *Where:* Adverbials of Place and Direction

> Let's take this chair *upstairs.*

Many adverbials answer the question *where.* These place adverbials usually come after the verb and its complements, and before time adverbials.

	VERB	COMPLEMENT	WHERE	WHEN
I'll	put	this chair	in the bedroom.	
Let's	move	the bed	upstairs	now.
	Put	the frame	over there	first.
	Put	the screws	into those holes.	

The adverbs *somewhere* and *anywhere* and their informal forms, *someplace* and *anyplace,* refer to indefinite places. *Somewhere* and *someplace* are usually not used after negative verbs, but *anywhere* and *anyplace* are.

> CORRECT Put that table *somewhere* in the living room.
> I can't find the screws *anywhere.*
>
> INCORRECT *I can't find the blue chair *somewhere.*

Prepositions of place and direction are discussed in section 9.2.

8.5 *How:* **Adverbials of Manner**

She learns her lines *quickly.*

Adverbials of manner answer questions that begin with *how.* Many adverbs of manner can be formed by adding *-ly* to an adjective.

ADJECTIVE
    ADVERB

Is Sylvia a *graceful* dancer?
    Yes, she dances *gracefully.*
Is she a *quick* learner?
    Yes, she learns her lines *quickly.*

Here are some common pairs of adjectives and their corresponding adverbs ending in *-ly*:

accurate	accurately	odd	oddly
bright	brightly	polite	politely
careful	carefully	quick	quickly
clear	clearly	severe	severely
delicate	delicately	sincere	sincerely
fortunate	fortunately	sweet	sweetly
light	lightly	weak	weakly
moderate	moderately	wide	widely

Sometimes there are spelling changes when the *-ly* suffix is added.

ADJECTIVE	ADVERB
easy	easily
simple	simply
automatic	automatically

The spelling rules for adding suffixes to words are in section 11.12.

In a few cases, the adjective and adverb forms of a word are the same.

ADJECTIVE
    ADVERB

Is she a *fast* worker?
    Yes, she works very *fast.*
Is he a *hard* worker?
    Yes, he works extremely *hard.*

Here are some words whose adjective and adverb forms are the same.

daily   early   fast   high   low
deep   far   hard   late   straight

Some of these adverbs may be confusing because there is an --ly form adverb with a different meaning.

ADVERB WITHOUT -*ly*
   ADVERB WITH -*ly*

She works *hard* (intensely).
   He *hardly* works at all. (He doesn't work much at all.)
She has never come *late* (after the appropriate time).
   He hasn't worked overtime *lately* (recently).
She tries to aim *high* (not low) in her career.
   He is *highly* (very) respected at work.

Prepositional phrases are often used as adverbials of manner.

Sylvia sings *like a bird*.
She prepares for a concert *with great efficiency*.
She speaks *in a low voice*.
She shows emotion *by changing her voice*.

Some prepositional phrases beginning with *by* refer to transportation or communication (see section 9.5). The articles *(a, an,* and *the)* are not used with these adverbials of manner.

CORRECT   I talked to Sylvia *by phone* yesterday.
             She arrived here *by plane*.

INCORRECT   *I talked to Sylvia *by the phone* yesterday.
             *She arrived here *by the plane*.

With phrases are often used to tell with what instrument.

She signed her contract *with a gold pen*.
She tipped the waiter *with a ten-dollar bill*.

Adverbials of manner come before or after the verbs that they modify but never between a verb and its object.

CORRECT   The director *quickly* offered Sylvia the role.

INCORRECT   *The director offered quickly Sylvia the role.

8.6 *Why:* **Adverbials of Reason, Cause, and Purpose**

We eat there *because of the location.*

Adverbial phrases beginning with *because of* answer questions beginning with *why.*

Jerry: Why do you eat in the cafeteria?
Pam: We eat there *because of the location.*

Phrases that begin with *despite* or *in spite of* explain an undesirable action or situation.

The food is terrible.
We eat there *in spite of the food.*
It's also noisy.
We go there *despite the noise.*

Because of, in spite of, and *despite* all introduce phrases, not clauses. (A clause contains a subject and a verb, but a phrase does not.) *Because* and *although* introduce adverbial clauses.

ADVERBIAL PHRASES

We like it   because of the people.
We eat there   in spite of the food.

ADVERBIAL CLAUSES
                          SUBJECT   VERB

We eat there   because   it   is   near work.
We go there   although the food is   bad.

Adverbial phrases beginning with *in order to* sometimes answer questions beginning with *why. In order to* is followed by the simple form of the verb. Sometimes *in order* is omitted and only *to* is used.

We are writing *in order to* complain about the food.
We are writing *to* complain about the food.
 (We are writing because we want to complain about the food.)

We would like to have a meeting *in order to* discuss the problem.

We would like to have a meeting *to* discuss the problem.

(We would like to have a meeting because we want to discuss the problem.)

8.7   *How Much*: **Adverbials of Degree and Emphasis**

She's *too* short to be on the basketball team.

a.   Defining Adverbs of Degree

Adverbs of degree answer questions beginning with *how much* or *to what degree.*

How much of the fence was painted?

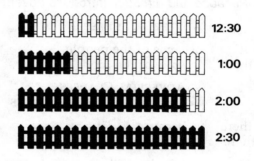

By twelve-thirty, the fence was *hardly* painted at all.

By one o'clock, it was *partially/partly* painted.

By two o'clock, it was *almost/nearly/practically* finished.

By two-thirty, it was *completely/entirely* painted.

Adverbs of degree can answer other *how* questions, such as *How tired were they?*

After five miles, the bicycle racers were not tired.
After ten miles, they were *hardly* tired.
After twenty miles, they were *rather/somewhat* tired.
After twenty-five miles, they were *fairly* tired.
After thirty miles, they were *quite* tired.
After thirty-five miles, they were *very* tired.
After forty miles, they were *exceedingly* tired.
After fifty miles, they were *completely* exhausted.

b. *Too* and *Enough*

He's *too* old for a child's ticket.

The adverbs *too* and *enough* have different meanings depending on the words that they modify. Look at these prices for movie tickets.

Child (under 12)	$4
Senior Citizen (over 65)	$5
Adult	$7

Henry is eleven years old.
He is young *enough* for a child's ticket.

Mr. Gonzalez is sixty-five years old.
He is old *enough* for a senior citizen's ticket.

Ellen is eighteen years old.
She isn't young *enough* for a child's ticket.
She isn't old *enough* for a senior citizen's ticket.
She is *too* old to buy a child's ticket.
She is *too* young to buy a senior citizen's ticket.

The adverb *too* comes before the words that it modifies; *enough* usually comes after the words it modifies.

This apartment is *too* small.
It isn't big *enough* for two people.

In many cases, phrases with *too* and *enough* are followed by complements beginning with *to* and *for.*

The closets are *too* small *for my clothes.*
They aren't large *enough for my shoes.*
The curtains are *too* old *to use.*
The kitchen isn't big *enough to move around in.*

c. *Too* and *Very*

These shoes are *too* narrow for me to wear.

The adverbs of degree *too* and *very* have similar meanings, but *too* suggests something negative or bad.

These shoes are *very* narrow.
They are *too* narrow for me. I can't wear them.
The heels are *very* high.
They are *too* high to walk in. I can't walk in them.
They are *very* expensive.
They are *too* expensive for me. I can't afford them.

Do not use *too* to mean *very*.

CORRECT The dress is *very* nice. (positive situation)
      The color is *very* attractive. (positive situation)

INCORRECT *This dress is too nice. (What is the negative
      situation?)
      *The color is too attractive. (What is the
      negative situation?)

d. *So* and *Such*

Why is it *so* expensive?

The adverb *so* (like *very, too,* and *enough*) can mean "to a greater degree" or "to a lesser degree" depending on the words it modifies.

Why is that green dress *so* expensive?
Why is the red dress *so* cheap?

In formal English, *so* is not used in statements to mean "very" unless it is followed by an adjective and a *that*-clause. In informal English, *so* can be used instead of *very* in statements; the *that*-clause is understood without being expressed.

FORMAL
 INFORMAL

That dress is *very* expensive.
 That dress is *so* expensive (that I can't afford it).

I like the dress *very* much.
I like the dress *so* much (that I'll buy it anyway).

The following sentences are good in formal or informal English:

Their prices are *so* high *that* I can't shop there. (Their prices are very high, and I can't shop there.)
The salespeople are *so* helpful *that* I never have to wait. (The salespeople are very helpful, and I never have to wait.)

The adverb *so* is sometimes confused with *such.* They have similar meanings, but they are used differently. *So* is used with adjectives or adverbs that are not followed by a noun. *Such* is usually used before an adjective followed by a noun.

		ADJECTIVE	NOUN
Why are these dresses	so	expensive?	
Why do you buy	such	expensive	dresses?
Why are the salespeople	so	helpful?	
How can they keep	such	helpful	salespeople?

When the noun phrase begins with *much, many, little,* or *few,* however, the adverb *so* is used, even when these quantifiers are followed by nouns.

There are *so many* departments that it is easy to get lost.
There are *so few* lines that you can shop quickly.

e. *Only, Even,* and *Especially*

I go to the movies *only* in the summer.

Some adverbs such as *only* are used to emphasize certain words or phrases.

I go to the movies *only* in the summer. (I do not go to the movies in any season except the summer.)

In spoken English, it is not always necessary to place these emphatic adverbs next to the words or phrases modified because the speaker's stress and intonation make the meaning clear. However, in written English, these words are usually placed before the words they modify.

SPOKEN ENGLISH   I only bought *SIX* candy bars.

WRITTEN ENGLISH   I bought only six candy bars.

When *only* is moved to a different part of the sentence, the meaning of the sentence can change.

> The children *only* went to the movies. (They did not do anything else.)
> The children went *only* to the movies. (They did not go anywhere else.)
> *Only* the children went to the movies. (No one else went to the movies.)

Other adverbial emphasizers that usually come directly before the words or phrases they modify are *even, especially, exactly, just, merely,* and *simply.*

8.8 Comparisons

> Betty paints *faster* than John.

When comparing two actions or events, the comparative form of an adverb is used for those adverbs that have a comparative form.

> John paints a house fast.
> He paints three rooms a day.
> Betty paints *faster* than John.
> She paints four rooms a day.

When comparing more than two actions or events, the superlative form is used. Adverbs that use -*er* for the comparative form use -*est* for the superlative form following the word "the."

> Sarah paints five rooms a day.
> She paints *the fastest.*

However, most adverbs form the comparative by using *more* or *less* before the adverb.

> Betty also paints *more neatly* than John.
> John paints *less neatly* than Betty.

Adverbs that form the comparative with *more* and *less* form the superlative with *the most* and *the least.*

> Sarah paints *the fastest* and *the most neatly.*
> John paints *the slowest* and *the least neatly.*

The following list shows the comparative and superlative forms of some common adverbs. (See section 11.12 for changes in spelling when -*er* and -*est* are used.) Except for the adverb *early,* adverbs of two or more syllables use *more/less* and *most/least* to form the comparative and superlative forms.

POSITIVE	COMPARATIVE	SUPERLATIVE
accurately	more accurately	the most accurately
	less accurately	the least accurately
early	earlier	the earliest
fast	faster	the fastest
long	longer	the longest
often	more often	the most often
	less often	the least often
slow	slower	the slowest

A few adverbs have irregular comparative and superlative forms.

POSITIVE	COMPARATIVE	SUPERLATIVE
badly	worse	the worst
far	farther	the farthest
	further	the furthest
little	less	the least
many	more	the most
much	more	the most
well	better	the best

The irregular comparative and superlative forms are used in the same way as the regular forms.

Sarah paints *better* than Betty.
Of the three painters, John paints *the worst.*
Sarah paints *the best.*

When a verb has a direct object, the comparative and superlative adverbs come after the direct object and not directly after the verb.

CORRECT	Betty can mix paint *more easily* than Sarah.
	Sarah uses a roller *the most.*
INCORRECT	*Betty can mix more easily paint than Sarah.
	*Sarah uses the most a roller.

To show a large difference between two actions or events, *much* or *far* is used before the comparative phrase.

Sarah paints *better* than Betty.
Sarah paints *far better* than John.
Betty also paints *much better* than John.
She paints *far more neatly* than John.
John paints *much less neatly* than Betty.

To show a small difference between two actions or events, *a little* or *a bit* is used before the comparative.

John drives *a little faster* than Betty.
Betty drives *a bit more carefully* than John.

Do not use *very* before comparative forms.

CORRECT   Betty paints *better* than John.

INCORRECT   *Betty paints *very better* than John.

However, *very* can be used before superlative forms, and *by far* can be used after superlative forms.

Of the three painters, Sarah paints *the very best*.
She also paints *the most neatly by far*.

When comparing two actions or events that are equal or almost equal, use the words *as...as*.

John works *as* hard *as* Sarah.
Betty drives almost *as* fast *as* John.

8.9 Sentence Adverbials

I will *probably* vacation in Europe this summer.

Sentence adverbs modify a whole sentence. They can come at the beginning, middle, or end of a sentence. Some sentence adverbs show probability. The sentence adverbs in the following sentences are arranged from high probability to low probability:

Obviously, Spain will be hot in August.
I *definitely* need to take summer clothes.
I can *probably* get tourist information at the consulate.
I can learn some Spanish before I go, *possibly*.
Maybe I can find a teacher.
Perhaps I will enroll in a course.

The punctuation of sentence adverbs depends on the pronunciation of the sentence. When there is a pause, a comma is used before or after the adverb. When the adverb occurs in the middle of a sentence and there are pauses before and after it, commas are used before and after the adverb.

Another kind of sentence adverbial indicates what the speaker thinks about the action or situation in the sentence. Adverbs such as *surprisingly, incredibly,* and *strangely* make judgments about how expected an event is. Adverbs such as *fortunately, happily,* and *luckily* give the speaker's opinion about a situation. These sentence adverbs are usually separated from the rest of the sentence by commas.

Unfortunately, the plane tickets will be expensive.
A rail pass, *luckily,* is still quite cheap.
I may not be able to stay all summer, *regrettably.*

8.10 Linking Adverbials

Cars are convenient; *however,* they are expensive to own.

A number of adverbs show relationships between ideas. These adverbs, called linking adverbials or conjunctive adverbs, are important cues for listeners and readers because they show how ideas are related.

It is very nice to own a car.
In fact, it is sometimes necessary.

Sentences with linking adverbials are sometimes punctuated with a semicolon and/or a comma.

There are many expenses besides the cost of a car.
For example, automobile insurance is very expensive.
Cars are convenient; *however,* they are also expensive.

Most linking adverbials are used only in formal speech and in writing. They can express many different kinds of relationships.

Linking adverbials such as *for example* introduce more information. Other linking adverbials that do this are the following:

also	further	in fact
besides	furthermore	moreover
equally	in addition	that is
for instance	indeed	too

Besides, which is a linking adverb, is sometimes confused with *beside*, which is a preposition.

> There are other expenses *besides* insurance. (There are other expenses *in addition to* insurance.)
> Put your signature *beside* the X on this form. (Put your signature *next to* the X on this form.)

Some linking adverbials show cause and effect.

> People under twenty-five have many automobile accidents. *As a result*, automobile insurance is expensive for young people.

Here is a list of linking adverbials that show cause and effect:

accordingly	then
as a consequence	therefore
as a result	thus
consequently	

Some linking adverbials compare or contrast ideas:

> Owning a car can be very expensive. *Nevertheless*, many people own cars.

Here is a list of linking adverbials that compare or contrast ideas.

by comparison	nonetheless
however	on the contrary
instead	on the other hand
likewise	otherwise
nevertheless	still

Some linking adverbials show the order of events:

> Last year, I saved some money. *Then* I started to think about buying a car. *First*, I read about the different makes and models. *Second*, I visited some showrooms.

Here is a list of some linking adverbials that show the order of events:

afterwards	later	second
earlier	next	simultaneously
first (of all)	now	subsequently
formerly	nowadays	then
last	previously	third

Some linking adverbials are used to show that what follows is a summary or restatement.

I shopped around; I borrowed money; finally, I did it.
I took the step.
In short, I became a car owner.

Here is a list of linking adverbials that are used to show that what follows is a summary or restatement:

briefly	in short	to summarize
in a word	in summary	

In most cases, linking adverbials come at the beginning of a clause. However, it is also possible for them to come in the middle or at the end of a clause.

Formerly, Americans preferred large cars.
Small cars, *however,* are becoming very popular.
Small cars are now big business, *in fact.*

8.11   Position and Order of Adverbials

Last night, the police caught a burglar *near here.*

Some adverbials, especially sentence adverbials, can come in a number of different places in a sentence.

INITIAL POSITION
Last night, there was a burglary near here.

FINAL POSITION
Someone robbed the grocery store *around midnight.*

When adverbials come in the middle of a sentence, they follow the verb *be* or the first auxiliary verb. If there is no verb *be* or auxiliary verb, the adverbial comes before the main verb. In negative sentences, adverbials can come before the negative word.

MIDDLE POSITION

The gas station was *recently* robbed, too.
Storekeepers should *definitely* take precautions.
They *probably* don't realize the danger.

Not all adverbials can come in all three positions. There are exceptions to the following general statements, but these statements can be used as guidelines for placing adverbials.

Sentence adverbs that describe a speaker's attitude or opinion are often in the initial position.

Fortunately, no one was hurt.

Adverbials of time that answer questions beginning with *when* sometimes come in the initial position, particularly when there are other adverbials at the end of the sentence.

Last year, the same store was robbed.
Six months later, the owner sold it.
At about the same time, a gas station was also robbed in the middle of the night.

In most cases, only one-word adverbs come in the middle of sentences. Adverbs of frequency and adverbs that refer to indefinite times usually come in middle position.

I *often* read about robberies in this area.
There have *already* been two robberies here this month.

Adverbs in middle position do not come between a verb and its object.

CORRECT   Thieves have robbed that store *often.*
               Some storekeepers know the danger *well.*

INCORRECT   *Thieves have robbed often that store.
               *Some storekeepers know well the danger.

Adverbs of frequency occur in the final position when they refer to definite times, such as *every day.*

The police now check the local stores *hourly.*
I see police cars going by the stores *every day.*

Sentence adverbs sometimes come in the middle of sentences.

Stores should *definitely* have burglar alarms.
They *certainly* provide some protection.

Many adverbials occur in the final position, after the verb and its complements. Adverbial phrases and clauses often come at the end of sentences.

Owners should leave some lights on *when their stores are closed.*
They should check all doors *before leaving.*

Sometimes there is more than one adverbial at the end of a sentence. When this happens, shorter adverbials usually come before longer ones.

	ADVERB	ADVERBIAL PHRASE
The thief entered	quietly	through the back door
		ADVERBIAL CLAUSE
		because it was easy to open.

In addition, adverbs that refer to shorter times or smaller places usually come before those that refer to longer times or larger places.

There was another robbery *one Saturday* last month.
The thief is now *in jail* in Cleveland.

Adverbials of manner, place, and time can occur in the following two patterns. (Place can refer to location or direction.)

	PLACE	MANNER	TIME
The burglar approached the store		slowly	at midnight.
He pushed a back window	up	carefully.	
He entered the store	from the back room		at about 12:15 a.m.
He filled a bag with merchandise		quietly	for about twenty minutes.

	MANNER	PLACE	TIME
Then he slipped	quietly	into the street	again.
He made his way	quickly	to a nearby bar.	

8.12   *Where, When, How Long*: Adverbial Clauses of Place and Time

a.   Adverbial Clauses of Place

Put the table *wherever you can find a place.*

Like single-word adverbs and adverbial phrases, adverbial clauses can answer the question "*Where?*". Adverbial clauses of place are introduced by the words *where, wherever,* and *anywhere.*

ADVERBIAL CLAUSE OF PLACE

Put the refrigerator	where the cabinet was.
Put those boxes	wherever you want.
Put the lamp	anywhere it fits.

Be careful not to use adverbial clauses as separate sentences. They are dependent clauses and cannot be used alone in formal written English.

CORRECT   Put it down *where the couch was.*

INCORRECT   Put it down. *Where the couch was.

b.   Adverbial Clauses of Time

Call me *when you arrive.*

Adverbial clauses that answer questions about time begin with *after, before, since, until, when, whenever,* and *while.* In these clauses, the *will* future tense is not used for future time.

CORRECT   Call me when you *arrive* at the apartment.
We can unpack after we *unload* the truck.
I will clean the place before the truck *arrives.*

INCORRECT   *Call me when you will arrive at the apartment.
*We can unpack after we will unload the truck.
*I will clean the place before the truck will arrive.

Adverbial clauses can come before or after independent clauses. In adverbial clauses of time, the introductory word *(before, after, when)* shows the order of events. The order of the clauses does not show the order of events. The following pairs of sentences have the same meanings:

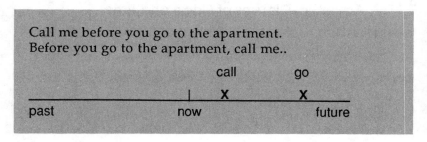

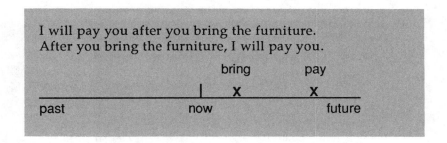

When an adverbial clause comes first in a sentence, it is followed by a comma.

After you bring the furniture, I will pay you.

Both *when* and *while* can be used in sentences about two events that happen at the same time.

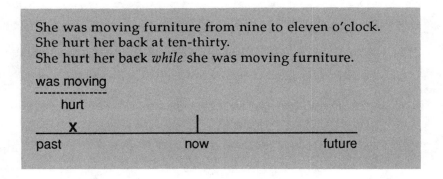

When two events happen at the same time, *while* is used before the longer event.

SHORTER EVENT	LONGER EVENT
She bumped her head	while she was carrying a big box.
She cut her finger	while she was putting away the knives.

While can also be used for two long events that happen at the same time.

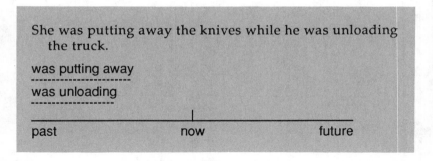

She was putting away the knives while he was unloading the truck.

When can also be used for two events that happen at the same time.

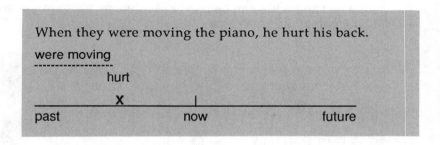

When they were moving the piano, he hurt his back.

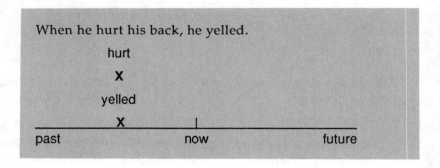

When he hurt his back, he yelled.

With adverbial clauses of time, it is often important to pay attention to whether the verbs in the sentence are durative (take place over a period of time) or punctual (take place quickly).

Continuous verb tenses have durative meaning. Compare the following sentences:

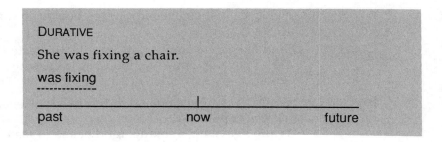

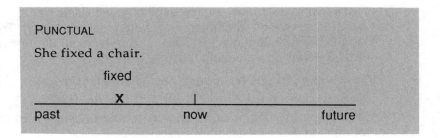

Some verbs are durative or punctual because of their meanings,P regardless of the tense of the verb.

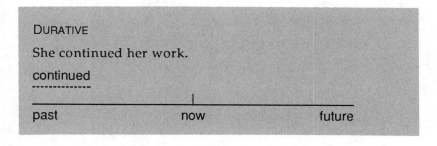

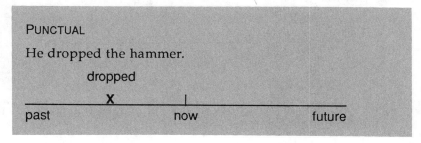

Punctual verbs usually cannot be used in clauses beginning with *while*.

CORRECT   *When* I began to smoke, I didn't like the taste.
           When I gave up smoking, food began to taste good.

INCORRECT *While I began to smoke, I didn't like the taste. (*Began* is punctual.)
           *While I gave up smoking, food began to taste good. (*Gave up* is punctual.)

Sentences with adverbial clauses beginning with *since* and *until* can answer questions beginning with *how long* and *when*. The verb in the independent clause (*since* and *until* begin dependent clauses) is usually durative in meaning.

She *has been losing* weight since she began smoking.
He *complained* loudly until she put out her cigarette.

Since refers to the beginning of an action, and *until* refers to the end of an action.

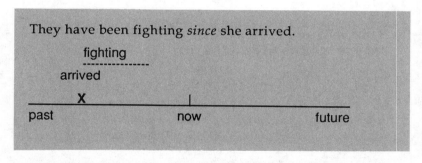

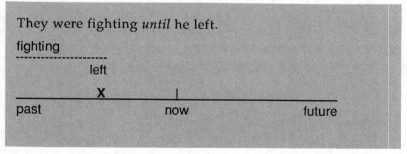

The verb that follows *since* or *until* is usually punctual, but the other verb in the sentence is not.

CORRECT	She has lost ten pounds since she *began* smoking. He coughed continuously until she *left* the room.
INCORRECT	*He coughed until she was leaving the room. *He began to cough since she started smoking.

8.13 *Why:* **Adverbial Clauses of Cause**

This umbrella won't keep you dry *because it has a hole in it.*

Some sentences with adverbial clauses answer the question "*Why?*" These sentences often state both the cause and the effect.

CAUSE	EFFECT
Because my umbrella had a hole,	I got wet.
Since this shirt is too small,	I want to exchange it.

It is possible for the effect to come before the cause in a sentence.

EFFECT	CAUSE
I want to exchange this robe	because it's too long.
I can't buy this blouse	since I don't have any money.

Adverbial clauses beginning with *so that* also tell why. Sometimes only *so* is used in this kind of sentence.

I bought a camera *so that* I could take it on my trip.
I need extra film *so* I don't run out.

Although and *even though* mean the opposite of *because.*

Although this camera is heavy, I like it. (This camera is heavy, but I like it.)
Even though I liked these sunglasses yesterday, I want to exchange them today. (I liked these sunglasses yesterday, but I want to exchange them today.)

Clauses with *although* and *even though* are similar in meaning to phrases with *despite* and *in spite of.*

I'll buy the camera *although it's expensive.*
I'll buy the camera *despite the expense.*
I'll buy it *even though* the carrying case is ugly.
I'll buy it *in spite of* the carrying case.

8.14 Conditionals with *If* and *Unless*

If you buy a new car now, you'll get a good price.

Conditional clauses describe one state or event (the condition) that must occur if another state or event (the result) is to occur.

CONDITION	RESULT
If we eat dinner early,	we can look at cars tonight.
If we buy a car this week,	we will get a rebate.

The result clause can come before or after the condition clause with no change in meaning.

RESULT	CONDITION
We will get a rebate	if we buy a car this week.

Unless is also used to introduce conditional clauses.

I won't eat at six unless I'm hungry. (I won't eat at six if I'm not hungry.)
We can't look at cars unless we eat early. (We can't look at cars if we don't eat early.)

In clauses with *if* and *unless*, the tense of the verb shows whether the speaker believes the condition to be probable or not. When the present tense is used, the condition is usually probable.

PROBABLE CONDITION	RESULT
If we *leave* now,	we will have plenty of time.
Unless we *go* by seven,	we won't have enough time.

When a past tense is used with *if*, it often shows that the speaker believes the condition is improbable or even untrue.

IMPROBABLE CONDITION	RESULT
If I *had* more money,	I *would buy* a sports car.
If I *had bought* a car,	we *could have gone* to the mall.

For further examples of conditional sentences, see section 4.23.

8.15 Summary: Adverbial Clauses and Phrases

Ideas that can be stated in adverbial clauses can sometimes also be expressed in prepositional phrases. In some cases, the prepositional phrases contain gerund phrases. Compare the following sentences:

ADVERBIAL CLAUSES
  ADVERBIAL PREPOSITIONAL PHRASES

After I had been looking for a job for two weeks, I became discouraged.
  After looking for a job for two weeks, I became discouraged.
Before I read the want ads, I thought that there were a lot of summer jobs.
  Before reading the want ads, I thought that there were a lot of summer jobs.

Although gerund phrases can be used after *when, while, since, before,* and *after,* they are not usually used after *because of, in spite of, until,* or *during.* The following chart gives a summary of different kinds of adverbial prepositional phrases and clauses. The adverbial phrases are below the adverbial clauses.

I went to a rock concert	*although* the tickets were expensive. *despite* the expense.
We arrived early	*so that* we could get good seats. *in order to* get good seats.
We couldn't talk	*because* the music was so loud. *because of* the music.
We couldn't see	*even though* we were in a good location. *in spite of* our location.
I liked rock music	*before* I went to that concert. *before* going there.
I didn't like rock music	*after* I went to that concert. *after* going there.
The singers danced	*while* they sang. *during* the song.

Everyone stayed on stage { *until* they sang the last song.
                           until the last song.

They smashed their instruments   *when* the concert ended.

I have had ear trouble { *since* I went to that concert.(time)
                         since that concert. (time)

I won't go to another rock concert   *since* I didn't enjoy the first
                                        one. (cause)

Chapter 9
Prepositions

9.1 Defining Prepositions

Prepositions connect nominals (nouns, noun phrases, and noun clauses) to other parts of the sentence. A preposition combines with a nominal to form a prepositional phrase. The nominal is the object of the preposition.

PREPOSITIONAL PHRASE

	PREPOSITION	OBJECT OF PREPOSITION
Is dinner	on	the table?
Please take this	to	the kitchen.

Some prepositional phrases show time and space relationships and answer the questions *when, where,* and *which one.*

We want to eat *before seven o'clock.*
The salad is *on the table.*
The dish *under the gravy* is too small.

Some prepositions show relationships among people, actions, and things.

That tablecloth was made *for* me *by* my grandmother.

Other relationships that can be expressed by prepositions are comparison, manner, cause, possession, and many others.

Prepositions may consist of one, two, or three words. Some common one-word prepositions follow.

above	beside	of	under
about	between	off	until
after	beyond	on	up
against	by	out	with
along	down	outside	without
among	during	over	
around	for	past	
at	from	since	
before	in	through	
behind	inside	till(informal)	
below	into	to	
beneath	near	toward	

Here are a few examples of two- and three-word prepositions (see section 9.7):

because of	next to
in back of	on top of
in front of	out of

Two- and three-word prepositions are used like one-word prepositions.

Put the salad *near* the potatoes.
Put the salad *next to* the potatoes.

The object of a preposition can be a noun (possibly a gerund), a noun phrase, or a noun clause.

Thank you for *the nice dinner.* (noun phrase)
Thank you for *coming.* (gerund)
After *what I ate,* I should walk home. (noun clause)

Many prepositions are used in the same way in most sentences, regardless of the verb or adjective that they are used with. For example, *by* is often used before the doer of an action.

The dinner was cooked *by* an expert. (An expert cooked the dinner.)
The decorations were made *by* a talented woman.
(A talented woman made the decorations.)

However, there are many special cases in which the choice of preposition depends on the other verbs and adjectives used in the sentence.

CORRECT	They are married *to* each other.
	They arrived *at* the party late.
INCORRECT	*They are married with each other.
	*They arrived to the party late.

It is useful to learn the basic meanings of prepositions. However, many of the special uses should also be learned. In section 9.9 there is a list of adjectives and the prepositions that follow them; there is also a list of verbs and associated prepositions.

9.2   Prepositions of Place and Direction

The cat walked *to* the table.

Some prepositional phrases answer the question *where.* These prepositional phrases begin with prepositions of place and direction.

Doug: Where is the cat?
Connie: I think he's *in the living room*.

The following sentences contain prepositions of place and direction with reference to a point, a surface, and an enclosure:

PREPOSITION OF PLACE
PREPOSITION OF DIRECTION

POINT: I saw the cat waiting *at* the door.
             Then he walked *to* the table.
             Suddenly, he ran away *from* it.

SURFACE: A lamp was *on* the table.
             The cat jumped *onto* the table.
             He knocked the lamp *off* the table.

ENCLOSURE: A fish was *in* the fishbowl.
             The cat put his paw *into* the fishbowl.
             He pulled the fish *out of* the fishbowl
             and ate it.

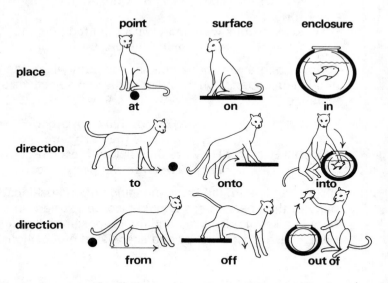

a. Prepositions of Direction

A mouse jumped *out of* the grass.

Many prepositions can be used with verbs of movement to show direction.

A cat walked *across* the street.

A mouse ran *through* the tall grass.

The cat ran *after* the mouse.

The mouse ran *toward* a tree.

It ran *around* the tree.

Then it ran *away from* the tree.

The cat ran *past* the tree.

The mouse ran *up* the stairs.

A dog ran *out* the door.

The dog ran *down* the stairs.

The cat ran *from* the dog.

The cat ran *to* the trash can.

It climbed *into* the trash can.

The dog ran *as far as* the fence.

The cat jumped *out of* the trash can.

The mouse jumped *off* the stairs.

The mouse jumped *into* the grass.

The choice between some pairs of prepositions, such as *over/through* and *onto/into,* depends on whether the speaker is thinking of a flat surface or a three-dimensional enclosure.

I pushed the lawn mower *over* the tall grass.
The mouse ran *through* the tall grass.

The cat jumped *onto* the box.
The mouse jumped *into* the box.

b.   Prepositions of Place: *at, on, in, inside, outside*

She lives *in* Canada.

The correct use of prepositions of place often depends on whether the speaker is thinking of a point, a surface or area, or a three-dimensional space. For example, *at* usually refers to a point; *on* usually refers to a line or surface; and *in* usually refers to something three-dimensional.

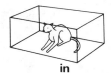

in   **at**   **on**

The cat sat *at* the window.
The cat sat *on* the floor.
The cat sat *in* the living room.

In most cases, *at* is used for specific addresses; *on* is used for streets; and *in* is used for buildings, cities, countries, and continents.

He lives *at* 231 Franklin Avenue.
He lives *on* Franklin Avenue.
He works *in* Powell Hall.
He lives *in* Chicago.
He lives *in* the United States.

However, sometimes *at* and *on* can be used for the inside of a building if the speaker is thinking of a place as a point or as a surface.

I'll meet you *at* the train station. (*at* = a point in the city)
Let's meet *on* the first floor. (*on* = a surface)

In some cases, the choice between *in* and *on* depends on how much of a space is enclosed. When three sides are enclosed, *in* can be used.

The potato is *in* the dish.

The potato is *on* the plate.

She is sleeping *in* her bed.

He is resting *on* his bed.

Sit *in* the armchair.

Sit *on* this stool.

When four sides are enclosed, *in* or *inside* can be used. There are many times when *in* or *inside* can be used in a sentence, but these words are not always used in exactly the same way.

IN OR *INSIDE*
Jim's *in* the house.
It's warmer *inside* the house.
What's *inside* the box?
There's nothing *in* that box.

IN ONLY
The dog is *in* the yard.

The opposite of *inside* is *outside.*

She makes her dog stay *outside* the house at night.
But she usually keeps her cat *inside* the house.

c.   Other Prepositions of Place

There's a lamp *over* her desk.

A number of prepositions express positions relative to the directions up and down. *On* and *on top of* are both "up" in relation to something else and are usually used when two objects are touching. *Under, beneath,* and *underneath* are "down" in relation to something else and can be used whether the objects are touching or not.

The plant is *on top of* that book.
Did you put the book *under* the plant?
My pencil was *on top of* the newspaper.
Did you leave the newspaper *on* the table?
Maybe your pencil rolled *beneath* the newspaper.
Look *underneath* the newspaper.

Over is usually, but not always, used for something higher in a vertical line. *Under* is the opposite of *over.*

Shirley has a light *over* her desk.
She is bending *over* her book while she reads.
Her dog is *under* the desk.

Above is often used in the same way as *over,* and *below* is often used in the same way as *under.* In some cases, *above* and *below* simply mean at a higher and lower level, not necessarily in a vertical line.

From the mountain peak we could see the stars *above* us.
We could also see the city *below* us.

The prepositions that express the ideas "up" and "down" are summarized in the following chart. *Above* and *below* cover a wider area than the other prepositions.

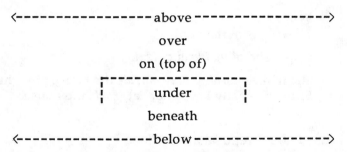

The prepositions *in front of* and *in back of* sometimes need to be understood from the point of view of the speaker.

Toshiko is *in front of* the car.
Carlos is *in back of* the car.

In this situation, someone standing behind Carlos could say, "Carlos is in front of the car," and "Yoshiko is in back of the car."

Ahead of and *behind* can also be used from the point of view of the speaker.

Betty and Sarah are walking
    ahead of us.
Ali is hiding *behind* a tree.

However, the more common situation is that the prepositions *in front of, in back of, ahead of,* and *behind* are to be understood in relation to the nouns in the sentence.

Alberto is *in front of* the car.
Julia is *in back of* the car.
Alberto is walking *ahead of* the car.
The dog is walking *behind* Julia.

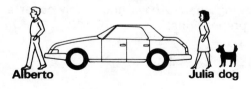

Beside, next to, and *by* can also be used either in reference to the viewpoint of the speaker or in reference to another person or object.

> Julia is standing *next to* the car.
>   (Julia's point of view)
> Julia is standing *in front of* the car.
>   (speaker's point of view)
> The dog is sitting *beside* Julia.
>   (Julia's point of view)

Julia dog

The meaning of *near* is similar to that of *next to* but is more general.

> The spoon is *next to* the knife.
> The glass is *near* the spoon.
> The napkin is *next to* the fork.
> It is *near* the edge of the table.

Far from is often used as the opposite of *near.*

> They are *far from* home. (They are not near home.)

The prepositions *among* and *between* are sometimes confused. *Between* is used to show a relation between a person or object and two others.

> The circle is *between* the two squares.
> The plate is *between* the knife and the fork.

Use *among* to show a relation between a person or object and more than two others.

The circle is *among* the squares.
There is a fork *among* the spoons.

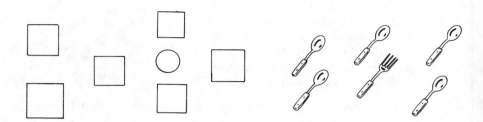

9.3 Prepositions of Time

She'll stay in Quito *from* Monday *to* Wednesday.

Some prepositional phrases answer the question *when*. These prepositions of time can refer to points *in time* or periods *of time*.

When will she arrive?
She'll arrive *at* five o'clock *on* Monday. (point in time)
She'll stay *from* Monday *to* Wednesday. (period of time)

a. Points in Time: *at, on,* and *in*

The prepositions *at* and *on* refer to points in time as well as points in space. *At* is used with specific times of day and other points in time.

The plane left *at* seven o'clock.
We arrived in Mexico City *at* midnight.
She often travels *at* the end of the month.

On is used before days, dates, and holidays.

She'll arrive at Machu Picchu *on* Saturday.
She has to return *on* July 1.
She plans to call us *on* Independence Day.

In is used for periods of time such as months, seasons, years, decades, or centuries.

He plans to go to Asia *in* September.
He'll visit Japan sometime *in* the fall.
He was there *in* 1983.
He traveled through the Middle East *in* the 1970s.

When a sentence has more than one prepositional phrase referring to time, shorter time periods usually come before longer time periods.

He promised to visit that church *at* sunrise *on* the first
Sunday *in* May.

In is also used for parts of the day, including the evening but not the night.

She studies *in* the morning.
She takes photographs *in* the afternoon.
She writes in her journal *in* the evening.

She likes to go out *at* night.

b. Periods of Time

He has been working on his car *since* eight o'clock.

The pairs of prepositions *from...to* and *between...and* are used to show periods of time when both the beginning and the end of the period are mentioned.

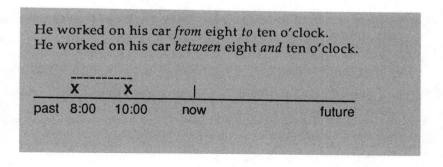

The preposition *until* is used for a period of time when only the end of the period is mentioned.

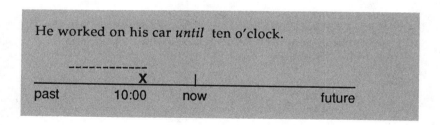

Since is used for a period of time when only the beginning point is mentioned.

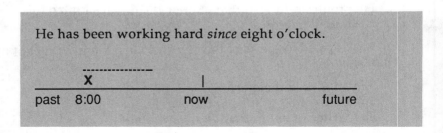

He has been working hard *since* eight o'clock.

past 8:00	now	future

Since is often used when an action or state is not finished. It usually occurs with the present perfect tense.

I *have lived* in New Orleans *since* 1972. (This state has not ended.)

Since is not used with the simple present or simple past tenses.

INCORRECT   *I work for this company since 1977.
*I worked for this company since 1977.

The preposition *for* is used for periods of time, but not when the beginning and end points are stated.

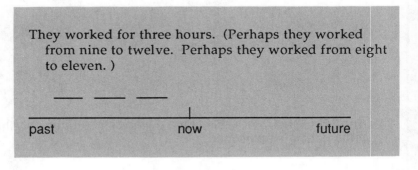

They worked for three hours. (Perhaps they worked from nine to twelve. Perhaps they worked from eight to eleven.)

past	now	future

When a *for* phrase is used with the present perfect tense, the end of the period is understood as the moment of speaking.

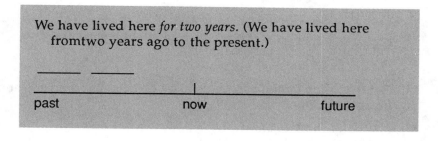

We have lived here *for two years.* (We have lived here
fromtwo years ago to the present.)

past   now   future

Notice the difference in the use of *since* and *for.* When the beginning point of an action or event is mentioned, *since* is used. When
the length of time is given, *for* is used.

It is November.
We have been in this house *since* July.
We have been in this house *for* four months.

Since is not used when the length of time is stated.

INCORRECT   *We have lived here since two years.

During refers to a period of time, but it is different from *since* and
for. During answers questions that begin with *when; for* and *since*
answer questions that begin with *how long.*

When did you work there?

I worked there { during the summer.
                during the week.
                during the morning.

How long did you work there?

I worked there { for three months.
                for five days.
                for four hours.

INCORRECT   *I worked there during three months.

c.   Relative Time

I always take a walk *before* breakfast.

Before and *after* show the order of events.

EVENT 1	EVENT 2
I took a walk at seven.	I ate breakfast at eight.
I took a walk *before* breakfast.	
I ate breakfast *after* my walk.	

Gerunds (-*ing* forms) can be used as objects of the prepositions *before* and *after*.

I took a walk *before eating*.
After walking, I ate breakfast.

When the preposition *by* refers to time, it has a meaning similar to that of *before*. *By* means "on or before," and *from...on* means "after" in the sentences that follow.

I must be at work *by* eight o'clock. (I must be at work on or before eight o'clock.)
I will be very busy *from* eight *on*. (I will be very busy after eight.)

9.4 Prepositions of Role

I threw a ball to my sister.

Prepositions can indicate who did an action and who received an object or action. The preposition *by* often tells who or what did an action.

A young man sold me this photograph.
This photograph was sold to me *by* a young man.

Ansel Adams took the picture.
The picture was taken *by* Ansel Adams.

The prepositions *from* and *to* have opposite meanings and are often used with verbs that have opposite meanings.

bought
took
borrowed
stole
} the stamps *from* my uncle.

sold
gave
lent
returned
} them *to* my brother.

The prepositions *to* and *at* both show who or what receives an action. However, they have slightly different meanings. *To* often suggests an "experiencer," but *at* does not.

CORRECT   I threw a ball *to* my sister.
                        I threw a ball *at* the tree.

INCORRECT   *I threw a ball to the tree.

In the following sentences, *to* and *at* do not have the same meanings.

To

Jack threw a ball *to* his sister. She caught it.
He shouted *to* her, "Wait a minute!"
He talked *to* her, and she listened carefully.

At

Susan threw a rock *at* her brother. She hit him.
She shouted *at* him, "I hit you!"
She was yelling *at* him, and he was crying.

The following sentences also show the difference between *to* and *at*:

To

He is being $\begin{cases} \text{kind} \\ \text{friendly} \\ \text{nice} \\ \text{polite} \end{cases}$ *to* her.

At

She is $\begin{cases} \text{angry.} \\ \text{annoyed} \\ \text{mad} \\ \text{furious} \end{cases}$ *at* him.

After linking verbs, *to* shows who receives or "experiences" the object or event.

It $\begin{cases} \text{feels} \\ \text{looks} \\ \text{seems} \\ \text{smells} \end{cases}$ like plastic to me.

It looks $\begin{cases} \text{expensive} \\ \text{good} \\ \text{old} \\ \text{ugly} \end{cases}$ *to me.*

The prepositions *for* and *to* both mark the indirect object of a sentence. The indirect object is often the one that receives the direct object.

	DIRECT OBJECT	INDIRECT OBJECT (RECEIVER)
I brought	these flowers	for you.
I wanted to buy	a cake	for you.
I'll give	this candy	to you now.
I'll show	something interesting	to you later.

Many verbs of communication are followed by the preposition *to*. Other verbs of communication are followed by *with*. When *to* is used, it places emphasis on one listener. When *with* is used, it suggests that there is more than one speaker.

To   A – – –> B

She will *announce* her engagement *to* her parents tonight.

Other verbs used with *to* are the following:

admit   explain
confess   mention
describe   report

WITH   A < – – –> B

She will *argue with* her parents about the engagement.

Other verbs used with *with* are the following:

agree	correspond	gossip	reason
confer	differ	jest	speak
consult	disagree	joke	(also used with *to*)
converse	fight	quarrel	talk
			(also used with *to*)

After verbs of communication, the preposition *about* can be used to show what was discussed.

She told her mother *about* her boyfriend.
Her father advised her *about* her money.
He lectured her *about* the responsibilities of parents.
They quarreled *about* the guest list for the wedding.

Other prepositions, such as *of, on,* and *over,* can also be used to show what was communicated, but these prepositions are much more limited. It is safer to use *about* before the subject of a communication.

CORRECT   They quarreled *over* the guest list.
               They quarreled *about* the guest list.

INCORRECT   *They quarreled on the guest list.

9.5   Prepositions of Method and Manner

Let's go *by* bus.

Several prepositions tell *how* or *by what method.*

Mary: How did he break the coconut?
Fred: I think he broke it *with* a rock.
         He did it *with* considerable skill.
         I can't break one *without* a hammer.
         Can you do it *without* smashing it?

The preposition *by* and a present participle are sometimes used to answer *how* questions.

Mario:	How can you get the coconut milk?
Sam:	You can do it *by drilling* a small hole.
Mario:	How do you drink it?
Sam:	I do it *by putting* a straw in the hole.

Manner is sometimes described by using the phrase *in a(n) . . . manner* or *in a(n) . . . way*. *Like this* and *like that* (with gestures) also refer to manner.

I learned how to break a coconut *in a new way*.
You hold it *like this*.

The preposition *by* is often used to describe a means of transportation or communication. In these cases, the determiner *the* is not used.

CORRECT	Let's go to the beach *by bus*.
	It's faster to go *by plane*.
	During your vacation, keep in touch *by phone*.

| INCORRECT | *Let's go to the beach by the bus. |

9.6 Prepositions of Cause and Reason

I did it *for* the money.

a. Cause

Some prepositional phrases answer the question *why*. *Because of* is a two-word preposition that introduces a reason. Do not confuse *because of*, which comes before a noun phrase, with *because*, which comes before a clause (see section 8.6).

| CORRECT | I'm considering the job because of the salary. |
| | I'm interested in it *because of* the location. |

| INCORRECT | *I'm interested in it because of I like the location. |
| | (*I like the location* is a clause, not a noun phrase.) |

Despite, in spite of, and *regardless of* mean the opposite of *because of.*

I may take the job *despite* the long working hours.
(I may take the job although it has long working hours.)
The benefits are good *in spite of* the one-week vacation.
(The benefits are good although there is only a
    one-week vacation.)
I would like the job *regardless of* its shortcomings.
(I would like the job although it has shortcomings.)

Except, except for, but, and *apart from* are used to show exception.

I like everything about the job *except for* the long hours.
Everything *but* the long hours appeals to me.
Apart from the long hours, it's the perfect job.

b.   Reason

The preposition *for* is used to give causes or reasons. It has a similar meaning to *so that* (see section 8.13).

Are you doing this *for* the money? (Are you doing this so
    that you can earn money?)

When the answer to a question beginning with *why* is a noun phrase, a phase beginning with *for* is used. When the answer to a question beginning with *why* includes a verb, an infinitive phrase is often used.

Claude: Why are you leaving so early?
Leslie: I'm going *for an interview.* (noun phrase)
Claude: Why are you so nervous?
Leslie: I'm going *to talk to the manager* today. (infinitive
             phrase)

Other phrases used to give reasons are *for the sake of, as a result of,* and *due to.*

I may take that job *for the sake of* my family.
As a result of inflation, I need a higher salary.
Due to this situation, I'm not very happy.

9.7   Phrasal and Participial Prepositions

a.   Phrasal Prepositions

Thanks to you, we found my watch.

There are some sequences of words that are considered two-, three-, and four-word prepositions. These phrasal prepositions are used in the same way as one-word prepositions.

> We found it *in back of* the dresser. (three words)
> It must have fallen *behind* the dresser last week. (one word)

Do not use one part of a phrasal preposition without the other part.

CORRECT
> *Thanks to* you, we found my watch.
> *In addition to* the watch, we found a necklace.

INCORRECT
> *Thanks you, we found my watch.
> *In addition the watch, we found a necklace.

Some common two- and three-word prepositions are:

according to	far from	owing to
ahead of	in addition to	previous to
along with	in back of	prior to
apart from	in front of	regardless of
as for	in relation to	relative to
as to	in spite of	save for
aside from	instead of	short of
away from	irrespective of	subsequent to
because of	next to	thanks to
contrary to	on account of	together with
due to	on top of	up to
except for	out of	up until

b. Participial Prepositions

> *Barring* any delays, the trial should end soon.

A few present participles are commonly used as prepositions. These are usually used in formal English.

> *Excluding* the lawyer's fee, it should not cost too much.
> *Considering* the damage to the car, you were lucky.

When using these participles, it is important not to forget the *-ing* ending.

CORRECT
> There are a number of dents, *including* one on the left rear bumper.

INCORRECT   *There are a number of dents, include one on
                the left rear bumper.

Some common examples of participial prepositions are:

barring	excluding
concerning	including
considering	pending
excepting	regarding

9.8   The Preposition *of*

The roof *of* this house needs repairing.

The preposition *of* shows that two noun phrases are related; however, it does not indicate what the relation is. The following sentences give examples of some of the relations expressed by *of*:

Of is sometimes used to show "having" or "belonging to."

The owner was a friend *of* mine. (The owner was my
   friend.)
She was an old friend of the family. (She was my family's
   old friend.)

When the possessor is not human, the possessive with *of* is usually used instead of the -'s form.

The roof *of* the house needs repairing.
One leg *of* this table is broken.
The price *of* this house is too high.

Of is used to connect a quantifier with a noun (see section 3.6).

Many *of* the windows in this house are broken.
A few *of* the stairs are missing.
Half *of* this board is gone.

Prepositional phrases beginning with *of* are sometimes used to show what something is made of or where it comes from.

MATERIAL   The desk is made *of* plastic.
             Auto bodies are usually made *of* steel.

ORIGIN   Antonio is the merchant *of* Venice.
             The llama *of* the Andes is related to the camel
               of Asia.

CONTENT   Put that basket *of* grapes on the table.
                  There is a plate *of* cheese over there.

From can also refer to material and origin, but it implies a distance" from the original in space, time, or transformation.

MATERIAL   Plastic is made *from* petroleum.

ORIGIN   He lives in Los Angeles, but he's *from*
                 New York.

Nouns, such as *admiration,* that are closely related to verbs, such as *admire,* are often followed by the preposition *of.*

VERB
     NOUN PHRASE + *OF* + NOUN PHRASE

He rejected her offer.
     His rejection *of* the offer was odd.

She disliked his work.
     Her dislike *of* his work annoyed him.

The book arrived late.
     The arrival *of* the book was welcome.

She hoped to win a prize.
     Her hope *of* winning a prize was foolish.

Many proper names contain *of.* When proper names include an *of* phrase, the determiner *the* is usually used.

the Avenue *of* the Americas	the Republic *of* China
the Fourth *of* July	the Statue *of* Liberty
the American Museum *of*	the University *of* the
Natural History	Pacific

9.9 Prepositions after Adjectives and Verbs

Everyone laughed *at* his joke.

Many prepositions have basic meanings that don't change.

The speaker came *into* the room.
He walked *to* the stage.

However, there are many special cases in which the choice of preposition depends on the adjectives and verbs that are used in the sentence.

CORRECT   The speaker *looked at* the crowd.
               He *spoke to* the people.
               He was *interested in* talking to them.

INCORRECT   *The speaker looked to the crowd.
               *He spoke at the people.
               *He was interested about talking to them.

In the lists that end this unit, some of the adjectives and verbs can be used with prepositions other than those given. The lists include only common verbs and adjectives and the prepositions that usually follow them.

The adjectives in the list are usually used after some form of the verb *be*.

She *was ashamed of* her old clothes.

Most of the verbs listed are followed by the same preposition in both the active and the passive voice. In active sentences, an object usually comes between the verb and the prepositional phrase. In passive sentences, the prepositional phrase usually comes directly after the past participle.

ACTIVE VOICE   He *accused* the mayor *of* dishonesty.

PASSIVE VOICE The mayor was also *accused of* greed.

The subject of an active sentence can always be used in a prepositional phrase beginning with *by* in the passive sentence. Since *by* can always be used in passive sentences, it is not included in the list.

ACTIVE VOICE   Everything he said *pleased* the crowd.

PASSIVE VOICE The crowd was *pleased by* everything he said.

The lists also indicate whether the object of the preposition is usually a person (somebody), a thing (something), or a place (someplace). These objects can also be plural, of course.

PREPOSITIONS AFTER ADJECTIVES

She was *absent from* school.
(her school = someplace)

ADJECTIVE	PREPOSITION		OBJECT	
absent	from		something	someplace
accustomed	to	somebody	something	someplace
acquainted	with	somebody	something	
afraid	of	somebody	something	someplace
angry	about		something	
	at	somebody	something	
	with	somebody		
anxious	about		something	
	over		something	
apparent	to	somebody		
appropriate	for	somebody	something	
ashamed	of	somebody	something	someplace
available	for		something	
	to	somebody		
aware	of	somebody	something	
bad	about		something	
capable	of		something	
certain	about		something	
	of		something	
confused	about		something	
conscious	of		something	
critical	of	somebody	something	
different	from	somebody	something	
difficult	for	somebody		
disappointed	about		something	
	in	somebody	something	
	with	somebody	something	
discouraged	about		something	
disgusted	about	somebody	something	
	at	somebody	something	
	with	somebody	something	
doubtful	about	somebody	something	
	of		something	
eager	for		something	
eligible	for		something	

ADJECTIVE	PREPOSITION		OBJECT	
enthusiastic	about	somebody	something	someplace
equal	to	somebody	something	
excited	about	somebody	something	someplace
	for	somebody		
	over		something	
faithful	to	somebody	something	
familiar	to	somebody		
	with	somebody	something	someplace
famous	for		something	
fit	for		something	
fond	of	somebody	something	someplace
friendly	to	somebody		
full	of		something	
generous	to	somebody		
	with	somebody	something	
glad	about		something	
	of		something	
good	at		something	
	for		something	
	to	somebody		
grateful	for		something	
	to	somebody		
happy	about		something	
	for	somebody		
homesick	for	somebody	something	someplace
immune	to		something	
independent	of	somebody	something	
inferior	to	somebody	something	someplace
intent	on		something	someplace
interested	in	somebody	something	homething
jealous	of	somebody		
kind	to	somebody		
loyal	to	somebody	something	someplace
lucky	at		something	
	in		something	
mad	about		something	
	at	somebody		
married	to	somebody		
patient	about		something	
	with	somebody		

ADJECTIVE	PREPOSITION		OBJECT	
perfect	for	somebody	something	
pleased	about		something	
	with	somebody	something	
polite	to	somebody		
present	at		something	
proud	of	somebody	something	
nervous	about	somebody	something	
ready	for	somebody	something	
resistant	to		something	
responsible	for	somebody	something	someplace
rid	of	somebody	something	
sad	for	somebody		
	over		something	
satisfactory	for		something	
	to	somebody		
separate	from	somebody	something	someplace
short	of		something	
similar	to	somebody	something	someplace
slow	at		something	
sorry	about	somebody	something	
	for	somebody	something	
successful	at		something	
	in		something	
suitable	for	somebody	something	someplace
superior	to	somebody	something	someplace
sure	of		something	
surprised	at	somebody	something	
suspicious	of	somebody	something	
talented	at		something	
	in		something	
tired	of	somebody	something	someplace
tolerant	of	somebody	something	
typical	of	somebody	something	
upset	about	somebody	something	
	with	somebody		
useful	for		something	
	to	somebody		

PREPOSITIONS AFTER VERBS

We couldn't *account for* some of the money.
   (*some of the money* = something)
The money was finally *accounted for.*
The bank *accused* us of carelessness
   (*us* = somebody, *carelessness* = something)
We weren't *accused of* dishonesty.

VERB	PREPOSITION		OBJECT	
account	for		something	
accuse(sb)	of		something	
adapt	to		something	someplace
add	to		something	
adjust	to		something	someplace
advise(sb)	about		something	
(counsel)	on		something	
advise (sb)	of		something	
(notify)				
agree	about		something	
	to		something	
	with	somebody		
apologize	for		something	
	to	somebody		
apply	for		something	
	to	somebody	something	
approve	of	somebody	something	someplace
argue	about		something	
	with	somebody		
arrive	at			someplace
	in			someplace
ask	about	somebody	something	someplace
	for	somebody	something	
ask(st)	of	somebody		
attract	to	somebody	something	
beg	for		something	
believe	in	somebody	something	
belong	to	somebody		
blame(st)	on	somebody		
(somebody)	for		something	
bore(sb)	with		something	
borrow(st)	from	somebody		

Verb	Preposition		Object		
brag	about		something		
buy(st)	from	somebody			
call	for		something		
	to	somebody			
care	about	somebody	something		
	for	somebody	something		
change	from		something		
	to		something		
collect	from	somebody			
compete	for		something		
	with	somebody			
complain	about		something		
	of		something		
	to	somebody			
confuse(sb,st))	with	somebody	something		
consist	of		something		
contrast	to	somebody	something	someplace
	with	somebody	something	someplace
convince(sb)	of		something		
cooperate	with	somebody			
correspond	to		something		
	with	somebody			
deal	with	somebody	something		
decide	on	somebody	something	someplace
defend	from	somebody	something		
depend	on	somebody	something		
differ	from	somebody	something	someplace
disagree	about		something		
	over		something		
	with	somebody			
dream	about	somebody	something	someplace
	of	somebody	something	someplace
eliminate	from		something		
end	in		something		
	with		something		
exchange(st)	for		something		
	with	somebody			
fill	with		something		
forgive(sb)	for		something		
help(sb)	with		something		
hide	from	somebody			

VERB	PREPOSITION		OBJECT		
hope	for		something		
impose	on	somebody			
	upon	somebody			
inquire	about	somebody	something	someplace	
insist	on		something		
introduce(sb)	to	somebody			
joke	about		something		
	with	somebody			
keep	off		something		
keep away	from	somebody	something	someplace	
know	about	somebody	something	someplace	
laugh	at	somebody	something		
	over		something		
	with	somebody			
lend	to	somebody			
listen	for		something		
	to	somebody	something		
object	to		something		
pardon(sb)	for		something		
participate	in		something		
pay	for		something		
pay attention	to	somebody	something		
persist	in		something		
plan	for		something		
	on		something		
prefer(sb,st,sp)	to	somebody	something	someplace	
prepare	for	somebody	something		
present(sb,st)	to	somebody			
profit	from		something		
protect(sb,st)	from	somebody	something		
quarrel	about		something		
	over		something		
	with	somebody			
question(sb)	about		something		
rebel	against	somebody	something		
recommend	against		something		
(somebody)	for		something		
(something)	to	somebody			
recover	from		something		
refer	to	somebody	something	someplace	
rely	on	somebody	something		

VERB	PREPOSITION		OBJECT	
remind(sb)	of	somebody	something	
remove	from	somebody	something	someplace
rescue(sb,st)	from	somebody	something	someplace
request(st)	from	somebody		
	of	somebody		
result	in		something	
	from		something	
retire	from		something	
(something)	to		something	someplace
return	from		something	someplace
	to	somebody	something	someplace
rob(sb)	of		something	
scold(sb)	for		something	
search	for	somebody	something	someplace
separate(sb,st)	into		something	
shop	for	somebody	something	
smile	at	somebody	something	
speak	of	somebody	something	someplace
	to	somebody		
	with	somebody		
steal(st)	from	somebody	something	someplace
stop(sb)	from		something	
submit(sb,st)	to	somebody	something	
substitute				
(sb,st)	for	somebody	something	
succeed	at		something	
	in		something	
suffer	from		something	
	with	somebody		
suggest(st)	to	somebody		
supply(st)	to	somebody		
(sombody)	with		something	
suspect(sb)	of		something	
talk	about	somebody	something	someplace
	to	somebody		
	with	somebody		
tell(sb)	about	somebody	something	someplace
thank(sb)	for		something	
think	about	somebody	something	someplace
	of	somebody	something	someplace

VERB	PREPOSITION		OBJECT	
translate	from		something	
	into		something	
	to		something	
turn	from		something	
	into		something	
	to	somebody	something	
vote	for	somebody	something	
wait	for	somebody	something	
wait	on	somebody		
warn	about	somebody	something	
watch	for	somebody	something	
	over	somebody	something	
wonder	about	somebody	something	someplace
work	for	somebody		
	on		something	
worry	about	somebody	something	

Chapter 10

Conjunctions and Coordinate Structures

10.1 Coordinate Conjunctions

Put in two dimes *and* a nickel.

Conjunctions are words that join. The coordinate conjunctions, such as *and*, join two or more words, phrases, or clauses that are related.

Pick up the receiver *and* listen to the dial tone.
Put in two dimes *and* a nickel.

When more than two items are joined, use *and* only between the last two. Use a comma after the other items. A comma can be used before *and*, or it can be omitted.

I've got a dime, a nickel, *and* five pennies.
I've got a dime, a nickel *and* five pennies.

But and *yet* are used to show contrasts. In the following sentences, *but* and *yet* have similar meanings. The conjunction *yet* is used more often in written English than in spoken English.

I need to call, *but* I hate to spend the money.
I need to call, *yet* I hate to spend the money.
Using a pay phone is easy *but* sometimes frustrating.
Using a pay phone is easy *yet* sometimes frustrating.

The conjunction *or* is used to show choices.

You can use dimes, nickels, *or* quarters in a pay phone.
You can pay *or* you can call collect.

Nor is like *or*, but it joins negative phrases and clauses. When *nor* begins a clause, use question word order.

I haven't used a pay phone, *nor have I* called collect.
(I haven't used a pay phone, and I haven't called collect.)
I didn't reach the number, *nor did I* get my money back.
(I didn't reach the number, and I didn't get my money back.)

The conjunction *for* means "because." Sentences with *for* are more formal than those with *because*.

It's important to call, *for* we need to make plans. (It is important to call because we need to make plans.)

The conjunction *so* means "as a result."

I came home late last night, *so* I didn't call you. (I came home late last night. As a result, I didn't call you.)
I've been too busy to write, *so* I decided to call. (I've been too busy to write. As a result, I decided to call.)

When coordinate conjunctions join clauses, a comma is used before the conjunction.

I got very lonesome, *and* I wanted to talk to you.
It's expensive, *but* I like to hear your voice.

10.2 Compound Phrases and Subject-verb Agreement

The land and the water *are* threatened by industrial waste.

Parts of sentences are compound when they are joined by coordinate or correlative conjunctions (see 10.5). Most parts of speech and parts of sentences can be joined by conjunctions.

This news story is *shocking* and *disturbing.* (compound adjectives)
It was *in the newspapers* and *on television.* (compound prepositional phrases)
I don't like to read about *waste* and *pollution.* (compound nouns)

When subjects are joined by *and*, the verb is plural.

The sports page and the crossword puzzle *were* in the sections of the paper that you threw away.
The movie schedule and the TV listings *are* in the third section.

With *or* and *nor*, the verb agrees with the part of the subject following these coordinators. *Either* is often used with *or*, and *neither* is often used with *nor* (see section 10.5).

CORRECT   Either the business section or the sports section *is* the first thing I read.
Neither the editorials nor the sports scores *are* in this section.

INCORRECT   *Either the business section or the sports
              section are the first thing I read.
              *Neither the editorials nor the sports scores is
              in this section.

10.3   Compound Sentences

Alan didn't make a good impression in the interview, *so*
Ms. Simon isn't going to hire him.

When two sentences are joined by a coordinate conjunction, they
form a compound sentence.

Yukiko can use the word processor, *but* she doesn't know
how to use the printer.

In compound sentences, a comma is used before the conjunction.

Alan didn't make a good impression in the interview, so
Ms.Simon isn't going to hire him.
He knows how to use the word processor, but he doesn't
dress well.

When the parts of a compound sentence repeat the same phrase,
it is possible to omit the repeated part of the compound sentence.

Ms. Simon interviewed Alan *and then Carlos.* (Ms. Simon
interviewed Alan, and then she interviewed Carlos.)

In the following compound sentences, part of the second clause
is omitted. *Too* is used with the affirmative sentence, and *either* is
used with the negative sentence.

Maria became quite nervous, and Alan *did, too.* (Maria
became quite nervous, and Alan became quite nervous,
too.)
Alan hadn't met the manager, and Maria *hadn't, either.*
(Alan hadn't met the manager, and Maria hadn't met the
manager, either.)

So and *too* have similar meanings in compound sentences.
However, their positions are different, and question word order is
used after *so*.

Maria seemed quite nervous, and *so did Alan.* (Maria seemed quite nervous, and Alan seemed quite nervous, too.)

She wanted to meet the manager, and *so did he.* (She wanted to meet the manager, and he wanted to meet the manager, too.)

Neither means "not either." It comes at the beginning of the second clause and is followed by question word order.

Alan has no work experience, and *neither does Maria.* (Alan has no work experience, and Maria has no work experience, either.)

Compare the following sentences with *too, so, either,* and *neither.*

AFFIRMATIVE

Alan wants a job, and *Maria does, too.*
Alan wants a job, and *so does Maria.*

NEGATIVE

Maria hasn't worked before, and *Alan hasn't, either.*
Maria hasn't worked before, and *neither has Alan.*

10.4 Parallel Structure

She likes *reading, hiking,* and *singing.*

Structures that are joined by conjunctions should always be similar structures containing related ideas. When two or more parts of a sentence joined by commas or conjunctions have similar structures, they are parallel. In the following sentence, the *-ing* phrases are parallel and, therefore, correct.

She likes *reading novels* and *singing popular songs.*

The infinitive phrases are parallel in the following sentence.

She likes *to read novels* and *to sing popular songs.*

When the structures are not parallel, the sentence is incorrect.

INCORRECT   *She likes reading novels and tennis.
             *She likes to read novels and playing tennis.

These sentences can be corrected so that they are parallel.

CORRECT	She likes *reading* novels and *playing* tennis.
	She likes to *read* novels and *play* tennis.

Notice that in infinitive phrases, the second *to* can be omitted (*to read and play*). The structures are still in the infinitive form and are, therefore, parallel.

When three or more words or phrases are joined, they should also be parallel.

CORRECT	Last summer, she spent her afternoons *in the office, at home,* or *at the beach.*
	Last summer, he spent his afternoons *at work, at the movies,* or *on the golf course.*
INCORRECT	*Last summer, she spent her afternoons working, reading at home, or at the beach.
	*Last summer, he spent his afternoons at work, going to the movies, or playing golf.

Coordinate and correlative conjunctions should not be used to join clauses to words or phrases.

INCORRECT	*She is a young woman of great intelligence and who has a lot of ambition. (phrase + clause)
CORRECT	She is a young woman of great *intelligence* and *ambition.* (noun + noun)

When phrases or clauses are joined by correlative conjunctions, such as *both...and,* be sure that the sentence parts following the conjunctions are parallel.

INCORRECT	*After school she is either doing her homework or must take care of her children (not parallel)
CORRECT	After school she is either *doing* her homework or *taking care of* her children. (parallel)

10.5   Correlative Conjunctions

Both the food *and* the service were wonderful.

Correlative conjunctions come in pairs. The correlative conjunctions are *both...and, either...or, neither...nor,* and *not only...but also. Both...and* can be used to join two words, phrases, or clauses.

I enjoyed *both* the food *and* the atmosphere.
Both the quality *and* the variety of the food were excellent.

Use *either...or* to state a choice.

You can eat *either* in the dining room *or* on the patio. (You
can eat in the dining room, or you can eat on the patio.)
You can order *either* a full dinner *or* separate items. (You
can order a full dinner, or you can order separate items.)

Neither...nor is the negative of *either...or.* It should not be used
with other negative words.

CORRECT   The waiters *neither* rush you *nor* keep you
waiting. (The waiters don't rush you, and
they don't keep you waiting.)

INCORRECT   *You shouldn't miss neither the appetizer nor
the dessert.

With compound subjects, the verb agrees with the noun phrase
that follows *or* or *nor.*

Neither the drinks nor the *food was* expensive.
Neither the food nor the *drinks were* unusual.

The correlative conjunction *not only...but also* can join words,
phrases, or clauses. *Also* is sometimes omitted.

The food was *not only* tasty *but also* attractive.
A great meal depends *not only* on what you eat *but* on how
it is served.

When *not only* comes at the beginning of a sentence, question
word order is used.

Don: We have eaten well.
Rudy: Not only *have we eaten* well, but also we have
learned a lot about French food.

10.6 Subordinate Conjunctions

Call me *when* you arrive.

Subordinate conjunctions introduce adverbial clauses and join
them to independent clauses. (An independent clause can be a
sentence by itself; an adverbial clause cannot.)

ADVERBIAL CLAUSE	INDEPENDENT CLAUSE
After we have unloaded the truck,	we can unpack.
When the truck leaves,	we can have dinner.

The following subordinate conjunctions are discussed in sections 8.12–14:

	SECTION
after (time)	8.12
although (contrast)	8.13
because (cause)	8.13
before (time)	8.12
even though (contrast)	8.13
if (condition)	8.14
since (cause)	8.13
so that (cause)	8.13
unless (condition)	8.14
until (time)	8.12
when (time)	8.12
whenever (time)	8.12
where (place)	8.12
wherever (place)	8.12
while (time)	8.12

There are a number of other subordinate conjunctions; many of them are phrasal conjunctions. Some of them are:

as	in case
as far as	in order that
as if	once
as long as	provided (that)
as soon as	seeing that
as though	supposing (that)
considering (that)	till
except that	

Clauses beginning with subordinate conjunctions cannot be complete sentences by themselves.

INCORRECT	There is no evening train. *As far as I know. It won't take long to drive. *Except that there maybe a lot of traffic.
CORRECT	There is no evening train *as far as* I know. It won't take long to drive, *except that* there maybe a lot of traffic.

Chapter 11

Numbers, Capital Letters, Punctuation, and Spelling

NUMBERS

11.1 Cardinal and Ordinal Numbers

I paid *five* dollars for a *ten-dollar* book.

Some of the cardinal numbers from one to two hundred two are:

1	one	21	twenty-one
2	two	22	twenty-two
3	three	23	twenty-three
4	four		
5	five	30	thirty
6	six	31	thirty-one
7	seven		
8	eight	40	forty
9	nine	50	fifty
10	ten	60	sixty
11	eleven	70	seventy
12	twelve	80	eighty
13	thirteen	90	ninety
14	fourteen	100	one hundre/a hundred
15	fifteen	101	one hundred one
16	sixteen	102	one hundred two
17	seventeen		
18	eighteen	201	two hundred one
19	nineteen	202	two hundred two
20	twenty		

Large numbers are written with a comma between every three numbers beginning at the right (1,000). Notice that *hundred, thousand,* and *million* do not end in *-s.*

1,000	one thousand/a thousand
2,000	two thousand
3,153	three thousand one hundred fifty-three
11,000	eleven thousand
25,234	twenty-five thousand two hundred thirty-four
100,000	one/a hundred thousand
185,465	one hundred eighty-five thousand four hundred sixty-five
425,000	four hundred twenty-five thousand
1,000,000	one million/a million
17,000,000	seventeen million

| 100,000,000 | one billion/a hundred million |
| 1,000,000,000 | one billion/a billion |

A noun after any cardinal number (except *one*) must be in the plural form. Uncountable nouns cannot, of course, follow numbers.

I paid *five dollars* for the book.
The tax was *twenty-five cents*.

However, if a number-plus-noun combination is used as an adjective before another noun, the combination is hyphenated, and the noun after the number is used in the singular form.

I also bought a *three-dollar* book.

Some of the ordinal numbers from first to two hundred second are:

1st	first	21st	twenty-first
2nd	second	22nd	twenty-second
3rd	third	35th	thirty-fifth
4th	fourth	44th	forty-fourth
5th	fifth	57th	fifty-seventh
6th	sixth		
7th	seventh	100th	one hundredth
8th	eighth	101st	one hundred first
9th	ninth	102nd	one hundred second
10th	tenth		
11th	eleventh	200th	two hundredth
12th	twelfth	201st	two hundred first
13th	thirteenth	202nd	two hundred second

When fractions are spelled out, the second part is an ordinal number. A hyphen (-) is sometimes used in writing fractions.

1/2	one-half (a half)
1/4	one-fourth (a fourth)
3/8	three-eighths
2/5	two-fifths
2 3/4	two and three-fourths
69 1/4	sixty-nine and one-fourth

Numbers with decimal points are usually written as figures. Zero is sometimes spoken like the letter O (oh).

WRITTEN SPOKEN

| 97.8 | ninety-seven point eight |
| 61.04 | sixty-one point oh four (sixty-one and four hundredths) |

11.2 Numbers in Time and Dates

a. Time

It's nine-thirty.

There are several ways to report the time.

9:00	It's nine o'clock.
9:05	It's nine oh five.
9:15	It's nine-fifteen.
	It's a quarter past nine.
9:30	It's nine-thirty.
	It's half past nine.
9:45	It's nine forty-five.
	It's a quarter to ten.
9:55	It's nine fifty-five.
	It's five to ten.
10:00	It's ten o'clock.
10:00 A.M.	It's ten A.M.
	(It's ten o'clock in the morning.)
1:30 P.M.	It's one-thirty P.M.
	(It's one-thirty in the afternoon.)

b. Dates

He was born on *March 5, 1945*.

Dates are usually written with cardinal numbers. The order is the same for both the long and the short forms.

MONTH	DAY	YEAR
January	8,	1984
1/	8 /	84
May	21,	1997
5 /	21/	97

In spoken English, ordinal numbers are usually used for the day and cardinal numbers for the year. The year is spoken in units of two numbers (19-38).

January eighth, nineteen eighty-four
May twenty-first, nineteen ninety-seven

Place a comma after the day when writing a date. When a date that includes the year occurs in a sentence, place a comma after the year, too.

She was born on August 10, 1965, in Chicago, Illinois.
On May 21, 1973, her family moved to Seattle.

11.3 Addresses and Phone Numbers

He lives at 2765 Sunset Place, Los Angeles, California.

In sentences, addresses are written with commas after the name of the street, the city, and the state.

The store is at 140 Granby Street, Norwalk, Connecticut.

In spoken English, building numbers are often given in pairs.

140 Granby Street	one forty Granby Street
1715 Colonial Place	seventeen fifteen Colonial Place

On envelopes, the address of the sender is in the upper left corner, and the address of the receiver is in the center of the envelope. No commas are used after the name of the street or the name of the state. Abbreviations may be used for states.

In spoken English, zip codes are given as a series of individual numbers. For example, 08540 is read as oh-eight-five-four-oh.

Official Post Office abbreviations for the fifty states and the District of Columbia, Guam, Puerto Rico, and the Virgin Islands are:

Alabama	AL	Montana	MT
Alaska	AK	Nebraska	NE
Arizona	AZ	Nevada	NV
Arkansas	AR	New Hampshire	NH
California	CA	New Jersey	NJ
Colorado	CO	New Mexico	NM
Connecticut	CT	New York	NY
Delaware	DE	North Carolina	NC
District		North Dakota	ND
of Columbia	DC	Ohio	OH
Florida	FL	Oklahoma	OK
Georgia	GA	Oregon	OR
Guam	GU	Pennsylvania	PA
Hawaii	HI	Puerto Rico	PR
Idaho	ID	Rhode Island	RI
Illinois	IL	South Carolina	SC
Indiana	IN	South Dakota	SD
Iowa	IA	Tennessee	TN
Kansas	KS	Texas	TX
Kentucky	KY	Utah	UT
Louisiana	LA	Vermont	VT
Maine	ME	Virginia	VA
Maryland	MD	Virgin Islands	VI
Massachusetts	MA	Washington	WA
Michigan	MI	West Virginia	WV
Minnesota	MN	Wisconsin	WI
Mississippi	MS	Wyoming	WY
Missouri	MO		

b. Phone Numbers

Operator, I want four-two-three, one-oh-eight-eight.

Phone numbers include an area code for a city or state or part of a city or state. Area codes which are used for long distance calls have three digits. Local numbers follow the area code and have seven digits. Phone numbers are spoken as single digits.

AREA CODE	LOCAL NUMBER	ENTIRE SPOKEN PHONE NUMBER
(609)	219-1668	Area code six-oh-nine, two-one-nine, one-six-six-eight.
(303)	322-3045	Area code three-oh-three, three-two-two, three-oh-four-five.

11.4 Money

May I borrow a *quarter*?

Money in the United States has the following values:

a penny	$	.01	1¢	one cent
a nickel	$	.05	5¢	five cents
a dime	$	.10	10¢	ten cents
a quarter	$	.25	25¢	twenty-five cents
a half dollar	$	.50	50¢	fifty cents
(half a dollar)				
a dollar bill	$	1.00		one dollar
a five-dollar bill	$	5.00		five dollars
a ten-dollar bill	$	10.00		ten dollars

Amounts of money are read in the following way:

$ 1.39   a dollar thirty-nine
$42.67   forty-two dollars and sixty-seven cents
         (forty-two sixty-seven)
$225.99 two hundred twenty-five dollars and
         ninety-nine cents

To ask about the price of something, the following questions can be used.

How much does this cost?
How much is this?
What does this cost?
Could you please tell me the price of this?

11.5 Measurement and Quantity

How *deep* is the aquarium?

Length, width, and height are qualities of three-dimensional figures, but these qualities can also be used for two-dimensional figures, such as the following:

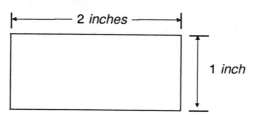

Teacher:	How high is the figure?
Student:	It's one inch high.
Teacher:	How long is the figure?
Student:	It's two inches long.

High and *long* are usually used for figures with two dimensions. When a figure has three dimensions, *long* is used for the greater horizontal dimension and *wide* for the lesser.

The aquarium is one and a half feet *high*.
It's three feet *long*.
It's a foot *wide*.

Deep is usually used for areas enclosed on at least three sides or for an uncountable noun, such as *water, mud,* or *grain,* inside an enclosed area.

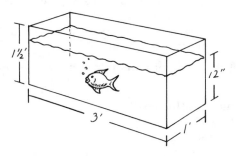

The aquarium is one and a half feet *deep*.
The water in the aquarium is twelve inches *deep*.

High always refers to a vertical measurement (Ā). *Long* and *wide* refer to horizontal measurements (À). When both terms are used, *long* is greater than *wide*. *Deep* can refer to horizontal distance (À) into an object or away from the speaker, or vertical distance (Ā) down from the speaker. The choice of term sometimes depends on what other terms have been used.

The drawer is twenty-four inches *wide*.
It is eighteen inches *deep*.
It is two inches *high*.

The word *thick* is used to describe solid objects.

The board is three feet *long*.
It is one foot *wide* and two inches *thick*.

When used with measurement, *tall* is usually used for people and buildings, and *high* is usually used for other objects.

Bill is six feet *tall*.
The fence is only three feet *high*.

Words such as *long, tall, wide,* and *high* are adjectives; measurement phrases with these adjectives can come before or after nouns. Notice that measurement words are plural after nouns but never before nouns. When used before nouns, measurement phrases are hyphenated.

I want a piece of chicken wire *four yards long*.
I want a *four-yard* piece of chicken wire.
I also need some nails *two inches long*.
I also need some *two-inch* nails.

Some adjectives can be used in measurement phrases, and other adjectives cannot, except as comparatives and superlatives.

CORRECT   She is four years *old*.

INCORRECT   *He is sixty pounds heavy.

Compare the adjectives that can be used in measurement phrases and those that cannot.

USED IN MEASUREMENT PHRASES

deep	tall
high	thick
long	wide
old	

NOT USED IN MEASUREMENT PHRASES

big	fat
expensive	heavy
far	large

In comparative and superlative sentences, any of the preceding adjectives may be used.

She is two years *older* than her brother.
Her brother is twenty pounds *heavier* than she is.

In questions and statements about measurements, the verb *be* is usually used and not the verb *have*.

Nina:	How old is your daughter?
Carlos:	She's nineteen years old.
Nina:	How tall is your son?
Carlos:	He's six feet tall.

INCORRECT	*She has nineteen years.
	*He has six feet.

The following units of measurement are used in the United States. Weight is given in avoirdupois units, the everyday system in use in the United States.

LIQUID

2 cups	= 1 pint	=	.47 liter
2 pints	= 1 quart	=	.95 liter
4 quarts	= 1 gallon	=	3.80 liters

WEIGHT

16 ounces = 1 pound = .45 kilogram

LENGTH

12 inches =	1 foot = 30.5	centimeters
3 feet =	1 yard = .9	meter
1,760 yards =	1 mile = 1.6	kilometers

CAPITAL LETTERS AND PUNCTUATION

11.6 Abbreviations

Dr. Sharma is my doctor.

An abbreviation is a shortened form of a written word. The meanings of many abbreviations and symbols (#, $, %) can be found in most English dictionaries. Some common abbreviations and their meanings follow.

A.D.	after the birth of Christ (anno Domini)
A.M.	before noon (ante meridiem)
Ave.	Avenue
b.	born
B.A.	bachelor of arts
B.C.	before the birth of Christ (before Christ)
B.S.	bachelor of science
cf.	compare
Co.	Company
cont.	continued
d.	died
D.D.S.	doctor of dental surgery
dept.	department
Dr.	Doctor
ed.	editor, edited by
e.g.	for example
et al.	and others
etc.	and so forth
ft	foot, feet
Gov.	Governor
i.e.	that is
in	inch, inches
Jr.	Junior
lb	pound
M.A.	master of arts
M.D.	doctor of medicine
mph	miles per hour
Mr.	man's title
Mrs.	married woman's title
Ms.	woman's title (rhymes with *his*)
M.S.	master of science

oz	ounce, ounces
p.	page
Ph.D.	doctor of philosophy
P.M.	after noon (past meridiem)
pp.	pages
Prof.	Professor
R.S.V.P.	please reply
St.	Street

Some titles are rarely used in the full form. *Mr.*, *Mrs.*, and *Ms.* are abbreviations and take periods. The title *Miss*, for an unmarried woman, however, is not an abbreviation.

> *Mr.* and *Mrs.* Stewart Brosky announced that their daughter would be married in August.
> *Miss* Alexandra Brosky will marry *Dr.* Alan Cooke.

Titles are abbreviated only when they come before proper nouns.

CORRECT	Alan Cooke is a *doctor*.
	Dr. Cooke will marry Alexandra Brosky.
INCORRECT	*Is the tall woman in the center the gov.?
	*Who is your chemistry prof.?

Some titles follow a name and are always abbreviated.

> Alberto Santos, *M.D.*
> Ruth Shore, *Ph.D.*
> Ann Sasaki, *D.D.S.*

Use the abbreviations *B.C.*, *A.D.*, *A.M.*, and *P.M.* and the symbols $ and ¢ only with specific times, dates, and numbers.

10:05 A.M.	A.D. 1066	$5
2:18 P.M.	44 B.C.	50¢

Do not use these abbreviations and symbols alone, and do not use the symbol *&* ("and") in formal writing.

INCORRECT	*They will be married in the A.M.
	*The bride & groom will live in Boston.

In formal writing, do not abbreviate the names of places, days, months, or holidays. However, the abbreviations *U.S.* (United States) and *U.S.S.R.* (Union of Soviet Socialist Republics) are commonly used, even in formal writing.

CORRECT   We left for *Nevada* on Friday.

INCORRECT   *We left for *Nev.* on Friday.

In formal writing, do not abbreviate units of measure unless they are long phrases, such as *miles per hour* (mph).

CORRECT   The painting is two *feet* long.

INCORRECT   *The painting is two ft long.

Familiar capitalized abbreviations for the names of people, organizations, and countries are often written without periods.

All the examples that follow are acceptable in formal writing except JFK.

(the) CIA   IBM   NATO
(the) FBI   JFK   UNESCO

11.7 Capital Letters

Next weekend, I plan to go to Chicago.

Capitalize the first word of every sentence in English.

There will be a school vacation next week.

Capitalize the first word of a quotation.

The announcement said, "Classes will be dismissed at noon."

Always capitalize the pronoun *I*.

Next weekend, I plan to visit Mom and Dad.

Capitalize the greeting and the closing phrase of a letter.

Dear Mom,

I will arrive by the evening train on Friday. See you then.

Love,
Tim

Capitalize proper nouns (the names of specific persons, places, and things) but not common nouns (the names of persons, places, and things in general).

298 NUMBERS, CAPITAL LETTERS, PUNCTUATION, AND SPELLING

PROPER NOUNS	COMMON NOUNS
California	state
Shakespeare	person
Museum of Modern Art	museum

There are many different kinds of proper nouns. Capitalize the following words:

1. Personal names used alone and with noble, military, religious, and customary titles.

Martin Luther King	Queen Elizabeth
Lady Anne	Madame Curie
General Jackson	Mother Teresa

2. Family titles used before a name or to replace a name.

I hope, Mother, that you talk to Aunt Judy and Dad.
My mother, my aunt, and my dad are coming.

3. Names of cities, states, countries, and continents. The word *the* is not capitalized in these names.

Asia	Massachusetts
British Columbia	the Philippines
Costa Rica	Rome

4. Names of regions, such as *South* and *Middle East,* when they refer to a specific area rather than a direction.

The North fought the South in the U.S. Civil War.
We walked north until we found the trail.

5. Names of oceans, seas, lakes, rivers, mountains, peninsulas, islands, deserts, and valleys.

Death Valley	Mt. Whitney
the Hawaiian Islands	the Pacific Ocean
the Iberian Peninsula	the Red Sea
Lake Superior	the Sahara Desert
the Mississippi River	

6. Names of streets, roads, squares, parks, zoos, bridges, and tunnels.

Alson Drive	the Golden Gate Bridge	the Lincoln Tunnel
the Bronx Zoo	Harvard Square	Rock Creek Park
First Street	Highway I-94	the San Diego Zoo

7. Names of organizations, institutions, and buildings.

the Boy Scouts of America	the Ford Foundation
Buddy's Market	Old Dominion University
the Democratic Party	the Rose Room
the Department of Defense	the Sistine Chapel

8. Names of groups of people, languages, and religions.

Buddhists	Christianity	Judaism	Old English
Chinese	French	Native Americans	Taoism

9. Well-known substitutes for names of deities, personal names, or geographic names.

the Almighty	the Loop (in Chicago)
the City (in London)	the Prophet
the Great Emancipator (Lincoln)	the Wizard of Menlo Park (Thomas Edison)

10. Names of ships, trains, rockets, airplanes, and other vehicles.

Apollo 11	Gemini 4
the Concorde	the Queen Mary
the DC-10	Skylab 2

11. Titles of newspapers, magazines, articles, plays, operas, songs, paintings, and other works of art. Short prepositions and conjunctions and the articles are not capitalized in titles except as the first word of titles of works of art (such as stories and books).

Carmen	"Jingle Bells"
Don Quixote	the *Statue of Liberty*
Hamlet	"The Three Bears"

12. Names of months, days of the week, holidays, historical periods and events, but not the names of seasons.

the Fourth of July   the Middle Ages   spring
Halloween   Monday   winter
January   World War II

13. Names of specific educational courses but not the names of general fields.

Contemporary French Civilization   humanities
Geology of the Moon and Planets   geology
Introduction to Psychology 101   psychology

Proper nouns and common nouns are sometimes confused in the following cases:

CAPITALS	NO CAPITALS
Dear Mother,	my mother
the Democratic Party	a democratic election
Dr. Alicia Novak	my doctor, many doctors
on Fifth Avenue	a lovely avenue
Geography 212	my class in geography
Howard University	a university I visited
President Baily	a college president
the Revolutionary War	a war of independence
industry in the South	walking south along this road
the Spring Festival	in the spring
the U.S. Army	neither an army nor a navy

11.8 Quotation Marks and Italics

You'll find " Fire and Ice" in *The Poems of Robert Frost.*

a. Quotation Marks

Use sets of quotation marks (" ... ") to enclose the exact words of a speaker or writer. A quotation can be interrupted by phrases such as *he said.* Each part of an interrupted quotation begins and ends with quotation marks.

" What's worrying you? " she asked.
" By next week, " he answered, " this term paper must be finished. "

The closing quotation marks follow a period or comma but come before a colon or semicolon.

> She said quietly, " Sit down " ; I hesitated, saying, "There doesn't seem to be room to sit down ."

Closing quotation marks sometimes go after a question mark and sometimes before, depending on the meaning of the sentence.

> Who said to me, " That course is easy "?

> I asked the professor, " May I turn in my term paper late ?"

The titles of relatively short works (articles, essays, stories, songs, poems, lectures, parts of books, and names of TV and radio programs) are enclosed in quotation marks.

> I'm reading " Anecdote of the Jar, " a poem by Wallace Stevens.

b. Italics

When a book is printed, some words are printed in italics. In hand-written or typed English, italics are indicated by underlining. The titles of relatively long works (books, newspapers, magazines, journals, plays, long poems, movies, and operas, and of works of art are italicized (underlined).

> I watched *Othello* on TV Saturday night.

Compare the use of italics and quotation marks in the following examples.

LONGER WORKS	SHORTER WORKS
Moby Dick (book)	" A Rose for Emily " (story)
The Magic Flute (opera)	" Silent Night " (song)
Reader's Digest (magazine)	" Selling Your House " (article)

11.9 Sentence Punctuation

> There's Colette .

Use a period (.) at the end of a statement. If the sentence ends with a direct quotation, put the period before the quotation mark.

He said, " I'm going to meet the president of the
company."

When a sentence includes a direct quotation that is also a sentence, use a comma after the quoted sentence unless the quotation ends the longer sentence.

" I'm going to meet the president of the company ,"
he said.

Use a question mark (**?**) after direct questions; do not use a question mark after indirect speech (see section 6.5). Do not use a question mark at the beginning of a sentence.

" Who is the president **?**" she asked.
She asked who the president was **.**
Have you heard the news **?**
Did he say, " It's a secret "**?**

Exclamation points (**!**) are used after words and sentences that show strong emotion. Do not use an exclamation point at the beginning of a sentence.

Wow **!**
I didn't know that **!**

Semicolons (**;**) separate independent clauses that are short and related. *And, but,* and *so* are not used after a semicolon.

She used to be a teacher **;** now she's an administrator.

A semicolon is often used before a linking adverb (see section 8.10).

She is very busy **;** however, she always has time for a
friendly word.

Do not use a comma in place of a semicolon.

INCORRECT   *She used to be a teacher **,** now she's an
administrator.
*She is very busy **,** however, she always has
time for a friendly word.

11.10   Commas and Apostrophes

As you know **,** a car is necessary in Los Angeles.

Commas (**,**)are used to separate or enclose parts of a sentence. They are often used where pauses are used in speech.

Use a comma before (not after) coordinate conjunctions, such as *and* and *but,* when they join independent clauses.

> CORRECT   We have a car **,** but we don't like it.
>
> INCORRECT   *We have a car but we don't like it.

Commas separate items in a series of three or more words, phrases, or clauses. The final comma in the series is optional.

> The engine is old **,** it leaks oil **,** and the brakes are failing **.**
> We've already replaced the carburetor **,** the fuel pump **,** and the brake drums.
> We've already replaced the carburetor **,** the fuel pump and the brake drums.

Commas set off many introductory expressions such as *yes, in addition,* and *for example.* Commas also set off long introductory phrases (four or more words).

> In addition **,** the car is ten years old.
> To make a long story short **,** we decided to buy a new car.

Commas can also set off expressions at the ends of sentences.

> We loved our old car **,** of course.
> The car dealer was happy that I decided to replace it **,** naturally.

Tag questions always have a comma before them.

> Buying a car isn't easy **,** is it?

Commas are also used in the following ways in dates, addresses, letter openings, letter closings, titles, and numbers:

1. Dates

> On June 29 **,** 1983 **,** my parents bought a car. They drove it to Florida on July 15.

2. Addresses

> At 1503 Colley Avenue **,** Greenfield **,** Massachusetts **,** you can buy a good used car.
> I bought a car in Greenfield **,** Massachusetts **,** before I moved to New Jersey.

304 NUMBERS, CAPITAL LETTERS, PUNCTUATION, AND SPELLING

3. Informal letter openings

Dear Mom **,**
Dear Uncle Bill **,**

4. Letter closings

Love **,**
Sincerely **,**
Yours truly **,**

5. Titles following names

June Meyer **,** Ph.D.
Robert Pearson **,** Ed.D.

6. Large numbers

1 **,** 465 **,** 293
2 **,** 985

Pairs of commas are used to enclose expressions that interrupt a sentence.

This car **,** you know **,** was especially modified.
I assure you **,** my friend **,** that this is a great car.
These old cars **,** the Swedish ones **,** are built to last.

Commas are used to separate nonessential phrases and clauses from the rest of the sentence (see section 7.8c).

A car **,** which is a necessity in Los Angeles **,** is a big expense.
This car **,** made in Germany **,** has cost me a fortune.

In direct quotations, commas separate a speaker's words from the rest of the sentence.

He asked **,** " What kind of car do you want? "
" I prefer a small car **,** " I said **,** " but I want one that's comfortable. "
" I have exactly what you need **,** " he exclaimed.

Commas are not usually used in the following cases:

1. Commas are **not** usually used between subjects and verbs.

INCORRECT   *The cars that I had driven before **,** were all old cars **.**

2. Commas are **not** used between verbs and their complements, unless the complement is a direct quotation. Commas are usually not used before reported speech or adverbial clauses.

INCORRECT   *I asked the salesperson **,** if I could drive the
car.
*He told me repeatedly **,** that the car was in
good condition.
*I bought the car **,** because it was a good value.

3. Commas are **not** used before the first item of a series or after
the last adjective before a noun.

INCORRECT   *The car came in earth colors such as **,** red,
brown, and tan.
*The company hires pleasant, ambitious,
hard-working **,** salespeople.

4. Although unnecessary commas should not be used, it is sometimes necessary to add a comma to avoid confusion.

CORRECT   For Harry **,** Martinez was a good source of
information.

INCORRECT   *For Harry Martinez was a good source of
information.

b. Apostrophes

The party was at Linda **'** s house.

Use an apostrophe (**'**) to show genitive relationships such as
possession. If a noun does not end in -s, add an apostrophe and
an -s. If a plural noun ends in -s, add only the apostrophe.

We laughed at Jack **'** s   jokes, and we enjoyed Fumiko **'** s
song.
The children **'** s   play was very funny.
We left before the girls **'**   dance.

If a singular noun ends in s, some writers add an apostrophe and
-s, but it is also correct to add only an apostrophe.

We enjoyed Chris **'** s   story.
We enjoyed Chris **'**   story.

The possessive is indicated differently for individuals and groups.

Jane **'** s and Linda **'** s   solos were wonderful.
(the solos of Jane and the solos of Linda)

Bob and Jim **'** s duet was awful.
(the duet of Bob and Jim)

Do not use an apostrophe with a pronoun except in a contraction. Apostrophes are not used to show possession with pronouns. Do not confuse the possessive adjective *its* and the contraction *it's* (it is).

CORRECT   This coat is *yours.*
              That one is *Jack* 's.

INCORRECT   *That coat is your 's.
              *It 's collar is different.

Apostrophes are used in contractions to show that letters have been omitted.

can 't = cannot   I 'd   = I had
don 't = do not   it 's = it is

Apostrophes are sometimes used to form the plural of letters, numbers, abbreviations, or words referred to as words.

How many *s* 's are in *Mississippi?*
I heard that joke in the 1970 's.
How many O.K. 's do we need?
You used too many *if* 's in that paragraph.

Apostrophes can also be used with some nonhuman nouns that modify nouns.

I spent a week 's salary on that dress.
It was a whole afternoon 's work to hem it.

11.11   Colons, Dashes, and Parentheses

Colons, dashes, and parentheses all separate a thought or idea from the main part of a sentence. The colon directs attention to something that follows it. A dash gives emphasis to material that interrupts the sentence. Parentheses set off nonessential material.

a.   Colons

A colon (:) can be used to introduce a list.

Many parts of the house need repair : the roof, the screens, the kitchen, the garage, the plumbing, and the wiring.

The colon can direct attention to an example, illustration, or explanation.

Finally he gave me his recommendation : Everything had
to be redone.
His advice was this : Roll up your sleeves and get to work.

Colons can be used to introduce quoted material.

Here is the opening line of a do-it-yourself manual :
"House repair can be a joy."

Use a colon after the greeting in a business letter.

Gentlemen and Ladies :

Dear Dr. Gomez :

Dear Credit Manager :

Use a colon in writing the time of day.

11 : 52 A.M.

7 : 09 P.M.

b. Dashes

I learned — to my absolute horror — that the house had
termites.

Use a dash to show an abrupt break in the thought of a sentence.

The sink didn't work — I was dismayed to discover —
and I was expected to fix dinner for six that night.
One of the workers — I'll call him Red — was able to help
me fix the sink.

Use a dash to set off nonessential material that already contains
commas.

The good things about the house — the location, the price,
and the garden — made up for everything else.

c. Parentheses

Parentheses (( )) set off nonessential material. They mark inter-
ruptions in the sentence that are not as abrupt as those marked
by dashes but more abrupt than those set off by commas.

The workers (I got them through an agency) did an
excellent job of fixing the roof.

SPELLING

11.12 Spelling Rules

a. "*i Before e*"

There are several spelling rules in English that are very useful. One rule that most people learn in school is, "*I* before *e*, except after *c*, or when sounded like *a*."

I before *e*	except after *c*	sounded like *a*
achieve	ceiling	eight
believe	conceit	freight
chief	deceit	veil
convenient	perceive	vein
field	receipt	weight
grief	receive	
niece		
piece		
relief		
view		

The following are exceptions to this rule.

ancient	foreign	leisure	protein	seize	weird
either	height	neither	science	species	

b. Adding Suffixes to Words Ending in Consonants

I'm *planning* on *dropping* this course.

In some cases, a consonant is doubled when the suffix *-ing, -ed, -er,* or *-est* is added. When the word has one syllable and ends in a consonant that follows one vowel, double the final consonant.

DOUBLE CONSONANT			NO DOUBLE CONSONANT		
big	+ est =	biggest	cheap	+ er =	cheaper
drop	+ ed =	dropped	join	+ ed=	joined
mad	+ er =	madder	poor	+ est=	poorest
plan	+ ing =	planning	talk	+ ing=	talking

When a word has more than one syllable and ends in one consonant following one vowel, double the final consonant only if the accent is on the final syllable.

```
CLEVer  +    er   =  cleverer
ENter   +    ing  =  entering
Open    +    ed   =  opened
ocCUR   +    ing  =  occurring
perMIT  +    ing  =  permitting
preFER  +    ed   =  preferred
```

Final *w, x,* and *y* are never doubled.

```
box     +  ing  =  boxing
gay     +  est  =  gayest
new     +  er   =  newer
play    +  ing  =  playing
plow    +  ing  =  plowing
```

When *-ly* is added to a word ending in *-ic,* add *-al* before the suffix. There is one exception to this rule, the word *public.*

```
automatic  +  ly  =  automatically
basic      +  ly  =  basically
frantic    +  ly  =  frantically
romantic   +  ly  =  romantically
public     +  ly  =  publicly
```

c.   Adding Suffixes to Words Ending in *-y*

The easy things get easier.

Many English words that end in *y* change the *y* to *i* when a suffix is added. When a word ends in a consonant and *y,* change the *y* to *i* when adding a suffix (except for *-ing*).

```
army   +  s     =  armies
beauty +  ful   =  beautiful
crazy  +  er    =  crazier
easy   +  ly    =  easily
funny  +  est   =  funniest
happy  +  ness  =  happiness
try    +  ed    =  tried
```

When a word ends in a vowel and *-y,* do not change the *y* to *i.*

```
boy    +  s     =  boys
enjoy  +  ment  =  enjoyment
lay    +  s     =  lays
play   +  ed    =  played
```

When *-ing* is added to a word ending in *-y,* do not change the *y* to *i.*

```
rely + ing  =  relying
try  + ing  =  trying
```

d. Adding Suffixes to Words Ending in Vowels

Are you *writing* this down?

When a suffix beginning with a consonant is added to a word ending in a vowel, there is usually no change in spelling.

```
care       +  ful   =  careful
encourage  +  ment  =  encouragement
entire     +  ly    =  entirely
fine       +  ness  =  fineness
```

However, when a word ends in *-ue,* drop the *e* before a suffix.

```
argue + ment  =  argument
due   + ly    =  duly
true  + ly    =  truly
```

When a suffix beginning with a vowel is added to a word ending in "silent *e*," drop the *e.* A "silent *e*" is an *e* at the end of a word that is not pronounced.

```
fame   +  ous   =  famous
guide  +  ance  =  guidance
like   +  able  =  likable
office +  er    =  officer
white  +  est   =  whitest
write  +  ing   =  writing
```

In some cases, a "silent *e*" at the end of a word is not dropped when it follows a "soft *c*" or "soft *g*." A "soft *c*" is a *c* pronounced with an *s* sound, as in *city.* A "soft *g*" is a *g* pronounced with a *j* sound, as in *angel.*

```
change   + able = changeable
courage  + ous  = courageous
notice   + able = noticeable
```

When the suffix *-ing* is added to a word that ends in *-ie,* the *ie* is changed to *y.*

```
die + ing  =  dying
lie + ing  =  lying
tie + ing  =  tying
```

e. Noun Plurals

I'll get pears, peaches, and tomatoes.

Most nouns form the plural by adding *-s* to the end of the word.

SINGULAR	PLURAL
one apple	three apples
one banana	two bananas
a carrot	several carrots

Nouns that end in *-s*, *-sh*, *-ch*, or *-x* form the plural by adding *-es* to the end of the word. Words that end in *-ch* that sounds like *-k* are exceptions.

SINGULAR	PLURAL
a box of eggs	some boxes of eggs
a peach	some peaches
a radish	some radishes
stomach	stomachs (*ch* sounds like *k*)

Many, but not all, nouns that end in a consonant and *-o* form the plural by adding *-es*.

SINGULAR	PLURAL
hero	heroes
potato	potatoes
tomato	tomatoes

There are many exceptions to this rule; many are words borrowed from other languages.

avocado	avocados	memento	mementos/oes
banjo	banjos/oes	piano	pianos
dynamo	dynamos	piccolo	piccolos
ghetto	ghettos/oes	solo	solos
gringo	gringos	two	twos
halo	halos/oes	zero	zeros
lasso	lassos/oes		

When a word ends in a consonant and *-y*, drop the *y* and add *-ies*.

SINGULAR	PLURAL
baby	babies
cherry	cherries
strawberry	strawberries

When a word ends in a vowel and *y*, do not change the *y*. Add *s* to the end of the word.

SINGULAR	PLURAL
chimney	chimneys
day	days

Index